SAGE was founded in 1965 by Sara Miller McCune to support the dissemination of usable knowledge by publishing innovative and high-quality research and teaching content. Today, we publish over 900 journals, including those of more than 400 learned societies, more than 800 new books per year, and a growing range of library products including archives, data, case studies, reports, and video. SAGE remains majority-owned by our founder, and after Sara's lifetime will become owned by a charitable trust that secures our continued independence.

Los Angeles | London | New Delhi | Singapore | Washington DC | Melbourne

RADICAL CITY

Thank you for choosing a SAGE product!
If you have any comment, observation or feedback,
I would like to personally hear from you.
Please write to me at **contactceo@sagepub.in**

Vivek Mehra, Managing Director and CEO, SAGE India.

Bulk Sales

SAGE India offers special discounts
for purchase of books in bulk.
We also make available special imprints
and excerpts from our books on demand.

For orders and enquiries, write to us at

Marketing Department
SAGE Publications India Pvt Ltd
B1/I-1, Mohan Cooperative Industrial Area
Mathura Road, Post Bag 7
New Delhi 110044, India

E-mail us at **marketing@sagepub.in**

Subscribe to our mailing list
Write to **marketing@sagepub.in**

This book is also available as an e-book.

RADICAL CITY

Imagining Possibilities for the Indian City

Edited by
Pithamber R. Polsani

Los Angeles | London | New Delhi
Singapore | Washington DC | Melbourne

First published in 2021 by

SAGE Publications India Pvt Ltd
B1/I-1 Mohan Cooperative Industrial Area
Mathura Road, New Delhi 110 044, India
www.sagepub.in

YODA Press
79 Gulmohar Enclave
New Delhi 110049
www.yodapress.co.in

SAGE Publications Inc
2455 Teller Road
Thousand Oaks, California 91320, USA

SAGE Publications Ltd
1 Oliver's Yard, 55 City Road
London EC1Y 1SP, United Kingdom

SAGE Publications Asia-Pacific Pte Ltd
18 Cross Street #10-10/11/12
China Square Central
Singapore 048423

Published by Vivek Mehra for SAGE Publications India Pvt Ltd. Typeset in 10.5/13 pt Bembo by Fidus Design Pvt Ltd, Chandigarh.

Library of Congress Cataloging-in-Publication Data Available

ISBN: 978-93-5388-714-8 (HB)

SAGE YODA Team: Arpita Das, Ishita Gupta, Tanya Singh, Amrita Dutta and Satvinder Kaur
Cover Design: Mizba Pathan

Contents

Part I: A Field of Inspirations

Part II: Palimpsest of Possibilities

Part III: Fractured Realities

Part IV: Material Manifestations

Part V: Potentialities and Probabilities

List of Figures

KIRANMAYI INDRAGANTI

NEELKANTH CHHAVA

SONAL MITHAL, ARUL PAUL AND FAHAD ZUBERI

MUSTANSIR DALVI

PITHAMBER R. POLSANI

SANKALPA

PRIVA JOSEPH

Acknowledgements

Just as it takes a village to raise a child, many people contributed to making this book possible. I am grateful to Dr Geetha Narayanan, Founder-Director, Srishti Institute of Art, Design and Technology, Bangalore, without whose commitment and enthusiastic support this book would not have been possible. I would like to thank the contributors to this volume for keeping the impossible deadlines I imposed on them during the preparation of the manuscript. My gratitude goes to the editors at Yoda Press, Arpita Das who enthusiastically accepted this book proposal when I first approached her, Ishita Gupta and Tanya Singh for their diligence and patience as well as for getting the copyrights cleared for the images used in this volume, and Aruna Ramachandran for the meticulous copyediting. Finally, but more importantly, I am grateful to my research assistant and cover designer Mizba Pathan, without whose dedication, enthusiasm, fortitude and creativity this book could not have happened.

Introduction
Should Our Cities Survive?

Pithamber R. Polsani

Modern city is nothing more than a problem which has not been solved ... it is a historical phenomenon which has not been objectively superseded.

—Achizoom Associati (2006)

Should Our Cities Survive? was the question that animated young avant-garde architects of Europe nearly a hundred years back. These architects, divided by ideology and politics, but united by belief in the socially transformative power of design, came together to form CIAM.

The founding of CIAM, the French acronym for International Congress of Modern Architecture, in 1928 was a watershed moment for city planning and architecture. Not only because it brought into vogue the word 'urbanism' to frame conceptually, deliberate design and planned development of large-scale habitations, but also in bringing to the fore the hitherto unknown idea of a 'Functional City', which subsists even today in the subconscious of all urban planners irrespective of their ideological positions. Although the members of CIAM popularised the concept of urban planning and rational organisation of city space, its antecedents go deep into the nineteenth century.

Urbanism signifies a phenomenon, a discipline as well as a practice. Spanish engineer and town planer Ildefonso Cerdá coined the term 'urbanism' (*urbanización*) from the Latin *urbs*. Cerdá in his *Teoría general de la urbanización* (*General Theory of Urbanization*), published in 1867, rejects the word 'city'[1] (*ciudad* in Spanish) in favour of *urbs* because 'city' in its etymological origins in Latin *civis* and its derivative *civitas* refers to citizenship. *Urbs* on the contrary refers to a demarcated grouping of buildings. Romans marked the perimeter of an area to be urbanised with *urbum*, a plough drawn by sacred bulls and thus converting an open and free land into an *urbs*. Cerdá's intention, openly articulated in his work, in coining the word 'urbanism' from the Latin *urbs* was to abstract structure from habitation. He defines urbanism—a new science for the new industrial civilisation—'as a set of principles, doctrines, knowledge and rules formulated to teach the way in which the buildings should be organised and grouped together so that the habitants can avail of services to live comfortably' (Cerdá 1867: 39, translation from Spanish is mine). What Cerdá was seeking to articulate in his new science of urbanism (*la ciencia urbanizadora*) was the centrality of infrastructure, because he deduces rationally that human beings are either in a state of movement or rest, and therefore the objective of urban planning is to enable habitants of a city to alternate between motion and repose. While the places of rest are demarcated based on the activity—work, family, pleasure—movement between the locations of repose acquires prominence. Although Cerdá wasn't known outside of Spain until much later in the twentieth century and his *Teoría general de la urbanización* wasn't read by any of the prominent urban planners and architects that followed, except another Spaniard and fellow town planner Arturo Sria y Mata, Cerdá was the first to pinpoint with precise formulation what would become the core of all urban planning—enabling movement and facilitating rest. In the new industrial civilisation propelled by steam and electricity, motor, motion, movement and circulation become the key operational concepts across the spectrum, including the arts. While the eighteenth-century mechanisation was mimetic, that is, the machines imitated life forms—for instance, Jacques de Vaucanson's automata—from the mid-nineteenth century onwards machines became the measure for living beings, as the productivism of the Industrial Revolution eliminated the difference between humans and machines since both are governed by the same force—energy converted to motion (Rabinbach 2018: 16).

By the second decade of the twentieth century, the trauma of industrialisation that was unleashed more than hundred years earlier had settled down. That is not to say the contradictions between capital and labour, tradition and modernity, past and future were resolved, but the ground on which these frictions would be played out had shifted and the terms of debate reframed. Capitalist modernity had triumphed. What the founding of CIAM signifies is that industrialism came to establish itself as the core and universal principle of reorganising of all life that was, to begin with, disrupted by industrialisation. Sigfried Giedion, one of the founders and most active members of CIAM, wrote years later that 'mechanization [today] is inextricably woven into the patterns of thought and custom' (1948: v). That is to say, the machine had entered surreptitiously into the consciousness of human beings.

During its three decades of existence until its dissolution in 1959, despite the irreconcilable differences, ideological conflicts between its members and organisational splits, what CIAM asserted time and again in its deliberations, planning and orientations, was that the organising principles of all life are Henry Ford's assembly plant and Fredrick Winslow Taylor's productive efficiency. What this means is that the very meaning of life was redefined. Now life no longer means living and being, but productivity and efficiency. This notion was not just advocated by capitalist Europe, it was firmly rooted in the communist Soviet Union—Lenin was a great admirer of Taylor—as well as liberal and left-leaning intellectuals. Almost all members of CIAM would fall into either one or the other of these camps. Progressives in Amsterdam, socialists in Frankfurt, communists in Moscow or liberals in Paris, all believed in the power of architecture and design to transform the social reality. Therefore, urbanism, as they defined it, is the total organisation of collective life irrespective of whether it is urban or rural. The reorganisation implied categorising life activities into four: working, dwelling, leisure and transportation. In order to achieve this vision CIAM advocated, vociferously and repeatedly, land subdivision, that is, zoning, building legislation and regulation of traffic. These ideas find their expressions in the utopic visions of cities of the immediate future. For example, one of the earliest to imagine a rational city of the future as well as accomplish it, to some extent, was the Spanish engineer and town planner Arturo Soria y Mata. His *Ciudada Lineal* (1882–83) is a long city with built forms extending five hundred metres on either side of a 40-metre central avenue that can accommodate trains and trams

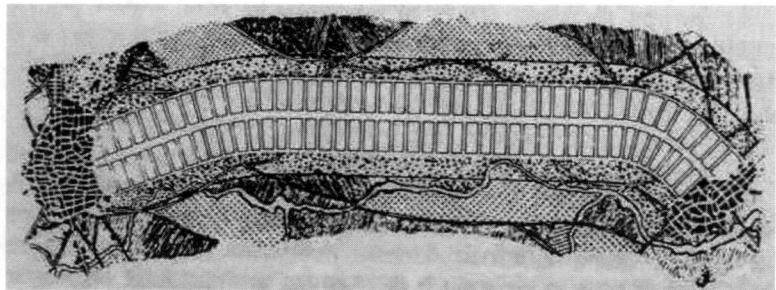

Figure I.1 *Arturo Soria y Mata*, Ciudada Lineal, *the preliminary drawing*
Source: https://commons.wikimedia.org/wiki/File:Ciudad_lineal_de_Arturo_Soria.jpg (accessed 22 August 2020).

(Figure I.1). The buildings along with the main avenue can extend infinitely in a repetitive pattern for hundreds of kilometres. Soria y Mata imagined one continuous long city stretching from Madrid to Berlin and beyond to St. Petersburg.

Tony Garnier's *Une Cité Industrielle* was remarkably ahead of its time. Although published in 1917 in a book form, Garnier imagined and drew *Une Cité Industrielle* while living in Villa Medici at Rome between 1899 and 1904 as a recipient of the prestigious Grand Prix de Rome (Figure I.2). *Une Cité Industrielle* as its name suggests is industry-centric with clearly demarcated zones of work, housing, entertainment. Le Corbusier who read *Une Cité Industrielle* in 1919 wrote to Garnier, 'It is a milestone clearly delimiting a past period and opening up all possible hopes.... In ten years, [your book] will be the foundation of all production and be the first rallying sign' (quoted in Tatke 2019).

Ludwig Hilberseimer's *Hochhausstadt* (1924), a vertical city, erases all distinctions between zones of activities and imagines identical structures differentiated only by height (Figure I.3). The Vertical City represents instrumental reason spatially manifested in its purest form as function. The inhabitants traverse through undifferentiated built forms up and down in elevators like shadows without bodies. Hilberseimer's geometrically rendered vertical city realises in architecture, in three-dimensional form, what D. H. Kahnweiler says about Cubism in visual

Figure I.2 *Tony Garnier,* La Cité Industrielle *(1901–04)*

Source: https://commons.wikimedia.org/wiki/File:GarnierTonyCiteIndus
trielle.png (accessed 22 August 2020).

Figure I.3 *A view of Ludwig Hilberseimer's* Hochhausstadt *(1924)*

*Source: https://www.artic.edu/artworks/101044/highrise-city-hochhausstadt-
perspective-view-north-south-street*

arts, 'a complete image devoid of the momentary and the accidental, and that retains only the essential and the durable' (quoted in Choay 1970: 47; translation from Spanish is mine).

Le Corbusier's *Ville Radieuse* (Figure I.4) is a culmination of the prior visions of Soria y Mata, Garnier and Hilberseimer. The Radiant City is a totalitarian vision of a god-like designer who obliterates the past and, on its ruins, brings forth, *ex nihilo*, a rational form of pure functions and circulation. If Piet Mondrian's paintings are an abstraction of a city laid in a grid, the radiant city is the realisation, in physical form, of Mondrian's canvases.

In all these projections of cities of the future, many of which, if not in their totality, continue to be realised across the globe, there are three important ideological tenets of industrial modernity and capitalism. First, abstraction, which is reflected in disassociation of structure from habitation resulting in pure technical consideration of structures and their spatial realisation through austere geometric aesthetics devoid of decorative elements, becomes one of the major concerns of urbanism, instead of living and the political and social organisation of life. Second, movement and circulation become the generalised condition of life and therefore urbanism's goal is to facilitate optimal movement of bodies and machines in and through space in the service of production, distribution and consumption. For Le Corbusier, circulation is an independent function abstracted and considered free-standing from the totality of built form in which it is embedded. He writes,

> there is a reciprocal independence between the constructed forms and channels of circulation. The highways are for transit and they will have most simple and direct forms; they will be totally connected to the ground and yet they will be perfectly independent from the buildings and objects that are around them. (Quoted in Choay 1970: 47; translation from the Spanish is mine)

Third, the indifference. As the thermodynamics frames all living and nonliving beings under the rubric of energy converted to motion and work, efficient production becomes the goal and the drive for efficiency leads to standardisation, defining a common and universal human type and functional typologies to reflect the logic of production.

At the founding of CIAM the advocates of modern architecture and city planning asked, *Should our cities survive?* The question was posed to their own context, the ideas of the neoclassical and Haussmannian city that dominated architectural thinking and were disseminated through the academies. Proponents of modern architecture were like the avant-garde artists who wanted to assassinate painting. They rejected everything that was historical, inherited and traditional. They were the Futurists who embraced industry, the automobile, rationalised production, efficient distribution of space and speed.

We are living today in the cities that the avant-garde architects of the twentieth century dreamt, which have become our nightmare. In the next few decades a billion people will be urbanised. There will be over 100 megacities—with more than 10 million inhabitants—most of which will be located in the 'global South', especially China and India. Cities already stretched to the seams will explode. The accelerated global warming and extreme weather events will only make the situation worse, resulting in unimaginable consequences. Currently, two predominant conceptual models to confront this bleak future are gentrification and the smart city. While gentrification is driven by certain notions of living, lifestyle and forms of leisure embodied in acculturative environments, the smart city believes in technological intelligence as an inevitable destiny and a singular solution, because of its ability to measure, monitor and apportion all resources, including human, in real time. But both these models—not incompatible with each other—are embedded in a broader idea of the city: a space of conglomeration of a large number of people who flow between distributed and demarcated zones of activity. The foundational blocks of this conception of city which was born with CIAM—planning, monitoring, measuring and intervening—have lost their effectiveness in the face of overwhelming growth and environmental challenges. So we ask this question again: *Should our cities survive?*

Cornelius Castoriadis observes that every human society imagines forms of its existence, and it is through these forms that a world of norms, values and objectives of collective as well as individual life are created. Into this world the society inscribes itself, imbibing it with 'social imaginary signification' (1993: 84). The forms imagined by the society are not static; instead, subjected to internal and external dynamics, they evolve and transform with time. European colonialism interrupts, often with violence, non-European societies' ability to imagine their possibilities and realise them in the world. It imposes on the colonised its own modes of imagination, its own forms and institutions that embody them. As a result, the colonised are deracinated from their sources of imagination and are only tangentially tethered to the coloniser's. Consequently, the forms imagined by the postcolonial societies and their people are, often, spasmodic and their spatial manifestation discontinuous. A good example of this condition was the Bombay Progressives, artists who embraced international modernism totally but were unable to find success in the Western capitals. Because the Western pictorial modernism, contrary to their assumptions and beliefs, was not a neutral and objective resource that everyone could appropriate and develop individual styles; instead it was deeply rooted in the experience of the Western cultures and the problem of representation—space, form and composition—that the Western modernists were grappling with (Polsani 2017: 1).

The city in modern India is a colonial inheritance. This legacy continues in post-independence India in the name of modernisation and development with the State embracing material modernity. The modern city came to India in many variants: railway town, company town, model town, new town, radiant city and garden city, and their radical appropriation by the Indian masses since their emergence shows the failure of design as harbinger of social change and transformation. Design as conceived in the context of the nineteenth-century Industrial Revolution and its subsequent role as 'a craftsman of synthesis, and hence as a programmatic mystifier' (Cacciari 1993: 36) may be adequate to sell expensive gadgets, but is inadequate to capture the fractured realities of Indian cities and provide any real solutions to the problems faced by the inhabitants. The activists, artists, academics and practitioners whose articles and personal reflections are brought together in this volume reflect on the ruptures and discontinuities of Indian cities in their historical evolution and contemporary manifestations. Although the writers in this book engage with multiple themes on and about Indian cities simultaneously, the essays have been arranged under five broad themes.

The first group of writings sees the city from an artistic and exploratory lens, be it that of film, street theatre, or simply through visual
images that are splattered across billboards. For instance, Namrata
Toraskar argues that Mumbai's idea of 'dwelling' thrives on visual
images unconnected to the ecological, historical and social context of
the city and traces how the visual culture propagated through hoardings, advertisements, and apartment apps shapes its urbanity. Whereas
Sudhanva Deshpande, drawing from his personal experience as a street
theatre actor and director, critically examines Peter Brook's idea of the
empty space of the city becoming a performance space. Because
the spaces where a street play is staged are never empty—instead they
are charged with histories of contestations and therefore a continuous
performance—Deshpande asserts that we have to contend with,
become part of, and be partisan in, this contestation over spaces in the
city. In her work on the city as the perceptual field of inspiration,
Kiranmayi Indraganti traces the history of a walled city through the
study of her students' films on Bidar in north Karnataka. She posits
that the city is something that is free-flowing, ever changing and
boundless—just like cinema, the city too lies beyond its materiality. In
contrast to looking at the city through an exploratory lens, Savyasaachi's
article explores the difference between two meanings of 'radical' with
reference to the urban. On the one hand, 'radical' refers to a radicalisation by means of adopting extreme social and economic positions not
inclusive of non-human nature, and, on the other hand, 'radical' refers
to conventions inclusive of non-human nature. In engaging with these
two extremes, he attempts to find a radical middle ground, where both
human and non-human can co-exist in the city.

The chapters in the second part engage with the city as a continuously evolving artefact. Neelkanth Chhaya, for example, examines the
city as an organic patchwork vis-à-vis its functioning as a streamlined
machine. He argues that, sadly, in the contemporary city, technocrats
keep on dreaming of absolute coordination and efficiency, aided
with the technologies of information. As a result, he writes, the idea
of 'collective' has become a huge, faceless, shapeless mass of urban
inhabitants—as the scale parity between the human and the machine
has vanished. The next article, by Sohail Hashmi, reflects on the transformation of a village into a city. Hashmi identifies the elements that

turn a village into a city and underscores the essence of a city as lying not merely in the size of the population, but in its character. He also identifies the essential features that distinguish the city from other human settlements, from the village, the mufassil town and the suburb. Next, Sonal Mithal, Arul Paul and Fahad Zuberi explore the possibility of looking at historical transformations of Lucknow through multiple layers all at once. Mithal et al. undertake a gendered reading of the city of Lucknow, a city, they argue, bred on liberal-minded, educated and highly skilled women with an adaptable spirit, women who defied the hetero-normative gender stereotypes, and took charge of not just their identity, but also wealth, profession, and sexuality. Similarly, the chapter also explores LGBTQ+ histories of the city, through the study of queer archives of Lucknow—books, biographical records, poetry, newspapers, photographs, paintings, illustrations, posters, and digital references. The authors argue that these archives are currently fragmented, and if pieced together they can reveal the gendered and sexual histories of the city. As part of a third layer in the palimpsest of Lucknow's history, the chapter chronicles violence in the city, which is not communal but sectarian. They argue that the conflict in Lucknow—that results in shifting neighbourhoods, identities getting ghettoised, and the emergence of a new urbanity—is one of the important frames through which all our cities must be viewed.

The next part of the book deals with modern imaginations of a city, from the Art Deco movement to recent decadence via model towns, that have transformed contemporary urban life. Pithamber Polsani, in discussing fractured realities of urban geography, employs ruins as an onto-epistemological category to frame the neoliberal urban phenomenon in India. In doing so, he brings it in sharp contrast with previous—modernist—forms of urbanism such as company towns, which lie in ruins now. The city has been a site of experiments, economic as well as social. The latter is aptly captured in the next chapter by Rachna Mehra. She writes about the new towns built in India post-1947 that were intended to exhibit the vigour and vitality embodied in the actions of the fledgling nation state. As a result, the objective was to create new human relations as a corollary to planning. This implied that people could transform civic life if they embraced and optimised the hard-won gains of citizenship over kinship ties. The third offering in this part is by Mustansir Dalvi, who examines Art Deco in Bombay, a movement which allowed radical reimagination of the city through its aesthetics. Dalvi argues that the transformation of early-twentieth-century Bombay was fuelled by the availability of new materials and technologies, and the stylistic trend was championed by many first-generation architects, who were educated in India. Transformation and reimaginations of a city therefore are not simply a result of economic development, but also a conscious choice that gets appropriated by architects and clients, who believe in keeping with the times.

A rational functional city of modernism could not have been possible without the materials produced by the Industrial Revolution, and yet the same materials because of their resource-intensive production pose a challenge to the future. The three chapters in the fourth part focus on the emergence, use and future of steel, cement and brick. In making an argument for a city in steel and timber, Sankalpa writes that focusing on constructional details of buildings, especially high-rise structures, could offer new direction in imagining future cities. Paying attention to how buildings could be dismantled and reused in their life cycle, could help to reduce pollution and decrease the pressure on resources, he argues. Further, he states that giving high priority to devising technological details could help in assembling flexible spaces in buildings, which can easily adjust to different, and often changing, needs of users. While Sankalpa pitches his focus on the modern use of steel and timber as materials that could drive the future of cities, Priya Joseph makes a case for the time-tested brick. Although seemingly an ordinary material today, brick was at the forefront of transforming cities in the past, argues Joseph. She explores the historic use of brick, through paradoxical cases and the events that led to the standardisation of brick in the nineteenth century, which changed the urban architecture that followed. The third chapter in this part by Gauri Bharat focuses on concrete, or rather, how advertisements allowed the mainstreaming of this material in British India of the twentieth century. Bharat focuses on cement and reinforced cement concrete from the moment of their introduction into construction practices in the 1920s. By examining the advertisements in technical journals and printed news media, she probes some early claims that the producers and suppliers made, which reveal that the early architectural potentials of concrete were considered as desirable and marketed accordingly.

The final two chapters in the book offer potential and useful ways in which our existing cities could be made tolerable by localised solutions to highly localised problems. In promoting the need for spontaneous urbanism, Ashish Ganju narrates the story of a village on the outskirts of Delhi that has transformed into an urban centre in the last three decades. Ganju makes a case for grounding urban theories around spontaneous settlements that are emerging on the margins of our existing cities. While accretive and spontaneous settlements on the margins continue to be governed informally, Tikender Panwar makes a case for strategies of managing cities through the provisions of law. The author reflects on the contemporary relevance of the 74th Constitutional Amendment that has directly affected governance of cities in India. While this amendment has led to positive change, Panwar argues that the law needs to be updated to match changing times, because issues like urban migration, street vending, urban poverty and homelessness, among others, are not adequately addressed in the scope of the 74th Amendment. Perhaps the telling sign of this disparity is how the city has failed to respond to the crises of migrants in the post-pandemic period. Although this was not the focus of the conference that led to the making of this book, that reflections coming from these essays could still help in understanding the city in these times makes them all the more relevant. Without a doubt, these wide-ranging reflections, critiques, and strategies of and for cities in India that are offered by the authors in this book, help in unpacking the complex idea that is shaping our contemporary urban reality. In putting works from authors, who hail from different backgrounds and fields of expertise, in conversation with one another, the book offers radical reimaginings of the city. The strength of these offerings is not so much in the individual reflections, but rather in understanding the idea of the city collectively.

As we gathered together artists, architects, writers, poets, designers, urban planners, social scientists, humanists—many of whom are repre-sented in the volume—at Srishti in Bangalore in the middle of December 2019 to enter into a dialogue that expanded beyond planners, infrastructure, zoning, transportation and automobiles and imagined the city as a space of representations, of events, objects, actions, celebrations, laughter and melancholy, the highly contagious and deadly novel Coronavirus 2, later to be named COVID-19, was quietly spreading through the human population in the city of Wuhan, China. In a little over a month of its appearance, COVID-19 became an outbreak and soon a global epidemic infecting and exposing the fragility of seemingly unstoppable supply chains and global networks of production, distribution and consumption that reach every corner of the world to harvest cheap labour and natural resources for economies of scale, for mass consumption and above all for maximisation of profit. Ironically, these very same networks of communication and transportation that rapidly moved people and products across the world enabled and augmented the spread of Covid-19. A panicked world shut itself up and in 120 days shrank to a bare essential life. The economy confined to producing only the basics was on the brink of collapse, revealing that it is the non-essentials that drive it. What the COVID-19 pandemic discloses is that the world that we have built as a global enterprise of production and distribution is not an inevitable destiny of humanity, but what it is, is a built form, and therefore the world can be reimagined. Such a reimagination should begin by overcoming deeply the entrenched ethos of productivism, because what is threatened is not the minimum dwelling that worried the modernist planners, but this earth as our dwelling.

NOTE

1   Cerdá also rejects other words (Cerdá 1867: 29–32).

REFERENCES

Achizoom Associati. 2006. *No-Stop City* (ed. Andrea Branzi). Paris: Librairie de l'architecture et de la ville.

Cacciari, Massimo. 1993. *Architecture and Nihilism: On the Philosophy of Modern Architecture* (trans. Stephen Sartarelli). New Haven: Yale University Press.

Castoriadis, Cornelius. 1993. *World in Fragments: Writings on Politics, Society, Psychoanalysis, and the Imagination* (trans. David Ames Curtis). Stanford: Stanford University Press.

Cerdá, Ildefonso. 1867. *Teoría general de la urbanización y aplicación de sus pricipios y doctrinas a la reforma y Ensanche de Barcelona*. Madrid: Española.

Choay, Françoise. 1970. *El urbanísmo: las utopías y realidades* (trans. Luís del Castillo). Barcelona: Editorial Lumen.

Garnier, Tony. 1917. *Une Cite Industrielle; etude pour la construction des villes*. Paris: C.H. Massine & Co.

Giedion, Sigfried. 1948. *Mechanization Take Command: Contributions to an Anonymous History*. Oxford: Oxford University Press

Hilberseimer, Ludwig. 1927. *GroBstadtarchitektur*. Stuttgart: J. Hoffmann.

Le Corbusier. 1933. *La ville radieuse*. Boulogne: Editions de l'Architecture D'aujourd'hui.

Polsani, Pithamber R. 2017. 'Shadows without Bodies: How Was Modernism in India?' Indian Cultural Forum, https://archive.indianculturalforum.in/2017/11/21/shadows-without-bodies-how-was-modernism-in-indian-art/ (accessed 10 August 2020).

Rabinbach, Anson. 2018. *The Eclipse of the Utopias of Labor*. New York: Fordham University Press.

Soria y Mata, Arturo. 1935. *Cosas de Madrid: Apuntes y comentarios municipals*. Madrid: Imprenta Augusto Boue Alarcón.

Tatke, Sukhada. 2019. 'Reviving the Utopian Urban Dreams of Tony Garnier'. Bloomberg CityLab, 11 November. https://www.bloomberg.com/news/articles/2019-11-11/why-architect-tony-garnier-was-ahead-of-his-time (accessed 10 August 2020).

PART I

A Field of Inspirations

Chapter 1

The City as Stage

Sudhanva Deshpande

When we think of theatre, of watching plays, we typically think of the built theatre. But if we look at the history of theatre in India, and particularly in our most theatrically vibrant cities like Bombay, or Pune, or even Delhi, we find that some of our best theatre spaces were actually not originally built for theatre. For instance, the Shri Ram Centre for Art and Culture in Mandi House, New Delhi. Now, this was built for theatre, and has a large auditorium on its second floor. But the more interesting space that enabled a lot of new and young theatre groups to function was a basement, which was not built for theatre. It was supposed to be a godown, and so it had a large, round pillar right in the middle of it. The ceiling height was too little for proper stage lighting. There was backstage space only on the right-hand side. And yet this space, which was entirely inappropriate for theatre, turned out to be one of the most exciting theatre spaces in Delhi. Sadly, for the last several years, about a decade and a half, this space has been shut down apparently because of some municipal regulation. It is no longer available for theatre.

Or take the Chhabildas School in Bombay—again a fantastic incubatory space for experimental theatre in Bombay. The entire Marathi so-called *prayogik rangabhoomi* (experimental theatre) would have been impossible to conceive of without this space. This was a school, with a hall on the third floor. There was no lift, so one had to climb four storeys to reach the hall. It wasn't built for theatre at all. It was supposed to be used as a marriage hall and for school functions. The theatre group Awishkar got it on lease in the late 1960s and early 1970s, and they in turn made it available to Bombay's theatre groups. I saw a lot of plays there as a child. One had to sit in the sweltering heat because there was no air-conditioning, and the fans had to be turned off for the plays. There was a street right outside, and the acoustics were not great, so the city always sort of seeped into the theatre via the sounds.[1] Or take the Sudarshan Rangamanch in Pune. Again, it was built as a marriage hall, so there is literally no backstage space, and the wing space is minuscule, hardly enough for four actors to make an entry. And with its low ceiling, all the lights are in your face.

Sometimes, then, the best theatre happens in spaces, even in built spaces, which are not meant for theatre. This is not just the experience of India, or of poor/third-world countries alone. This is the experience all over the world. Theatre architects have written at length about how, as opposed to the movie hall, where comfortable seating is a pre-requisite—today, in premium multiplexes, the seats are so luxurious that I wonder how people don't fall asleep in them—in theatre you require a little bit of discomfort, that is, the seating should not be so comfortable as to make people really relax.[2] It should be the kind of seating where your elbow touches your neighbour, where the spectator has to sit straight, sometimes even bend forward a little. Some of the best theatres in the world actually follow this as a conscious architectural design principle.

But I am not going to talk about the 'built' theatre. As someone who does street theatre, I am going to talk about the 'unbuilt' theatre—the city as theatre. Sometimes this can be literally true. Like recently, where I come from, Delhi, the entire city, it appeared transformed into a grand stage for a theatre of protest. It was exhilarating to see so many people out on the streets, protesting, occupying various spaces within the city, turning them into spaces for protest and for the art of protest. It was street theatre of a kind, on a grand scale, utterly spontaneous, unscripted, and all the more beautiful for it.

I do street theatre that is scripted and rehearsed—for the most part, at any rate.[3] Today street theatre is fairly ubiquitous, and most of us are likely to have seen a street play performance at some point in our lives. But there was a time when street theatre was not so common. In the mid–1970s, this thing that we call 'street theatre' today didn't really exist. It was groups like Jana Natya Manch (Janam) in Delhi and Samudaya in Karnataka which pioneered the form of modern street theatre that we know today. The main impulse behind this theatre was not so much an artistic or aesthetic but an immediate, political impulse. This kind of theatre was a direct response to the Emergency, imposed by the Congress government from 1975 to 1977. It is interesting that both Jana Natya Manch and Samudaya, the pioneers of this form, performed their first plays, *Machine* by Janam and *Belchi* by Samudaya, in the same year, 1978; in fact in the same month, October. It was not as if they were corresponding with each other; in fact, each first saw the other group's plays only about three years later. So it's interesting that in two different parts of India, unknown to each other, young people 'invented' this form, simultaneously. I say 'invented', not because street theatre had not been done anywhere else in the world before, but because they invented it for themselves. In other words, they had never done this kind of theatre before. They had done theatre which was more formal, involving a stage—whether this was a pro-scenium space or in the open, the audience was essentially on one side. Stage theatre comes with a backstage, green rooms, and so forth. Street theatre changed all of that. In street theatre the actor is in the centre and the audience is all around her. Therefore, there is no notion of a backstage or a front curtain, or of an exit or an entry. Of course, there is still the notion of an entry and exit theatrically speaking, but the idea of the actor being hidden in the wings and then revealing themselves by their entry does not exist in street theatre. All the actors are always seen.

What I find fascinating is this. In a street play, when the audience is sitting in a circle and watching the play in the middle, the audience on any side is able to see the audience opposite them as they watch the play. Yet when we are actually watching the play, we don't see that audience. That audience which is on the other side of the acting area becomes invisible to us because there is something happening in the circle that occupies our attention. We stop seeing beyond; we stop listening to extraneous noises. One reason why recordings of street theatre on video are terrible is because one suddenly realises how much extraneous noise there is. It's amazing how when we are actually watching a street play, all of that seems to disappear. The human body is actually a very bad conductor of sound. Now when a built theatre is filled up with human bodies, the actor has to project her voice in order to reach the last person. In street theatre also, of course, the actor has to project her voice, and so training in voice culture is very important. But what happens is that the extraneous noise of the city is somehow sealed off if you are able to create a circle of spectators. In such cases, if the circle of spectators is three to four rows deep, then there is a way in which a well of relative silence can be created in the middle of the circle, even as the noisy city enfolds us (see Figure 1).

Figure 1 *A photograph of Janam performing in the early 1980s. When spectators gather around the actors in a tight circle three or four rows deep, it helps create a well of relative silence in the middle, aiding acoustics.*

Source: Photo courtesy Jana Natya Manch.

There has been much comment about the fact that these kinds of performances, which occur in spaces not normally meant for performance —in other words, spaces where people work, live, commute, shop and so on, what performance studies discourse might call 'found space'— convert such spaces temporarily into theatrical space, and, in a sense, 'stop' time. Time stops because the people who are passing by, going about the business of their lives, stop and watch the play, and then carry on with their lives. But I find it fascinating how, outside this play of space and time, there is also the play of sound, how one can create a circle or well of relative silence in the middle of the acting area. In this well, the human voice can traverse quite strongly, and one can play with silences in a way that seems counterintuitive.

I say counterintuitive because, in a number of plays, for instance, plays done by students in universities, the assumption is that you have to be loud. Because the city is so loud, performers have to be louder still, since that is the only way to catch the attention of spectators. In our experience, however, we have found the opposite. Of course one needs strong voices, but we find that if we work with silences, it some- times works better because we are able to get the audience to focus in quite a special way. To be able to communicate through silence is an important skill to learn if you do street theatre.

Even though it's called street theatre, we actually don't like to perform on a street, because of the noise and the hustle-bustle. In the performance in Figure 2, for instance, the man driving by in a tow- truck decided that he had the best seat in the house, so he stopped his truck right on the road and started watching the play. Within half a minute, we had a traffic jam and people were honking. I had climbed up somewhere on a ladder to take this picture, and I had to rush down, run to him and request him, 'Bhaisahab please *thoda aage ho jaiye, peechhe* traffic jam *ho raha hai*' (Sir, please could you move up ahead a little, there is a traffic jam behind you). A little reluctantly, he did move, and the play carried on. That's the beauty of street theatre—you can really do street theatre almost anywhere.

Not all street theatre happens in localities or areas that are poor. A lot of it can also happen in spaces that are not-so-poor. Figure 3 is a photograph of a performance on the front steps of the Reserve Bank

Figure 2 *Janam performing in NOIDA*
Source: Photo courtesy Jana Natya Manch.

Figure 3 *Janam performing outside the Reserve Bank of India*
Source: Photo courtesy Jana Natya Manch.

of India (RBI), on Parliament Street in New Delhi. I doubt very much if we would be able to do this today, given the present dispensation, but there was a time when we used to perform here regularly. It is a wonderful space, because with the stairs going up all the way, everyone can see clearly, but we could also use the stone wall at the back as a kind of a bouncing board for sound. We love spaces like these to perform.

The Empty Space is a famous book by Peter Brook, the great British theatre director who has been working in Paris for many years now. The book was published in 1968, and consists of four chapters, on 'The Deadly Theatre', 'The Holy Theatre', 'The Rough Theatre' and 'The Immediate Theatre'. The book begins with a striking sentence: 'I can take any empty space and call it a bare stage. A man walks across this empty space whilst someone else is watching him, and this is all that is needed for an act of theatre to be engaged' (Brook 1968: 9). In the 1960s, this was an arresting thought—that at the minimum, all you needed for theatre to happen was an empty space, one performer and one spectator.

The fact is, however, that there are no empty spaces. All spaces are spaces of contestation. This is especially the case in cities. For instance, in a Dalit *basti* (settlement) such as in Figure 4, the statue of Ambedkar is an act of assertion—an assertion that is political, social, and also spatial. It lays claim to space. This is why, across the country, every time that dominant groups have tried to put down Dalits, one of the potent ways of doing this has been by desecrating statues of Dr Ambedkar. Such a desecration is a symbolic reclaiming of space, or a symbolic effort to erase and deny space that has been won by Dalits through organising and struggle.

If you are performing in the city, if you are using the city as a space for performance, then you have to be alive to the fact that every space is a space of contestation, a space of assertion. Even the act of performing in front of the RBI only becomes possible when there is a strong Left trade union inside the RBI. I cannot go today and perform there just like that. For many years, even prior to 2014 when the Narendra Modi–led Bharatiya Janata Party government came to power, large parts of central New Delhi have been under Section 144, which forbids

Figure 4 *No empty space—all spaces are contested*
Source: Photo courtesy Jana Natya Manch.

the assembly of groups of people in specific areas designated by the administration. This is not very well known. There used to be a time when we could go and perform at the Boat Club lawns at India Gate whenever we wanted (Figure 5). In the winters especially, we would often go and perform at lunchtime because thousands of central government employees came here during lunch to play cards and lounge about. Today we cannot do this. It was as far back as 1992, after the demolition of the Babri Masjid, that the Boat Club lawns were made off limits for any kind of political protest or similar activity.

Which Delhi are we speaking of? Sohail Hashmi in his chapter writes about the different cities of Delhi, some of which became cities in the true sense, while others remained administrative centres or garrison towns. There are many, many cities, many parts of Delhi, and not only in the geographical sense. Sohail also mentions the move towards 'smart cities'—sealed-off enclaves of the rich, the elite.

Figure 5 *Janam performing on the Boat Club lawns, November 1988*
Source: Photo courtesy Jana Natya Manch.

Yet they also need people to work for them, and where are these people going to come from?

Figures 6a and 6b are pictures from a slum cluster called Kusumpur Pahadi. Kusumpur Pahadi has Vasant Vihar on one side, the Jawaharlal Nehru University (JNU) campus on another side, and Vasant Kunj on the third side. With these enclaves of relative affluence on three sides, it's interesting how Kusumpur Pahadi itself is completely invisible. It sits on top of a hillock, and you can drive past this slum cluster and never see it. It is literally hidden from view, and, to me, it has always been a kind of metaphor for the city itself: that you have large numbers of poor people, working-class people who keep the city going, and without whose presence the city would just collapse—these are the people made invisible in the city. That's the city that we try to reclaim through our street theatre. This is the city that we try to give a voice to.

Figure 7 is another picture from Kusumpur Pahadi, from a perfor-mance we held there. The act of performing in such spaces is fundamentally a democratic act, because we are laying claim to a space,

(a)

(b)

Figure 6 *Janam actors walk to the performance space in Kusumpur Pahadi, New Delhi*

Source: Photos courtesy Jana Natya Manch.

Figure 7 *Janam performs in Kusumpur Pahadi, New Delhi*
Source: Photo courtesy Jana Natya Manch.

saying that voices have validity, that no voices can be suppressed and erased. But there is also a very lovely and not-so-exalted way in which the democracy of the street takes over. I love how, for instance, animals walk through your acting area. I love how children sit and enjoy the play. When they lose interest, they start playing with each other. I love how women stand around and, at whatever time they need to go home to cook or do housework, they just leave.

So, what I love about street theatre—apart from the act of performing itself, which I, being an actor, absolutely love—is also this lovely democracy of a lack of etiquette. There is a particular etiquette that marks the conventional theatre, where we go to watch a play, having bought our tickets, and take our seats in a row of 10–15 people. We might not like the play, we might be bored by it—yet we don't just get up and walk away. It's even worse if the performers are your friends—you have to even go backstage after the performance and say fake, polite things like 'Really interesting, how did you think of this,' or 'Wow, that's a lot of work you put into that,' so that you say something that sounds nice but you don't actually say you liked it. We are constrained by the conventions, the etiquettes of bourgeois theatre. The whole thing is too damn polite—but only on the surface, because in our head we are cursing. Street theatre does not participate in these conventions. It is truly democratic. In street theatre, spectators vote with their feet. If the play works, they stay. If the play doesn't work, they walk away. I think it's really lovely that you have this kind of an open space where anybody can come, where there are literally no barriers—social, economic, cultural, political—against anyone watching and enjoying an act of theatre.

The choice of where you perform and how you perform will also dictate the choice of what play you do, whose stories you tell. The photograph in Figure 8 is from a performance in Sahibabad in Ghaziabad, Uttar Pradesh, bordering Delhi. In an industrial area called Site 4 Industrial Area in Sahibabad, there is a very large factory, which was recently declared bankrupt, with the owner being sent to prison. Now, this factory specialised in processing scrap metal from across the

Figure 8 *Performing outside the scrap metal factory, Ghaziabad*
Source: Photo courtesy Jana Natya Manch.

world; the metal was segregated, smelted, and so on, and then reused. Now, since it is in war zones that the largest volumes of scrap get produced, there are these containers shipping scrap from Iraq, Afghanistan, and so on, into countries like India, and the metal is segregated in factories like these. Now, the scrap that comes in consists not only of construction material from demolished and destroyed buildings, but also a lot of war debris, which includes artillery shells and other ammunition. While most of this ammunition is just empty shells, the scrap includes live shells that for some reason don't explode, and they get shipped all the way here. And when they are being offloaded or processed, they explode, leading to deaths. There have been at least two recorded instances of workers dying at this factory.

A worker from this factory told us this story, which we then converted into a play. He told us about an injured worker who is taken to the hospital, where he dies. Another worker is sitting there and crying, and when the trade union people go to him and ask, 'Why are you crying? Who is he to you? Who are you? How are you related to him?' he says, 'No no, nothing, it's all fine. I'm okay.' And then a friend of his goes up to him and says, 'Why are you saying this? These are union people, they'll stand by you, they'll fight for you. Tell them who you are.' And he says, 'Yes, I am his brother.' Now, this terror of losing one's job forces a man to deny that the dead man is his brother. This is a story that we have to tell, not just because of its human poignancy, but also because it comes to us as a result of the choice we make in terms of deciding what spaces we choose to perform in.

Sometimes spaces also disappear. Figure 9, for instance, is a picture from a large slum cluster that used to be located right next to the Yamuna River, adjacent to Nigambodh Ghat. A number of the slums in central Delhi or nearby have been demolished in efforts to 'beautify' the city, and people living there have been thrown out. This particular performance took place literally just one month before the entire slum was demolished.

In Figure 10, as you can see, there's a main road on the far side, where you can see buses. On the near side, behind the (invisible) photographer, there is a railway line. And behind the railway line is the Okhla Industrial Area. Workers get off the bus on the main road and

Figure 9 *This slum no longer exists*
Source: Photo courtesy Jana Natya Manch.

Figure 10 *Performing* Machine *in a loop*
Source: Photo courtesy Jana Natya Manch.

walk to their factory, crossing the railway line. We performed our play on this path with temporary shops, which is not even a paved road because we knew that the workers use this path to get to work and back. But because it's a thoroughfare, we knew that nobody would linger there for any length of time. So the challenge was to grab their attention in this little time. Normally, we talk to the audience a little bit before the play, introduce ourselves and the play, speak a bit about why we've come, and so on. This gives the time for the audience to settle down and be comfortable. Here, though, we had to dispense with all that and get right down to the performance. The play we did is called *Machine*, and it's a powerful and short play—just 13 minutes long! So we ended up doing eight performances one after the other, with barely any gap, as if on a loop. For every performance, we'd have a new lot of workers. I like to think of this as a kind of drive-through street theatre—except that nobody in the audience has a car!

As I said earlier, all spaces are spaces of contestation: they are socially contested and therefore politically charged. Figure 11 is from Parliament Street, at a protest of survivors and victims of the Bhopal gas tragedy. They have come to Delhi numerous times over the decades, and it is a shameful blot on our republic that they have not got justice. We have performed for them as a mark of solidarity on numerous occasions, both in Delhi and in Bhopal. On one of these occasions, we suggested doing something together with them. They said, 'Well, what can we do? We are not actors.' We said, 'Let's stage something.' So in the photograph, the women who are sitting and mourning and the 'bodies' under the white cloths are all actual survivors of the gas tragedy. We invaded an intersection on Parliament Street without any warning, taking the traffic and pedestrians by surprise. We had sent out invites to the media in advance, but even they didn't know what was going to happen. The actors wearing masks moved silently amongst the 'dead bodies' and the grieving people. It became a spectacle, holding up the traffic and getting media attention. But what was interesting was that because it was wordless, silent, and because the image created was poignant, the police found it hard to be rough with us. In the past, on numerous occasions, for different causes, we have been hounded out by the police. But the fact that the 'actors' included the real victims and survivors of the gas tragedy made things hard for the police.

Figure 11 *Occupying a busy intersection in New Delhi with victims and survivors of the Bhopal gas tragedy playing themselves*
Source: Photo courtesy Jana Natya Manch.

And, mind you, this is the Delhi Police, not exactly a shining beacon of civic compassion. There was something particular to *those* bodies, of the victims and survivors, that made it hard for the police to use their batons and water cannons on us.

Figure 12 is a photograph of JNU's Azadi Chowk. As is well known, JNU has been under siege for the last five years. The students, teachers, and *karamchari*s (staff) of JNU have led a valiant struggle to keep alive the spirit of intellectual inquisitiveness, the spirit of criticality. One of the physical spaces that has come to symbolise this struggle is what has been christened the Azadi Chowk (Freedom Square), right outside the vice chancellor's office. The play we performed was *The Last Letter*, based on Rohith Vemula's final note. In Janam, as in the rest of the country, everyone who read that note could not help but be deeply moved by it. We converted that note, along with anti-caste poetry, into a performance. So this was an act of bearing witness in a double

Figure 12 The Last Letter *by Jana Natya Manch, being performed at Azadi Chowk, Jawaharlal Nehru University, New Delhi*
Source: Photo courtesy Jana Natya Manch.

sense—on one side, it bore witness to the JNU struggle, and on the other to Rohith Vemula's institutional murder.

Figure 13 is a picture of a performance at Dr Ambedkar Park in a place called Jhandapur, in Sahibabad, Ghaziabad. We had gone there to perform for the Centre of Indian Trade Unions (CITU) on 1 January 1989, when we were attacked by anti-social goons who wanted to suppress the workers' struggle. Two people were killed in the attack. One was a worker called Ram Bahadur, and the other was an actor called Safdar Hashmi.[4] Safdar died in a Delhi hospital on 2 January 1989. On the next day was his funeral, an incredible moment when 15,000 people spontaneously came out into the streets of Delhi to march as a mark of protest. Then on 4 January, less than 48 hours after Safdar had died, we went back to the same space—the actual location of the attack—and performed the play that had been interrupted three days earlier. This is a photograph of that performance—to my mind, perhaps the single most important street theatre performance in the history of India. The fact that Janam was led by Moloyashree Hashmi,

Figure 13 *Janam, led by Moloyashree Hashmi (extreme right), returns to the very spot where Safdar Hashmi was killed less than 48 hours after his death, to complete the interrupted performance of* Halla Bol *on 4 January 1989*

Source: Photo courtesy Jana Natya Manch.

actor, organiser, and Safdar's wife, made it more symbolic still—not to mention stirring and inspirational. Subsequently, every year on 1 January, we go back to Dr Ambedkar Park, Jhandapur, Sahibabad, and perform. Over the years, this has become a huge affair, with thousands of workers turning up with families and children to enjoy the play and be part of what is more a people's festival than a political rally. In this way, thousands of workers, along with theatrepersons, lay a claim to Jhandapur and its radical history.

I will end with these questions: What does it mean to perform in non-empty space? If spaces are not empty of meaning, of histories, of contestation, what does it mean to perform in these spaces? I have offered some examples of what it might mean, but of course there are so many other ways in which we can infuse meaning into non-empty spaces. But we can only do so if we are aware of the struggle around these spaces, and if we are partisan with respect to it. If there is a contestation, we cannot be neutral in that contestation; we have to take a partisan position.

It does not matter whether or not one is a victim or a survivor. We cannot choose our histories. We are who we are, and we can choose who we want to become.

NOTES

1   For more on the theatre spaces of Bombay, see Gokhale (2015).
2   See, for example, Mackintosh (1993).
3   For more on street theatre, see Deshpande (2007) and Hashmi (1989).
4   For more on Safdar Hashmi, the attack, and the early history of Jana Natya Manch, see Deshpande (2020).

REFERENCES

Brook, Peter. 1968. *The Empty Space*. New York: Scribner.
Deshpande, Sudhanva (ed.). 2007. *Theatre of the Streets: The Jana Natya Manch Experience*. New Delhi: Janam.
———. 2020. *Halla Bol: The Death and Life of Safdar Hashmi*. New Delhi: LeftWord.
Gokhale, Shanta (ed.). 2015. *The Scenes We Made: An Oral History of Experimental Theatre in Mumbai*. New Delhi: Speaking Tiger.
Hashmi, Safdar. 1989. *The Right to Perform: The Selected Writings of Safdar Hashmi*. New Delhi: SAHMAT.
Mackintosh, Iain. 1993. *Architecture, Actor and Audience*. London: Routledge.

Chapter 2

'Belonging' in a City of Unbelongers

Namrata Toraskar

Wind-blown hair undone from the hair band,
loosening itself in the light cold,
breathing its own bat.
Amidst early-morning snores, whispers and grunts,
the cramped backpack gets shuffled,
comforting the tired legs on the upper berth of the bus.
The body adjusts with exaggerated suspirations,
synchronising with the vehicle's squeaky wheels.
The spindles of the 18-hour road journey unwind deliberate considerations to
    move to Mysore
and whorl on the shores of memories from Mumbai.
Memories that escape indwelling and which throw upon the windowpane the
    arrivals:
of engagements, compromises, of reflections, of judgements, of discussions, of
    dialogue.

'Bombaiyyy Girlaaa?'—a pertinent question from my middle-aged Mysorean landlady who not only immediately paints a certain degree of fantasy and insouciance about the world I had departed from, but also questions my ability to belong in her quaint, orthodox *mohalla*.[1]

Her *mohalla*, her territory saw a lesser frequency of new arrivals than that of departures. Fuelled by my ruffled tight T-shirt that read 'Yours truly' and an over-sized skirt, her fire of curiosity about my arrival in her *mohalla* was soon doused by the fresh aromas of filter coffee in steel tumbler that she soon offered and the ominous ticking of an ancient grandfather clock, peacefully shoving the heavy wheels of time and change.

———

My world of arrival is Krishnaraja Mohalla in Mysore. Reminiscing about the time bygone, the landlady gloats,

We are from the city of maharajas & palaces.
We had gold that shone to the southern sun,
Our glory glinted in our eyes as the anointed elephants strode our streets,
We amused ourselves under the wide, arched courtyards.
We worshipped Chamundi with hopes and a full heart.
Ours was a singular song in a singular voice.

Now, it is only the landlady's singular voice that has been conversing since I occupied their upper-storey apartment christened as her son's 'marriage flat'. With her son working in an IT multinational in Bengaluru and husband hushing her voice, hers is a quintessential household typical of Mysuru, wherein the youth often venture out to Bengaluru in search of lucrative jobs.

———

My world of departure happens to be Bombay-Bambai-Mumbai however one relates to it. While trying to strike a conversation of familiarities, the landlady paints a fantasy picture of the city of dreams,

Sky-rocketing apartments having windows opening to the pristine Arabian sea,
Amitabh Bachchan waving from his Jalsa balcony to the vada-pav[2] *eaters and*
*   chai-drinkers across the street.*

Indeed, Mumbai is a fantasy city in which the fundamental aspect of 'dwelling' thrives on a culture that is formed out of images which have no connection to the ecological, historical and social context of the city. Just glance at the humungous billboards put up by the builders, developers of the upcoming luxurious skyscrapers while commuting along the Western and Eastern Express Highways of Mumbai. There seems no stone left unturned to project the xBHK ($x = 1$, 1.5, 2, 2.5, 3 ...) apartments untouched by reality to the aspiring 'arrival' in the city.

It is also a city of negotiations as the 'arrival' gets used to the black hole of the *chalta hai*[3] attitude. Daily conventions—like the fourth seat in train travel which allows only a single buttock to rest on a bench built for three—force an acknowledgement of other people's needs. The daily commute from Bandra station to a sprawling 21st-floor glass-walled corner office in BKC takes one through faeces on sidewalks and sidewalks on streets. But yeah, such habitual observations are happily brushed aside at the arrival in the sparkling BKC office keeping the stench of the adjoining, choked Mithi river away but still 'reflecting sunlight back and forth into infinity' (Lopez 2019). Such behavioural negotiations of utilisation and occupation further feed on the spatial narratives of dwelling that are offered involuntarily to the arrivals in Mumbai.

Owing to the economic fluidity in the city of Mumbai, the visual culture propagated through hoardings, advertisements and apartment apps shapes the urbanity and marks certain dwelling geographies, often of a rental nature, accompanied by a set of evolved spatial and dwelling narratives catering to the offer of a feel of 'belongingness to the unbelongers—the new set of arrivals'. The narratives of the unbelongers referred to herein are not through the accounts of migrant labourers, hawkers or slum neighbourhoods but though the lens of educated, middle-income groups migrating into new cities with aspirations bigger and better.

Capturing the dwelling trends in Mumbai, what call for a deeper examination are the questions of perceptions of dwelling here. How has the visual culture of these places shaped the current notions of dwelling within them? Adopting Ingold's (2000) dwelling perspective, how does the dwelling environment embody these notions? Does this idea of 'dwelling' thrive on visual images unconnected to the ecological, historical and social context of the city? And, most importantly, how do such shifting geographies feed into the local and global dwelling perceptions of these cities—is it an evolved sense of belongingness or alienation that is left behind?

Located at the intersection of visual culture and the acts of dwelling, this chapter questions the idea of 'belongingness' that is propagated through the city's visual culture. The chapter is centred around the concept of 'image production' of dwelling processes and the relationship of the mechanisms of image production to the perceptions of dwelling in a city. The focus herein is on the tools of popular image production, that is, literature and visual and mass media. These media reinforce the image produced, till it is established as the defining image of a dwelling process eventually leading to habituation of the portrayed image for the city dweller—both the natives as well as the new arrivals.

Though this popular image production enhances a few chosen patterns in dwelling processes, more often it leads to neglect and degradation of others. So, in the context of a city's survival, how can harmony be created between elements for ensuring a continuity of patterns that nurture a city's growth in tandem with its ecological and social context?

Based on Heidegger's idea of dwelling, Tim Ingold in his book *The Perception of Environment* (2000: 186) describes the 'dwelling perspective' as follows: 'the forms people build, whether in the imagination or on the ground, arise within the current of their involved activity, in the specific relational contexts of their practical engagement with their surroundings.' Now a question that arises here is whether the city dweller's practical engagement with the surroundings is of an inclusive and sharing nature, or of an exclusive and possessive nature, and in this context, how does the idea of belongingness evolve?

Weaving the warp and weft of the narrative across accounts both personal and from anecdotal sources on the city of Mumbai, the chapter attempts a reflective deliberation on the identities of a dwelling, the sense of shifting city dwellers' geographies and their belonging in the winds of unbelongingness.

Holding the country in a state of thrall for hundreds of years, Mumbai has many varied cities within 'Mumbai'—

there is the city of high-rises and the city of shanty towns,
the city of derelict mills and the city of flashy malls,
the city of *koliwadas*[4] and the city of Bollywood,
and also, the binary of the city of *adivasis*[5] and the city of Devendra
    Fadnavis.[6]

Naresh Fernandes in his book *City Adrift* (2013) describes Mumbai as a metropolis reclaimed from ocean and iniquity that has effortlessly manufactured the dreams that captivated a nation and drew fortune-seekers to it by the millions. Over a period of time, the seven conjoined islands that the city is comprised of were occupied by the most varied set of people from the Indian subcontinent. The cocktail culture that was thus created was a product of their heterogeneity eventually rendering the city its unique brio.

Mumbai's heterogeneous nature however would be glorified through catchphrases like 'City that never sleeps', 'City of Dreams', 'Mayanagari',[7] and so on. Are these catchphrases an epitome of our understanding of the city's reality or are they the manufactured reality pulling in thousands of people? Kaiwan Mehta, curator of *The Shifting City* (2019), calls this phenomenon the 'accumulation of arrival' (Mollan 2019).

In this atmosphere of arrival it is worth noticing, for a change, stepping back and understanding, the visual setting that is conjured up to trick the displaced fresh graduate from a smaller town, newlyweds working in call centres, into aspiring eventually to find a footing in the foreign land of Mumbai, to eventually feel belonging in the diaspora of unbelongers, into eventually 'thinking they've "arrived"' (Mehta 2019).

For months, years in fact, the newspapers have been trying to squeeze in warnings of the inevitable catastrophe that Mumbai has been burdened with owing to its population and pollution. In the year 2019, these warnings in the newspapers spiked due to the efforts of the Aarey activists against the metro car shed in the middle of Aarey Colony, located to the south of Mumbai's 1,300-hectare forested Sanjay Gandhi National Park. However unnerving these warnings could be, they are somehow 'contained in full-page advertisements aimed at getting people to pay outrageous amounts of money to actually live in Bombay' (Fernandes 2013).

Housing complexes christened as:

Marathon NexZone: Next-generation eco-friendly Xtra utility homes,
Marathon NexWorld: Buy with confidence,
Sai World Empire: Live like Kings & Queens,
Vasant Oasis: Reside on newer heights of happiness,
Lodha The World Towers: See Luxury in a Whole New Way, and
    so on.

The sparkling 3D projection of the building with an infinity pool on the uppermost deck, photographs of grinning families occupying the apartments, never mind that the building would further contribute to the city's concrete jungle and be built right on a reclaimed mangrove or next to a stinking, choked nullah, a chawl, a defunct mill or a slum.

The city of Mumbai is a prototypical site of anonymity and estrangement, it is a place

of frequent comings and goings,
of inclusions and of exclusions.

Feeling belonging can be difficult in a city, even more so for the newcomer—the arrival—who needs to negotiate his or her position on various aspects. Hence the dilemma of 'being without belonging' crops up: it is easy to feel isolated in the midst of the crowd and hence get lured by all the luxuries and promises that the visual culture around bombards one with. This culture propagated by the ubiquitous advertisements, hoardings and billboards conveys the city's culture of desire, how it changes, and the medium through which the aspiring arrivals are manipulated. The geographies in Mumbai that are shifted and created due to such arrival settings meant for the new-age unbelongers often play at the behavioural level to ensure that they feel and belong to a global economic and cultural network that Mumbai seems to offer. The city itself eventually becomes a visual language with a pictorial cacophony that the arrivals eventually become used to.

In 2011, the suburbs grew faster than the island city for the first time in history. There was a sudden surge of new IT arrivals in areas on the Kandivali-Malad-Goregaon link road stretch. For accommodating these new arrivals, certain geographies evolved through peculiar dwelling narratives—spaces of consumption and work—which saw a range of architectures to house malls, call centres, head offices and so on. The set of new infrastructures like the metro, commercial hubs, supermarkets, and townships in the suburbs of Goregaon, Malad, and the way they pull these arrivals into settling into compact high-rises, are an epitome of the city's recent flux—

the old is demolished to make place for profitable ventures, the FSI (floor space index) being traded as a commodity.

Also, to add to these dynamics, a mixture of faceless service systems such as home delivery systems, security systems, is formalised via apps to further distance the new arrivals from the city and its habitants.

The skyrocketing high-rises in the suburbs contain these unbelongers' interaction with lucrative club-house offers, jogging tracks on the podiums which are often left unused owing to the global time that their offices function for. The only unit that they are ultimately left with is within the four walls of their own homes. The owners are happy with the small parcel of air-space from their 21st-floor balcony looking out to the starry nights minus the stars. They are happy with headphones with blaring music in their ears oblivious to the chirps, chaos and everything around them. Happier still with lounge chairs and their armrests encrusted with Swarovski diamonds, interiors with fake fireplaces, feature walls made of imitation resin and plastic brick patterns, a painting of Niagara Falls or an autumn scene along the dining table wall.

Neither do such dwelling patterns hint at the home belonging to the land that it is built on, nor is any attempt made to bring the occupying unbelongers out of those walls and tinted windows for tuning them with the natural and cultural context of the surroundings. Well, not to forget the tag lines of the billboard and newspaper advertisements:

it is all in good faith,
all for a good cause,
all for living life like kings and queens,
all for residing on newer heights of happiness,
all for the well-being of their next generation—'the future inheritors
    of a dead metropolis' (Bhatia 2002).

The new developments in the suburbs of Mumbai seem to cater
through voluntary and involuntary attempts for changing dwelling
patterns to accommodate the shifting unbelongers and make them
feel as if they belonged. This entire spectrum of such shifting geographies resembles a hall of mirrors, some intact, some broken, squares
and shards that infinitely reflect their images back at each other, very
much like a shifting kaleidoscope that continuously conjures images
and perceptions of what it means to dwell and where it means to be
a belonger.

The dangers of such a shifting kaleidoscope for perceiving belongingness come into being when the spatial and cultural narratives of
the city start being morphed and reinforced by the bombardment
of mass and visual media. 'These means reinforce the image produced,
till it is established as the defining image of place, eventually leading to
habituation of the portrayed image' (Kumar 2016: 17). 'If we examine
the general laws of perception, we see that as it becomes habitual, it
also becomes automatic. So eventually all of our skills and experiences
function unconsciously—automatically' (Bartelt 2010). The image
production of the variety of consumerist objects one needs to own
and the life one needs to aim for, for feeling belonging, acts seductively
on India's middle class which starts believing that 'greed is good, that
empathy for the less fortunate is unnecessary, that extreme individualism
is a virtue' (Fernandes 2013).

If such a culture of images and the resulting individualism 'has official sanction it begins to justify its presence over time into a subjective
consciousness' (Bhatia 2002) and slowly starts seeping its way into the
cities' dwelling patterns which have no contact with their natural, social
and cultural contexts. Intervening in such morphed and multilayered
cityscapes of arrivals and departures often goes much beyond the

architecture fraternity with its narrowed and stereotypical reading, mapping and analysis of architectural typologies. The challenge of the hour in the context of reimagining cities lies in exploring alternatives for having dialogues not through the architect's lens, but minus it. A multidisciplinary mode of understanding and expression through means like theatre, art, literature and so on can be adopted for addressing the aspect of unbelongingness at its very core and, at the very least, trigger a question in the shifting unbelongers regarding the way the notion of belongingness is offered to them.

NOTES

1   The residential neighbourhood of Mysore founded by the Wodeyar Maharaja in proximity of the Mysore palace.
2   A vegetarian fast food dish native to the state of Maharashtra. The dish consists of a deep-fried potato dumpling placed inside a bread bun (*pav*) sliced almost in half through the middle.
3   Attitude of brushing off everyday things because people think they don't matter.
4   The fisherfolk colonies in Mumbai.
5   The aboriginal people residing in the forests.
6   This has reference to the proposed felling of 2,700 trees in Mumbai's Aarey Colony to make way for a Metro car shed by the former chief minister of Maharashtra, Devendra Fadnavis. What is in debate here is Fadnavis's binary claim that Aarey doesn't fall under the forest area in spite of the fact that it is the sole green pocket in the city, thriving with many species of flora and fauna and numerous forest tribes.
7   A colloquial reference to Mumbai as being a city of opportunities and dreams.

REFERENCES

Bartelt, G. 2010. *N. Scott Momaday's Native American Ideology in House Made of Dawn*. Lewiston: Edwin Meller Press.
Bhatia, G. 2002. *A Moment in Architecture*. New Delhi: Tulika Books.
Fernandes, N. 2013. *City Adrift*. New Delhi: Rupa Publications.
Ingold, T. 2000. *The Perception of Environment*. New York: Routledge.
Kumar, K., 2016. 'Defragmenting Patterns of an Imagined Landscape: Case of Melukote, Karnataka'. Ahmedabad: Faculty of Architecture, CEPT University.
Lopez, R. 2019. 'Mumbaiwale: Can you See Past the Clichés?' https://www.hindustantimes.com/mumbai-news/mumbaiwale-can-you-see-past-the-cliches/story-9GiHywINzA2JuHRjvfMNqN.html (accessed 2 September 2019).

Mehta, K. 2019. *The Shifting City*. http://www.tarq.in/wp-content/uploads/2019/11/2019_05_01-Domus.pdf (accessed 29 August 2019).

Mollan, C. 2019. 'Giving Shape to a Shifting City'. https://www.asianage.com/life/more-features/070419/giving-shape-to-a-shifting-city.html (accessed 28 August 2019).

Chapter 3

City
The Perceptual Field of Inspirations

Kiranmayi Indraganti

The idea of 'city' in relation to cinema has a history of less than 150 years. If one excluded cinema, the 'city' has been something like an elastic mass of interlacing, a sponge, for centuries, serving dynasties and democratic mandates. Cities have absorbed technologies, diffused chromatic fields of perception for their inhabitants to experience life on its exponential curve: with the entry of cinema, cities have truly become a project of modernity, bound by geographies and histories with imperialist, colonial influences and rationalisations from broad patterns of differentiation in society. They have emerged as peculiar phenomena of industrialised masses with tenuous links to traditional notions of homogeneity where the boundaries of class, caste, resources and religion have woven painful histories. Conversely, cities have also been liberating for the same reason—growth-oriented, mobile, and giving scope and hope to accommodate the 'high-class' and 'low-class' (modern/provincial), and all the agro-literate communities in between. With the widening net of technology, it can be argued that the city is more a 'position' than an apparent fixed entity (alone). The constant negotiation between opposing systems of masses and the individual, the spatial and temporal, the standard and the special has afforded cities this inconstancy as a departure from the traditional notions of fixity.

Into this nebulous entity enters cinema, a non-physical mode of entertainment and interaction.

The concern of this chapter is to examine the possibilities of the technology of cinema, its application to the context of filmmaking as a 'perceptual field of inspirations', to use an idea of Hugo Munsterberg, a twentieth-century film theorist, psychologist and philosopher. The very act of responding to a city forms the basis of this chapter, where young student filmmakers, in the act of filming in a community, recorded their inspirations of the city. Such responses to and encounters with the city of Bidar in north Karnataka unveiled multiple contexts of the city for their films, which this chapter ruminates over, drawing inspiration from student work that showcases a means to understand the 'city'.

Hugo Munsterberg uses the exceptionally useful idea of cinema as something that is made in the mind: all cinematic properties are mental, according to him, as perceptual fields of experience and inspiration. For Munsterberg (1916: 38), the mind is where the experience of any encounter lends motion to emotion. For a filmmaker, this encounter is both modern, calling for negotiation, and inspirational to use technology to record.

WHAT IS A CITY?

In *The Art of City Making*, Charles Landry gives a useful definition of the city:

> The city is a multi-faceted entity. It is an economic structure—an economy; it is a community of people—a society; it is a designed environment—an artefact; and it is a natural environment—an ecosystem. And it is all four of these—economy, society, artefact and ecosystem—governed by an agreed set of rules—a polity. Its inner engine or animating force, however, is its culture. Culture—the things we find important, beliefs and habits—gives the city its distinctiveness—its flavor, tone and patina. (2006: 6)

Landry believes that making cities is not a formula but an art and it can be done only by revitalising and by the use of culture. While on the one hand, there are increasing concerns about whether a city is viable, sustainable and an urban form, some scholars view its intangible nature as potentially 'intelligent': so, for example, an 'intelligent city' has social equity as its focus and solves issues through technology. And, importantly, adaptability is key to the intelligent city along with indicators to measure and monitor change to ensure long-term sustainability. The arguments around the city inspire utopic and dystopic visions of human existence (more comprehensively so, amid the scale and scare of COVID-19), yet cities are the most radical of outfits to challenge the human intelligence of binaries and its by-products. Cities are the most negotiated and mediated spaces just as any other modern enterprises are because they are 'rationalised' spaces.

'Modernity theory', Andrew Feenberg (2004: 73–75) points out, 'relies on the key notion of rationalization to explain the uniqueness of modern societies. Rationalization refers to the generalization of technical rationality as a cultural form, specifically the introduction of calculation and control into social processes with a consequent increase in efficiency' (ibid.: 73). However, this 'reduction' does not entirely serve its purpose due to its inadequacy to account for our relation to the world. Technology studies posit that there are multiple players in the creation of technology, and therefore it constitutes or is characteristic of social complexity. Feenberg explains further: 'Rationalization depends on a broad pattern of modern development described as the "differentiation" of society. This notion has obvious applications to the separation of property and political power, offices and persons, religion and the state and so on' (ibid.: 74). However, what is important here, as Feenberg points out, is that 'technology is a social phenomenon through and through, no more and no less significant than any other social phenomenon' (ibid.). This differentiation rationalises our life in cities to an unquestionable extent of satisfaction and contentment until control and calculation begin to fail, encouraging us to look for alternatives.

As modern entities of rationality, cities are neither exclusively technologically intelligent nor purely based on calculation and control, but they rely on internal relations of societies, *micro contexts*, as it were, that they inhabit, for growth. It happens with the help of technology or the market, either of which is socially specific. Arguably, cities are intertwined saturations of expansions, perceptions and historic memories, deeply engraved in colour, pattern and patina, as pointed out by Landry (2006: 6), quoted earlier. Both characterised by linguistic and regional specificities and as part of a larger, particular national history, north Karnataka and, within it, the city of Bidar, exemplify this 'position' curiously.

To start with, the city of Bidar did not originate as a settlement but as a negotiation for a capital city: as an alternative to Daulatabad, which was itself seen as a historical alternative to Delhi. Ahmad Shah Wali or Ahmad Wali al Bahmani, as the founder of the Bidar-based kingdom in the 1420s, considered several factors: economy, society, ecosystem and culture. Bidar promised a city for a new kingdom with a new polity. The subsequent years witnessed a pre-modern form of advancement and sophisticated understanding of quality of life. There was a rare confluence of arts, literary traditions and cultures, architecture, religious and social practices, despite political intrigue and the occasional upheaval.

Bidar was one of those early examples of pre-modern technologies travelling from Persia—a rationalisation that facilitated new engineering systems, water conservation methods, education systems and training centres. What could be more radical than having *taleem* (education or training) as a physical entity, as a block—embalming the memory of a philosopher or spiritual master? The old city of Bidar is divided into *taleem*s, as it were, and the film students were quickly cognisant of this distinct marking in their travels within the city. Bidar, one could argue, was a radical city at a time of expansionist politics of annexation and territorial gain, with an espousal of equanimity and the spirit of heterodoxy through its various forms of 'culture'.

To the thematic concerns of 'Silvern Motives', the undergraduate pre-thesis film project on syncretism, the historic city of Bidar proffered many possibilities: it took students close to various monuments, beliefs and practices, worship places, eateries and crafts and vocational centres to which almost all communities belonged. This opened a 'field of inspirations' for students to enter and document.

THE SEVENTH SEMESTER PRE-THESIS FILM PROJECT

The pre-thesis project (which spans the seventh semester of four months, a crucial learning period in the four-year professional undergraduate programme at Srishti) aims to fulfil various needs of film-major students by taking them through specific, critical components of film-making, including production management, production design, principles of film directing (among others), engaging in smaller hands-on exercises and investigating a new site of enquiry, in this instance, Bidar. The overall aim is to facilitate comfortable handling of technology, critical thinking about contexts and components of filmmaking, and strive for short, nuanced articulations of cinematic narratives—fictional and non-fictional. Here the learning methods include workshops, group work, classroom lecturing and discussions and readings of critical texts: print, aural and visual (see Figure 1).

Figure 1 *Framing the city*

Source: The Silvern Motives Project Group 2019.

The seventh semester film project thus alerted students to various possibilities of non-fiction and fiction filmmaking in specific contexts. For non-fiction, it attempted to engage a few webs of questions about *syncretism* in India through a journey of Bidar where research (and intervention) groups, importantly, Deccan Living Labs (DLL),[1] with Bidar-based teams such as Team Yuva, have been working with communities towards co-learning and co-creating frameworks for improved community experience. With a preliminary understanding of this research, the students had learned to explore issues and anxieties of modern life in Bidar, its surviving forms of art and craft. The larger argument here became: if there was a culture of inclusivity in India—the kind of inclusivity that one witnessed in Bidar, in its syncretic living—how would or could a young filmmaker approach and represent it? What does the learning space of a city do to students' understanding of the medium for an inspiration of its architectural, cultural and religious non-uniformity, its creativity and its various expressions and discontents (Figure 2)?

Figure 2 *The dargah of Ahmad Shah Wali in Bidar—from the film* Do Nadiyon ki Tehzeeb *by Niladri Mukherjee*

Source: The Silvern Motives Project Group 2019.

So, at the heart of the project was a city, its dissonances, 14 students, and their own ways of responding to diverse inspirations.

HUGO MUNSTERBERG

How does one encounter the question of the city—its peculiar modernity, history and pre-colonial technologies and rationalisations for film? The ideas and observations of Hugo Munsterberg, his film theory, on an emergent medium of the early twentieth century, are of compelling significance and value here. Munsterberg, identified as one of the founders of modern psychology, was an eminent philosopher, and in his well-known work *The Photoplay: A Psychological Study* (1916), he dwelt on the matter and means of 'photoplay'. His curiosity stemmed from his desire to learn about the medium of cinema with perhaps a question: 'What do I want to examine?' He identifies the development of the medium as being of two types: film's 'inner' and 'outer' developments, between the technological history of the medium and the evolution of society's uses of the medium. Munsterberg argued that technology had provided the body of this phenomenon, and society had animated it (that body), forcing it to play many actual roles. 'Without technology there would be no moving pictures and without psycho-sociological pressures, these pictures would sit un-projected in attics and museums. It is society's craving for information, education and entertainment that allows cinema to exist at all' (Andrew 1976: 18–19). The propulsion was from the first stage of toying with visual gadgetry to the second stage of serving important societal functions of education, information and construction of narratives, and finally to the seat of emotion—the human mind. Only when the gadget worked on the narrative capacity of the mind did the photoplay come into being, and through it the artistic wonders of film, for Munsterberg (ibid.: 19). At its primary level, the mind animates the sensory world with motion. 'The complex machinery (cameras, projectors and all processing gadgetry) producing intermittent still pictures has been developed to work directly on the raw material of the mind. The result is motion pictures' (ibid.: 21).

STUDENT FILMS

As one walked through the city of Bidar, along the marked spaces of monuments of tolerance and celebration, in the form of mausoleums, tombs, worship places, water channels and forts, one was struck by an inspiration to define the city. 'Could this really have been a city? Is it possible to have cities like this anymore?' All the 14 students asked similar questions with a different inclination while running from pillar to post to capture details of their films on Canon C100 cameras and H6N recorders. They had never seen in their young lives a Hindu/ Lingayat priest and a Muslim maulvi occupying a space of worship to prostrate before a tomb such as Ahmad Shah Wali's at Ashtur, outside Bidar. *Do Nadiyon ki Tehzeeb* (roughly translating as the Culture of Two Rivers) brings to life the culture of 'making' a city; what we have inherited as a good custom should be carried forward, affirm the characters in young filmmaker Niladri Mukherjee's film. City for the filmmaker is the quiet spaces of monuments that extol the lofty ideals of great minds.

In her youthful, asymmetrically nostalgic portrait, Maanvi Chowdary makes an effort to represent the city as a plaque of three tiles: a self-developed mosaic of small visual units, like three tiles to 'capture', while collaborating *with*, the city: She calls it, *The City: A Theatre, a Legacy and a Passion*. Maanvi's reflexes were more about the perception of past as a loss, where cinema theatres were beset by worn-out chairs, pulled upholstery, disturbed rows, humbly undecorated façade and less formally maintained ticket counters. Feroze Theatre, therefore, comes alive in a series of shots of 'fixity' and 'mobility' that covers the alleys, stairs, billboards, rusted chairs, electricity boards and bulky projectors as we move through the space of the theatre. The next visual unit shows a collection of objects of importance—antiquated, embalmed in history—as being more a burden to its collector Liaqat Ali Khan, than of any gain; she listens to his self-evaluation of wasted time in collecting the legacy and a lack of recognition from government. This asymmetrical rendition of the city was at the heart of the architecture of her documentary, which she identifies as a personal response to Bidar (see Coffman 2009). As a filmmaker, her struggle has been to find connections, until she decided to leave the camera alone to do its job of capturing what she perceived. Her editing, to this effect, was deliberately disconnected and unobtrusive (see Figure 3).

Another similar film titled *Ehsaas* (Experience) by Bornil Anurag attempts to rationalise the encounter with the city along the lines of the human body's sensory perception of deriving pleasure out of

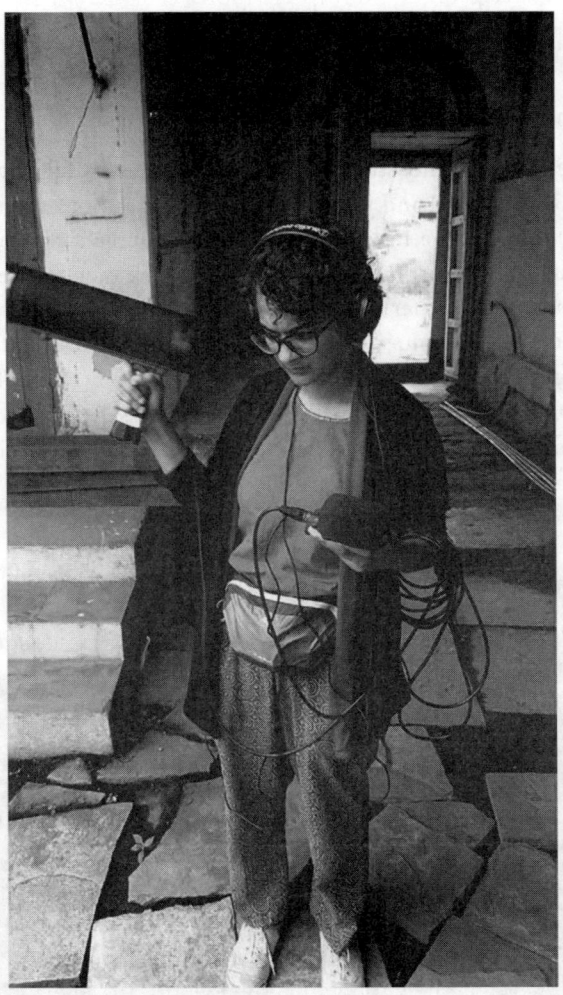

Figure 3 *Maanvi Chowdary checking the sound on location*
Source: The Silvern Motives Project Group 2019

external stimuli: as if a city could be animated as an embodiment of five senses. It could perhaps be argued or reckoned that a city *is about* five senses to evoke an emotional response. Bornil's images take one through the touch of Bidri craft, the taste of gurudwara langar food, the sounds of the city, the smell of incense inside Ahmad Shah dargah, and their 'connections'. The culture of the city is organised as a body that stimulates the mind and relentlessly animates it towards emotional responses. *Ehsaas* exemplifies the young filmmaker's striving to experience the city as a set of quiet oddities and subtle shifts: in flavour, colour and sound.

Nidhi Binu, another student, follows a shy brass-band player, a polyglot who leads the band, who declares that it is not easy to manage a girlfriend and to be in love. Her endearing subject flawlessly shows what is unique about his city: 'It's hassle-free, easier to live.' City, as Nidhi discovers with her funnily ironic hero, is a place where aspirations and dreams are harboured in its inhabitants' minds to transform them into a fuel to run mundane chores smoothly. Family, caste, friendship, community, one's professional group—all bind the individual to an abject surrender of dreams. The city is its people and their scape of dreams, as unspoken by their real life (Figure 4).

Figure 4 *Nidhi Binu and Sha Shwat filming a procession in Bidar*
Source: The Silvern Motives Project Group 2019.

Purnima Bhutoria solemnly follows the observance of the Moharram festival for her 19-minute film, *Razakar-e Muharram*, through different *taleem*s to discover that austerity significantly belongs to men; Aashrita Raju plonks herself amid a large male gathering of qawwali audiences, her own direct import of the Sufi musical form until then being from the Bollywood films, which quite contradicts this reality. Purnima identifies disparate sects in one seemingly unified religion, as Aashrita discovers the love of a city for a particular musical form. City is about its culture of in-memoriams, death and praising of the divine in song.

Srujana Dake traces the class divide between two households of over a hundred years of history. The city for her is the absorption of time by the walls and porches of old manors (Figure 5). Generations come and go, and the value of the house is determined (ironically) by the least experienced of the later generation, who prefer larger cities and refuse to live 'here'. Shalini Ray tries to map the missing histories of female aristocrats; Arjun Gonsalves cooks the dishes of nawabs and common people; Nisha Satpute sees rationale in the Lingayat struggle over identity politics and religious recognition. Nimisha Venugopal goes under the tunnel to film the water channelling system that the

Loving someone is not an ordinary thing to do

Figure 5 *A still from* Bidar ka Mauli, *a film by Nidhi Banu*
Source: *The Silvern Motives Project Group 2019.*

Persians brought five centuries ago which still works. Sha Shwat records the history of a history-writer, Samad Bharati, for whom Bidar is its history. Eshna Benegal's search for poetry and language moves through the uneven ground of gender politics, identities and questions of power. Jai Wadkar sees the struggle of potters, the Kubharas, in slushing through rainy waters while the wheel spins and shapes a moist jar to the resonance of their mythologies.

Figure 6 *All for a city*
Source: The Silvern Motives Project Group 2019.

CONCLUSION

As mentioned at the outset, examining the possibilities of technology (the gadgets of recording, its processes) in the context of filmmaking, in an act of responding to city, allows one to signify perception and inspiration as pivotal to representing external stimuli. The student films are creative ruminations about both the city and cinema, the origins of both being the seat of emotion, the mind: as a learning context, city is to film students as cinema is to city (Figure 6). This chain of perception expands curiously when a recorded reality embalms the history of the moment unequivocally.

NOTE

1   For more information about DLL, visit https://www.facebook.com/DeccanLabs/

REFERENCES

Andrew, J. D. 1976. 'Hugo Munsterberg', in *The Major Film Theories: An Introduction*, pp. 18–19. London: Oxford University Press.

Coffman, E. 2009. 'Documentary and Collaboration: Placing the Camera in the Community'. *Journal of Film and Video*, 61(1): 62–78.

Feenberg, A. 2004. 'Modernity Theory and Technology Studies: Reflections on Bridging the Gap', in P. Brey, A. Feenberg and T. Misa (eds), *Modernity and Technology*, pp. 73–75. Boston: MIT Press.

Landry, C. 2006. *The Art of City Making*. London: Routledge.

Munsterberg, H. 1916. *The Photoplay: A Psychological Study*. New York: D. Appleton and Company.

Chapter 4

Non-human Nature and City Life
Exploring the Radical Middle Ground

Savyasaachi

I know the city neither as an urban sociologist nor as an urban designer nor as an urban planner, but as someone who returned to live in it after spending several years trying to learn from forest dwellers about the forest universe as a living space.

I observed that all elements of the forest landscape—human beings, plants, trees, insects, rivers, mountains, hills, earth … and spirits, that is, human and non-human nature—were internalised in their mind, body, spirit and world view, to make up the being of forest dwellers. In their sparse homes, I found handmade objects for daily use. These did not weigh more than they could carry when shifting residence from one place to another.

In contrast I observed that the elements of non-human nature were either minimally present or totally absent in the urban landscapes and for this reason were not internalised to constitute the mind, body, spirit and world view of city dwellers. Instead, machine-manufactured material objects for daily use were internalised. These weighed several truckloads; several thousand times more than a city dweller could carry when shifting residence from one place to another.

Further, I observed that non-human nature was living, self-active, capable of self-regenerating and self-reproducing, and that machine-manufactured objects lacked these attributes, the limits of their life being set by the time for obsolescence. The worlds of manufactured objects are made from human effort. This effort is instrumental human labour or the work human beings do for wages. In contrast, the worlds of forest landscapes exist independently (are not a product of) of human labour. This world expresses the work of nature as reflexive labor. In contemporary English, 'labour' and 'labor' are used interchangeably, perceived to be alternate spellings with the same meaning: 'labour' in British English and 'labor' in American English. However, a close reading shows that there are two qualitatively different kinds of work that are clubbed, namely the work of nature—childbirth, the delivery of a baby—and manual physical work, wage labour. It is necessary to keep these distinct. Towards this end I use 'labor' to characterise expressive-reflexivity in the work of nature, and 'labour' for the instrumentality of wage labour.

A wholesome way of elaborating this distinction is by looking at the difference between H_2O and Water. These look alike and are necessary for metabolism. However, a closer look shows different metabolisms associated with each. H_2O metabolises industrial manufacturing systems and processes to generate large quantities of waste water that is poisonous for non-human nature (forests, plants animals …). The city is founded on the metabolism of H_2O. In contrast, Water metabolises to bring together the three realms of human and non-human nature—the Sky, the Earth and the Underground.

This difference determines different imaginations.

As a person or a group living in the forest mainstreams and moves to live in urban settlements (towns and cities), non-human nature (forest landscapes) shifts either to the periphery or is totally excluded from settlements and world views. Consequently their minds, bodies, spirits and world views are de-forested.

The teleology of de-forested beings works relentlessly towards the exclusion of non-human nature from settlements and world views. This radicalises urban life with progressive increase in toxicity, persistent social apathy and mounting grief.

The toxicity of everyday city life comes from the continuous release of pollutants into air, with depleting clean drinking water, with drying up groundwater and with the accumulation of non-recyclable waste. Cities are now the epicentre of toxicity and can be graded accordingly. The cumulative outcome is climate change and social degeneration.

Everyone in a city does not suffer similarly on account of toxicity. All classes do not contribute equally to the production and distribution of toxicity. These sharp, dramatic differences infuse toxicity into inter-personal and inter-community differences.

Toxic social relations generate persistent apathy across all classes and communities. For instance, in 2019, Delhi witnessed extreme congestion and pollution for the third year in a row. Children continue to suffocate from asthma every year in the city. It is common knowledge that water is heavily polluted. Consumerism in non-recyclable goods is proliferating. And, by and large, people learn to live with it—some with green technologies, some looking towards good governance, and the rest remaining ignorant of its seriousness.

Anonymity, an important attribute of city life, is a camouflage for grief, a condition to suffer in isolation. This anonymity is a mix of freedom and opportunity; security and vulnerability tempered with rumour, lies and deception. From here comes a propensity for radicalisation—to escalate social and cultural differences into conflict, conflict into violence and violence into fearsome terror. This manifests in fluctuations of city social life between two extremes: individual pursuit of self-interest to the detriment of the collective good; and the assertion of collective interest to the detriment of individual good.

The sum total of this radicalisation (with progressive increase in toxicity, persistent social apathy and mounting grief) is monopoly of the understanding that 'to be human is to disregard non-human nature' in social life. The non-negotiability of this understanding has become much more than dehumanisation, it is now irreverence for life.

Against this radicalisation a middle ground is created with the shifting of non-human nature to the centre of the urban world view. Here efforts are being made to see that the individual and the collective mutually benefit—to try and ensure what is good for the individual is good for the collective and vice versa. It is represented by people, randomly dispersed in urban spaces, who allocate time and space in their daily routine for care of the homeless and the abandoned living human and non-human beings (animals, plants, features of a natural landscape). This inclusion of non-human nature is a radical departure from radicalisations as it positions reverence for life at the centre of the world view. The time and space created with this inclusion are healing.

The potential of this radical middle ground comes forth with recognising that only when grounded in labor can the social division of labour 'continue' to fulfil our needs. Here it is acknowledged that the labor of non-human nature is the basis of our living-being on the one hand and that the objective world of things and people produced by human labour 'is nothing' without contributions from non-human labor. Recognition of this kindles an epic energy of compassion. It heals by detoxifying the mind, the body and the spirit. It is necessary for us to take this energy and legitimise inclusive social space and time.

Water metabolism is the foundation of this radical middle ground.

PART II

Palimpsest of Possibilities

Chapter 5

What Is a City

Sohail Hashmi

What exactly is a city? Is it just a large settlement? Is the size of the population living within a definable area the only criterion? Is it merely a centre of production, exchange and transport? How does one distinguish it from a village or a small town?

Such questions have engaged scholars cutting across diverse disciplines. Naturally, a large number of definitions of a city exist. Some definitions have relied on the demographics while others have taken into account systems of centralised civic administration, centres of production, centres of political power or the history of existence of an urban settlement cutting across centuries.

A city, however, can be all this and more. This 'more' can consist of many things, a history, for example of migration and exchanges—cultural, economic, technological and social—and the synthesis of all these into new expressions in a clearly defined area may define the emergence of a city. Let us explore this thought through Delhi.

It has been said that Delhi is the site of seven cities, namely Lal Kot or Mehrauli, Siri, Tughlaqabad, Jahanpanah, Ferozabad, Deenpanah or Shergadh, and Shahjahanabad. Indeed, some go to the extent of calling New Delhi the eighth city. Let us first look at these seven capitals closely and consider New Delhi later.

The first of the seven capitals was Lal Kot, also known as Mehrauli; the capital of the Slave Kings (1192–1290) and of Jalal-ud-Din Khalji (1290–96). This was followed by Siri, the new capital commissioned by Ala' ud-Din Khalji (1296–1316), established primarily as a fortified garrison town located at the present-day site of the Siri Fort Auditorium and Shahpur Jat. It was built to settle bulk of the Khalji army at one location to aid and ease quick movement against the Mongols who had begun their incursions into India from the late thirteenth and early fourteenth centuries.

The third capital to come up was Tughlaqabad, built by Ghazi Malik, an erstwhile Khalji governor of Punjab who took on the title of Ghyas-ud-Din Tughlaq (1321–25) after deposing Khusrau Khan, the last Khalji king. Mohammad bin Tughlaq (1325–50), son and successor of Ghyas-ud-Din, built the fourth capital of Jahanpanah, but he moved the capital to Daulatabad in the Deccan in 1329 and then moved back to Delhi in 1335. Mohammad Tughlaq's cousin Ferozeshah Tughlaq (1351–88) built a new capital and named it Ferozabad, popularly known as Kotla Ferozeshah.

Amir Temur sacked Delhi in 1398. After his departure three Syed kings ruled between 1398 and 1451; the last abdicated in favour of one of his commanders, Bahlol Lodi (1451–89). Bahlol was succeeded by Sikandar Lodi (1489–1517). Sikandar moved the capital to Agra and his son Ibrahim (1517–26) ruled from Agra before being defeated by Babur (1526–30). Babur ruled from Agra as well but his son, Humayun, brought the capital back to Delhi and built Deenpanah, the sixth capital. Humayun's son Akbar took the capital back to Agra in 1556.

The capital eventually returned to Delhi during the reign of Akbar's favourite grandson, Shahjahan, 92 years later in 1648. Shahjahan built one of the most magnificent capitals in the mediaeval world and named it Shahjahanabad, the seventh capital. Shahjahanabad remained the capital of the Mughals till 1857, when the British shifted the capital to Calcutta only to bring it back in 1912 and to eventually build the eighth capital.

Out of the seven medieval capitals, it is only the first—Mehrauli, or Lal Kot—and the seventh—Shahjahanabad—that remained capitals for long periods; the former for 104 years and the latter for 209 years. The very short life of the other five capitals ensured that these sites never had the time to even begin to resemble a city. Most of them were in fact deserted once the founder died or the successor chose to build another capital. The three Tughlaq kings, for example, raised three capitals within a span of 30-odd years. Clearly, none of them had the time or leisure to grow into a city.

Let us, thus, look at just Lal Kot or Mehrauli and Shahjahanabad to see if they meet the criteria—migration, trade, settlement and the coming together of diverse cultural resources—that we have laid down for a city.

Mehrauli developed into a city due to several reasons. It was not deserted when Ala' ud-Din Khalji built the garrison camp of Siri. The installation of the Iron Pillar, the expansion of the Jami Mosque, the start of the Alai Minar, the construction of the Alai Darwaza, the repairs carried out at the Hauz-e-Shamsi—all initiated in the reign of Ala' ud-Din Khalji—point to the fact that Mehrauli continued as the true capital. All this activity would have led to people of all trades and crafts flocking to Mehrauli.

The technology of building with rubble masonry, held together with a mixture of slaked lime and crushed bricks, was introduced to Delhi by the Turks and Central Asians in the late twelfth century. This would have led to the establishment of brick kilns and lime kilns. The true arch and the dome were introduced in the late thirteenth century and all this came together to transform architecture. The Indian mason began to be identified by the term *sangtarash*, and many terms for measurement, for weighing and for names of tools used by artisans in Persian, Turkish and other Central Asian languages became a part of the language spoken in the streets.

Mehrauli, thus, became a centre where different crafts that drew upon diverse resources began to come together. Turks, Persians, Uzbegs, Tajiks, Pathans, Moroccans, Ethiopians, Arabs, Armenians and others came to travel, trade and to settle down. They brought with them their own culinary traditions, which in due course mixed with the local food to evolve eventually into what became the Mughalia cuisine.

The Turks and the Central Asians also brought with them paper that they had learnt to make from the Chinese. They also brought the Persian wheel that had a profound impact on agriculture in a semi-arid region like Delhi. They brought the pit-loom and the spinning wheel and introduced the technique of carpet making. The art of glazing ceramics originating in China travelled through the Silk Route to Turkey and to the Central Asians who brought it to India—to Mehrauli.

The synthesis of diverse crafts and arts from Central Asia and South Asia led to the evolution of newer forms and techniques of building, weaving, and creating music. New attires emerged on the scene— *pairahan, qaba, jubba, dastar, shalwar, qameez, kurta* and the *paijama*. It was in Mehrauli that some of the first large-scale *karkhana*s (workshops) were set up to produce robes for the court. A large number of craftsmen belonging to different castes, religions, regions and linguistic groups worked together, perhaps for the first time, in large *karkhana*s. They began to learn from each other and to draw from all the languages they knew to construct a Creole that was to be known as Hindavi or Dehlavi, the ancestor of Rekhta, Urdu and Hindi.

All of this together marked the beginning of a new work culture and of what was eventually to develop into urban cosmopolitanism, something that has always been absent in a village.

The continuation of the settlement in Mehrauli through the reign of the Mamluks and the Khaljis contributed in no mean measure to helping the area develop into a city. This process was aided by an unlikely group of people—the Sufis. The shrine of Khwaja Qutub-ud-Din Bakhtyaar Kaaki and perhaps the even older Temple of Jog Maya ensured the continuing importance of Mehrauli despite the rise of Siri, Tughlaqabad, Jahanpanah and Ferozabad in quick succession. The fact that the two shrines are the focus around which the so-called Phool Walon ki Sair (the Procession of the Flower Sellers), started in the nineteenth century, is celebrated to this day clearly points to the continuing importance of Mehrauli.

The presence of the Sufis in Mehrauli continued to attract people from far and wide and many devotees and several Sufis began to settle down in this area. With them came new languages and new crafts. The kinds of cultural inputs being introduced through the Sufis were being reinforced through the arrival of large numbers of traders, artisans and others not only from different parts of the subcontinent but also from Turkey, Afghanistan, Iraq, Iran and parts of Africa like Ethiopia and Morocco among others.

Bakhtyaar Kaaki arrived in Delhi in the reign of Shams-ud-Din Altamash. Among the most important Chishti Sufis in India, he was the disciple and successor of Moin-ud-Din Chishti of Ajmer. Regarded as the patron saint of Delhi, he was the first Chishti to settle down in Delhi. It was at the hospice or *khanqah* of Bakhtyaar Kaaki that the qawwali in its nascent form began to evolve as the *qaul*. Many of the characteristic principles of the Chishti tradition, including love of music and keeping one's doors open for all faiths, were ideas that owe much to Bakhtyaar Kaaki. Bakhtyaar Kaaki was the preceptor of the highly venerated Fareed-ud-Din Ganj-e-Shakar or Baba Fareed, who in turn was the preceptor or *peer* of Nizam-ud-Din Auliya.

It is through the Sufis that the discourse of inclusion began to be propagated, just as it was being propagated by the *nirgun* poets of the same era—Kabir, Raidas and later *nirguni* saints like the Nathpanthis, Dadu, Namdev, Guru Nanak and others.[1]

The constant influx of Sufis and devotees led to the creation of a diverse range of facilities. Caravanserais, residential accommodations and shops catering to the daily needs of devotees began to come up. All this added further to the population mix and continued well into the nineteenth century when the rich and powerful of Shahjahanabad began to build their summer retreats in Mehrauli. Many Mughal-era and earlier buildings were cannibalised initially by the British and then by those who chose to imitate the colonisers. Mehrauli has, thus, seen ceaseless construction over eight centuries.

It needs to be asserted that cities have no native populations; they are made by migrants. A settlement that is composed only of the daughters and sons of the soil is a village. Any city that begins to divide its residents into natives and outsiders is no longer behaving like a city but is fast regressing into the opposite of the cosmopolitan.

Large-scale migrations resulted from conquests, but also from rural strife, famine, or from major political upheavals. Traders and artisans travelled to places where they saw good business or work opportunities. Sufis, preachers of new faiths, travellers and mendicants arrived to settle down and explore these new territories. The introduction of new products, skills and crafts and new philosophical ideas was a natural corollary. The transformation of a village into a city is thus a process that unfolds over time, a few hundred years at least.

If one were to remove all the migrants from Mehrauli, in fact from all of Delhi, we would be left with the natives of the villages of Delhi—Jats, Gujars, Sainis, Banias and Brahmins carrying on with age-old assigned roles and status. This would go on endlessly as long as an outsider does not bring in new technology and implements. Ideas of urbanism begin to grow only when two traditions establish a dialogue—the most essential ingredient in the recipe that transforms a village into a city.

Work on building Shahjahanabad began in 1639 and it was formally inaugurated in 1648. The trajectory followed by Shahjahanabad in growing from a capital into a city was radically different from the one that Mehrauli had followed. Mehrauli had grown from a small settlement, nestling on the eastern slopes of the Aravali. Shahjahanabad on the other hand came up as a capital with a palace fort surrounded by residential and commercial areas.

As opposed to Mehrauli that had grown gradually, Shahjahanabad was planned from the ground up. In Mehrauli, new residents arrived constantly and began to contribute to what was to become a city, but in Shahjahanabad, a readymade city culture was bought from Agra, along with a large urban population. Some of those who relocated had roots in this region; their ancestors had gone to Agra from here in the sixteenth century; their language and culture had mixed with that of Agra and was returning a hundred years later only to evolve further. The exchange between the two cities was common. Nazeer, the nineteenth-century people's poet from Agra, was born in Delhi. Meer and Ghalib, both quintessentially Delhi poets, were born in Agra but came to Delhi in their teens.

Shahjahanabad was a city that was organised along professions. Specific parts of the city gradually grew to house specialised activities, not unlike mediaeval cities all over the world. An idea of the crafts and professions that took root in Shahjahanabad can be gleaned from the names of its localities—Gali Sangtarashan, Gali Gandhi, Kucha Qabil Attar, Gali Saqqe Wali, Gali Hakimji, Gali Bataashaan, Gali Kababiyan, Gali Jootewaali, Sirkiwalan, Chooriwalan, Suiwalan, Gadhey Walan, Ballimaran, Dareeba Kalan, Kinari Bazar, Qasabpura, Chawri Bazar for paper and kitchenware and now hardware and wedding cards, Naya Bazar for grains and lentils, Khari Baoli for nuts, dry fruits, spices, pickles and preserves and so on, Nai Sarak for bridal finery, sewing machines, second-hand books, stationery and art material. Some of these businesses are of relatively recent origin but have, nonetheless, been around for a while to be built into their own traditions.

When Akbar moved the capital to Agra, he had begun a major project of patronising Braj and commissioning large-scale translations from Persian into Braj and from Sanskrit into Persian. The language of Delhi had also travelled to Gujarat, Maharashtra and the Deccan in phases and was to return to Delhi as Deccani, enriched by words, expressions and literary forms that drew from Gujarati, Malvi, Telugu, Marathi and from Persian poetic forms like the *masnavi*, the ghazal, the *marsiya* and the *qaseeda* as well as the *barahmasa* and the *nakh-shikh varnan*.

As the capital shifted from Agra to Delhi, so did those associated with the court. Shahjahan made provision for scholars of Sanskrit and Persian to be on hand to translate old documents and records from Sanskrit to Persian. People who knew both languages—Kashmiri Pandits, Kayasths, Khatris, Sindhis, Multanis and others—shifted too. Khatri traders, both Hindu and Muslim, shifted from Punjab especially in the late seventeenth and early eighteenth centuries. Afghans who traded in dry fruits and nuts came every winter and stayed through winter to lend money for short duration on high-interest loans, before returning home—a practice that continues to this day.

Shahjahanabad attracted the finest calligraphers, miniaturists, poets, skilled craftsmen and others that included yogis, Sufis and travellers from far and wide. The French traveller and jeweller Tavernier and the French physician Bernier were in Delhi in the reign of Shahjahan and Aurangzeb. They saw and wrote about the city, its court life and the empire, and it is through their writings that we get an idea of the intellectual engagements of the educated elite of the city with European philosophical concerns of the time and the efforts made by the Europeans to understand the Yogic and Sufi traditions of India.

The Indian style of Persian poetry (Sabk-e-Hindi), only recently recognised by Iranian scholars as an important school of Persian poetry, evolved in Shahjahanabad. Those who wrote this Persian were not only those mentioned above like Abdul Qadir 'Bedil', Shah Mubarak Abru, Siraj-ud-Din Ali Khan-i-Arzu and Shah 'Hatim' but also Kayasths, Sindhis, Multanis and Kashmiris, including Girdhar Das who translated the Ramayan into Persian, Chandra Bhan Brahmin who authored a biography *Chahr Chaman*, Banwari Das Wali, associate of Dara Shikoh and author of a mystical anthology and a philosophical *masnavi*, Mathura Das who authored an anthology and two *masnavis*, Lala Shivram Das, Lala Amanat Rai 'Amanat', Lala Sukhram 'Sabqat', Basawan Lal 'Bedaar', Anand Ram 'Mukhlis', Vrindavan Das 'Kosgo', Laala Tek Chand 'Bahar', Sialkoti Mal 'Vaarasta' and Har Gopal 'Tafta', disciple of Mirza Asad Ullah Khan 'Ghalib'.

The other major development, rather the most significant, was the evolution of Urdu. It had started in Delhi in the thirteenth century, had travelled to Gujarat, Maharashtra, the Deccan and Karnataka with the Khaljis, the Tughlaqs and Sufi derveshes like Banda Nawaz Gesu Daraz, and had returned as Deccani in the eighteenth century through the earthy poetry of Wali Deccani or Wali Gujarati. Deccani then grew from the mixed language or Rekhta of the time of 'Bedil', 'Abru', 'Arzu' and 'Hatim' to become the language of literary discourse through the writings of Meer, Sauda and others in the eighteenth century and Ghalib, Momin, Zauq and a galaxy of others in the nineteenth century and later.

Shahjahanabad was a city with its own way of life, language, cuisine, literary and musical tastes, its own crafts, produce, its own working class, markets and educational institutions. It had many madrasas and pathshalas where, aside from religious matters, secular disciplines like mathematics, geography, calligraphy, languages, logic and philosophy were also taught. The foremost among them was the Madrasa Ghazi-ud-Din Haider, set up in 1692, an institution that continues 327 years later, today, as the Delhi College.

It is the mixing of people, their languages and cultures, an unending influx in search of enhanced status, livelihood or for spiritual solace that creates a city. This is how two of the seven capitals became cities.

And this is why the eighth capital did not become a city. New Delhi was designed to be a showpiece. It was never meant to be a city. A city has to have a resident population—New Delhi had none; there were the white Sahebs who came for a fixed tenure while the natives all lived in Shahjahanabad and came into New Delhi to work and returned to Shahjahanabad in the evening.

New Delhi continues to be like that even today. The only permanent residents are the cooks, gardeners, drivers and other household staff of the ministers, senior bureaucrats and top brass of the armed forces. The officers, ministers and members of Parliament arrive and depart; none of them live in New Delhi permanently. Those who come to work in New Delhi now live primarily in the large number of localities that either came up after Partition or after the 1970s. New Delhi has no wholesale market and it does not produce anything. It does not have a cuisine that it can call its own. It has no music—the Dehli Gharana has nothing to do with New Delhi—no culture and no lifestyle.

This brings us to the so-called smart cities being planned today. They will be watertight, sealed compartments, where people will come to work and leave. The other model proposes places secured on all sides with residents never needing to step out.

This is how the 'city' and cosmopolitanism will be killed. This is how the democratic impulse will be erased and the dream of an egalitarian society will cease to be. The sons of the soil will rule and those who are different will have no right to exist; if nothing else they can be declared non-citizens, the untouchable mlechhas of yore.

In the words of Robert Bevan (2014), writer on architecture and a regeneration consultant:

Ultimately, perhaps the true definition of a city can be found in the phenomenon of 'urbicide'—the deliberate destruction of cities. In war and in peace, this happens where the cosmopolitan is treated with suspicion and where strangers, differences and otherness cannot be tolerated. True cities should never have such smalltown mentalities. Their inhabitants are worldly citizens, not parochial townsfolk.

NOTE

1   The *nirgun* poets were part of the Bhakti movement. Almost all of them were artisans or peasants who were not allowed to enter temples, and they celebrated a formless, inclusive God who did not reside in temples but lived in the hearts of people. Espousing values of non-discrimination, rejecting empty rituals, serving the poor and helping the needy were acts that pleased God. The *niguni*s can therefore be described as those venerating the *nirakaar* or formless God.

REFERENCE

Bevan, Robert. 2014. 'What Makes a City a City—And Does it Really Matter Anyway?' *Guardian*, 8 May. https://www.theguardian.com/cities/2014/may/08/what-makes-city-tech-garden-smart-redefine (accessed 21 May 2020).

Chapter 6

City as Organic Patchwork, City as Streamlined Machine

Neelkanth Chhaya

Cities grow at particular locations. Human responses to conditions of geography create distinct patterns that get woven into the physical, social, economic and political structures of the city. These patterns, both tangible and intangible, become part of the 'codes' that subsequent events have to take into account. Initially, the responses are often 'organic', in the sense that they are not planned or centrally controlled, but evolve through trial-and-error responses of diverse actors in the environment, eventually forming patterns of custom and belief, languages and other expressive modes, spatial and formal characteristics, and so on.

Ahmedabad is a good example to study this process. It is a good example because while it is an important city in the region, historically it did not have to carry the burden of monumentality that imperial cities had to cater to. Similarly, during the British colonial period, Ahmedabad again did not have the symbolic role that the large metropolises of Kolkata, Delhi or Mumbai did. Nor did it ever have the symbolic status in the sacred geography or pilgrimage routes of India that temple cities responded to. So we can see geographical conditions and economic realities play a more significant role in the shaping of the city. The fact that until very recently Ahmedabad did not make any claims to symbolic importance has allowed a pattern of settlement that was affected mainly by contextual conditions. Thus the idea of an 'organic patchwork' of small-scale, piecemeal, almost opportunistic responses to context can be very clearly studied here. A particular kind of pragmatic reason is visible.

Yet Ahmedabad, in recent times, has developed larger ambitions. It attempts to show national leadership in planning and urban design ideas, as well as in political and economic forms. In its very recent history, large-scale urban design moves (notably the riverfront project, the bus rapid transit [BRT] system, and the new subcentres of GIFT city and Dholera) have been taken forward. These activities have needed the existence of concentrated political power and have been facilitated by a high concentration of techno-managerial mind-power. In effect, the city has projected itself as an example of an efficiently governed, streamlined machine. This model of development, the so-called 'Gujarat Model', is now promoted at the national scale, and has affected ideas of what a city should be, who it should cater to and how it should be governed.

Therefore, Ahmedabad might be an object lesson for those who wish to think about urbanity in India. Lessons learnt here can make us pause and consider more carefully what kind of cities we wish to make.

PRELUDE: PREHISTORY OF AHMED SHAH'S NEW CAPITAL

Prior to the establishment of Ahmed Shah's new capital city, the Ahmedabad region was a set of small settlements along the middle reaches of the Sabarmati river valley. The Sabarmati, rising in the hills to the north at the Gujarat–Rajasthan border, is here a meandering sandy bed during the greater part of the year, a small stream of water flowing within this bed in the dry seasons. Rainfall is low in this area as well as in the upstream catchment areas of the river. During the monsoon, however, the river flows from bank to bank, sometimes flooding beyond. For hundreds of years, the river has moved over the generally flat but gently undulating land, changing course at times. On both sides of the river, water has deposited silt and shaped the land into low mound-like formations between which rainwater drains towards the river, ultimately feeding the main flow (Figures 1a and 1d). It is a landscape where scant water and fertile silty soils together create a particular land-water pattern.

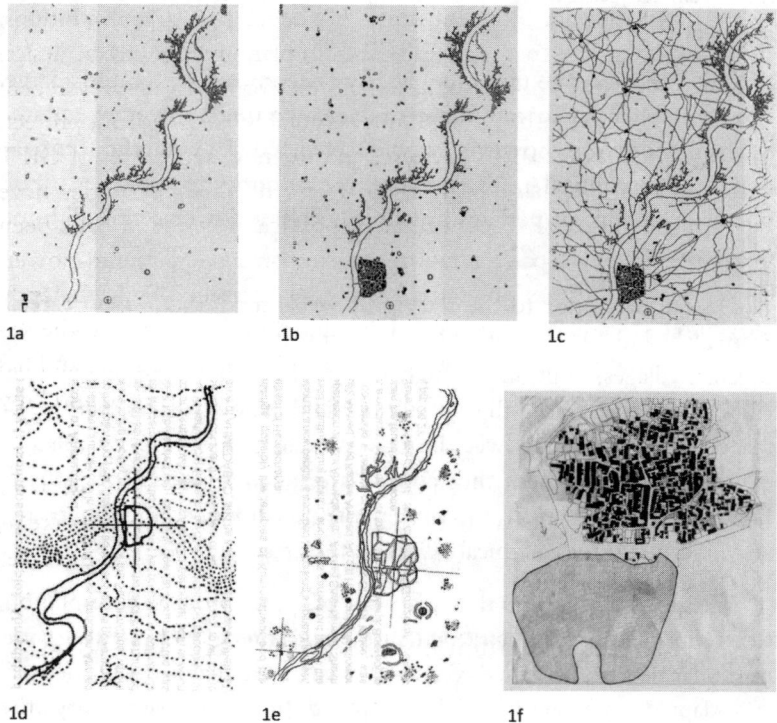

Figure 1 *The river Sabarmati near Ahmedabad*

1a: The river, watercourses debouching into it, and villages in the area
1b: Villages, lakes, the river and the future Ahmedabad
1c: Network of villages in the Ahmedabad area, connecting paths, and the lakes
1d: Topography of the area
1e: Interconnected pattern of settlements
1f: A typical village and lake in the Ahmedabad area: Naroda

Sources: Figures 1a, 1b and 1c: Mehrotra (2001). Figures 1d and 1e: Menghani (2000). Figure 1f: Tayyibji (1996).

It is in this challenging landscape that the inhabitants of this area found ways of surviving and prospering. By making earth dams on the slopes along the watercourses, reliable storage of water could be managed. Lakes formed by this method gave some water around the year for a little bit of agriculture (most crops continued to be rain-fed), were useful for animals, and most importantly, recharged the aquifer from year to year. Wells could then provide drinking water to people (Figures 1b and 1e).

One can speculate that it might have been possible to build a large and comprehensive irrigation system to create a mighty riverine empire. Such an endeavour, however, would have needed a powerful, centralised, unified political/military/economic authority to actualise it. For whatever reason, or perhaps by choice, such a power centre did not come about.

Historically, prior to the setting up of Ahmed Shah's new capital Ahmedabad in 1411, a definite settlement pattern emerged. A network of small villages, built on the higher mounds, each having one or two lakes at its edge, dotted the agricultural land. These villages were connected by tracks that followed the seasonal watercourses. This reticulation of water and movement thus created a distinctive settlement pattern. Figure 1c shows the river, the villages, the network of connecting roads; and Figure 1f shows a typical village in the area.

We see here a pattern that arises out of a slow process of adaptation to circumstances. It is a pattern that depends on developing a *language* of similar yet locally varied responses, a language that is freely adopted and adapted, emergent rather than imposed. In any language, a vocabulary and a grammar are held in common, but each speaker may speak sentences as desired while accepting the semantic and syntactical rules.

Importantly, such a pattern works with small-scale components while achieving coherence and unity at a large scale. Specificities are not flattened out, differences are taken into account, diversity is maintained—yet a subtle and workable order emerges.

Equally important is the fact that in order to survive and prosper in this area of few resources, people had to develop ways of carefully husbanding whatever was available. At the same time, cooperation within and between communities was required in order to govern the use of such resources. Thus, thrift was given greater value and the vulgar display of wealth was discouraged.

Thus, the physical pattern of settlement, as well as the pattern of social structure, can be seen as a language of human interaction that allowed both a shared similarity at the scale of the region, and great diversity of spatial and social organisation at the scale of the village.

AHMED SHAH'S CITY

Sultan Ahmed Shah moved his capital from Patan to Ahmedabad in 1411 CE. This move was necessitated by his desire to have greater control over both overland and seafaring trade. Moving his capital southward for this objective, he could also build the city *ex novo*, as opposed to the older city of Patan that he had conquered.

It is interesting to observe the layout of the new city. First, the city is located so as to connect to several existing villages. To the south-east was the village of Ashaval, already important as a centre in the indigo trade. To the north was Asarva, an ancient village on the trade route going northwards. By locating the new city here, advantage could be taken of the already developed trade networks (Figure 2a).

Second, the city layout took advantage of topography, but at the same time inserted a clear and visible spatial structure. The location of the palace precinct on a slightly elevated plateau on the eastern bank of the Sabarmati allowed its defence needs to be satisfied. Then the ceremonial Bhadra square to the east of the palace was connected through the monumental Teen Darwaza (triple gate) to the wide ceremonial avenue to the Jumma Masjid (Friday mosque). The mosque along with the king's and queen's tombs created a carefully composed geometrical composition in the centre of the city (Figures 2b and 2c). Streets radiated out from this centre to connect to Ashaval, Asarva, as well as other nearby villages. Finally, the Manek Chowk between the king's and the queen's tombs formed the main financial centre of the city. The Manek Chowk also connects to Maneknath temple. Thus, state, religion (both Islam and Hinduism) and trade are all given expression in the design of the city.

Ahmed Shah populated the city by inviting all kinds of traders and artisans to settle in the city. Each group was given land to make their houses and workplaces, forming a series of neighbourhoods around the centre (Figure 2c).

The city fortification wall and gates were built slightly later, during the course of the fifteenth century. A north–south route connecting Delhi Darwaza in the north to Jamalpur Darwaza in the south, intersecting the east–west route from the palace to Manek Chowk, completed the composition (Figure 2d).

It should be noted that the city plan takes into consideration the topography of the land where it is built. Figures 2a and 2b show both the Sabarmati flowing north–south and the seasonal watercourse flowing north-east to south-west debouching into the Sabarmati slightly south of the palace. This watercourse skirts Manek Chowk and the queen's tomb, and is woven into the street patterns beyond both upstream and downstream (see Figures 3a and 3b). Interestingly, most of the walled city area never experiences floods, even in the most severe rains, in contrast to widespread inundation in the 'new' city!

Note that the 'four-way intersection or crossing'—which is an imposition of a conceptual and geometrical principle by a ruling authority—combines here with the 'forked path' or V-junction—which is typically created by pre-existing surface drainage streams, not imposed by human will; both these coexist here (Figures 2a and 2b, 3a and 3b).

Figures 4a and 4b show the interplay of the large monumental installations, geometrically organised, and the very small incremental and non-geometrical texture of the residential neighbourhoods.

We see therefore a very careful, complex and subtle interweaving of two modes of thinking: on the one hand, the irregular existent context—natural topography and man-made features including villages—and on the other, the conceptual thinking of regular geometrical spatial organisation. On the one hand, decision making by the governing authority, on the other the scope offered for small individual initiatives and decisions. On the one hand, the monumental rectilinear central axis, on the other the intricate, irregular weave of streets and lanes following the topography. No erasure of the existent, yet full creative expression of the new.

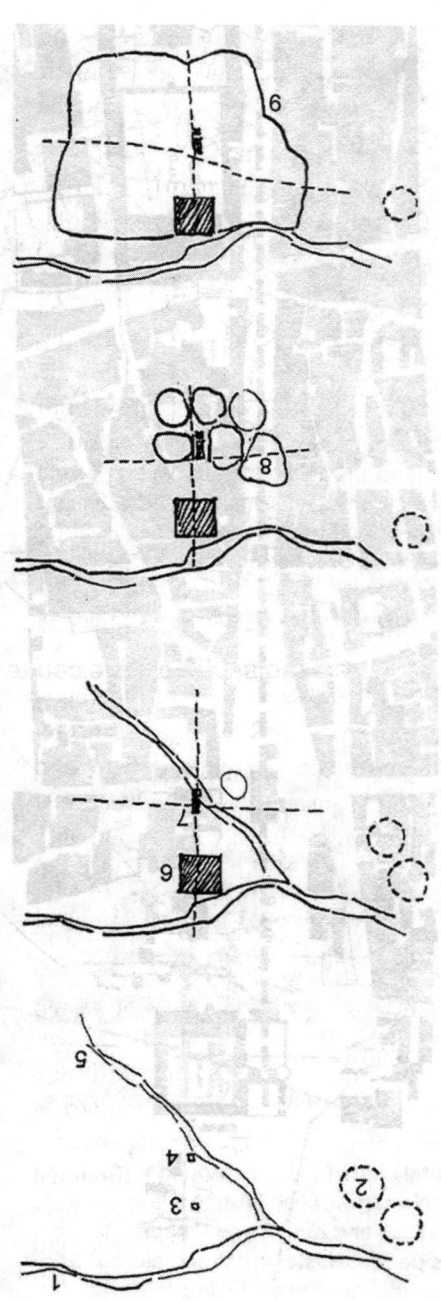

Figure 2 *Ahmed Shah's Ahmedabad: Context and sequence of development*

2a: The river Sabarmati running north–south, seasonal stream north-east to south-west

2b: The palace precinct built on the banks of the Sabarmati, and the Jumma Masjid built to its east

2c: The first residential clusters developed

2d: The north–south and east–west main thoroughfares and the city wall established

Source: Author's sketches.

Note: All maps with north upwards.

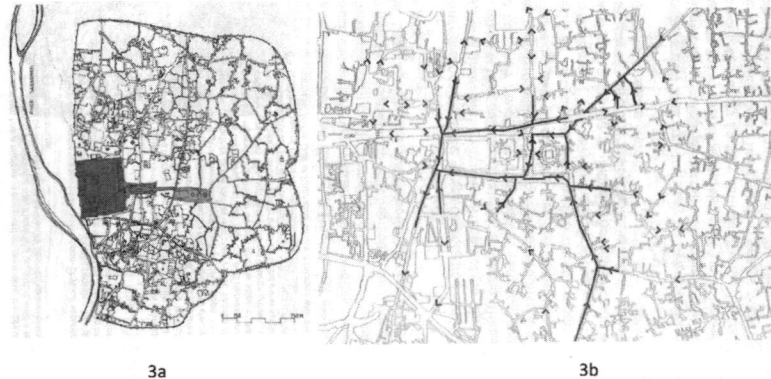

3a   3b

Figure 3 *Walled city of Ahmedabad*

3a: Fully developed street pattern and urban spaces: palace precinct (large rectangle on left); Bhadra ceremonial square (small adjacent rectangle); mosque and tomb precinct and Manek Chowk market square (shaded area in centre); other market streets bordering urban blocks (shaded).

3b: Streets aligned diagonally to follow the path of rainwater drainage (darker lines with arrows).

Sources: Figure 3a: Author; Figure 3b: Laheri (2005).

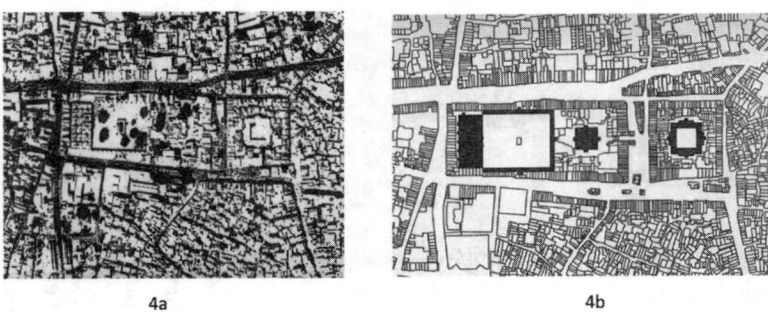

4a   4b

Figure 4 *The monumental symbols and the humble everyday coexisting*

An aerial view (4a) and an architectural plan of the area around the Jumma Masjid at the centre of Ahmed Shah's capital (4b). Notice the geometric regularity and large scale of the mosque and King's and Queen's Tombs, in contrast to the tiny houses in residential clusters that are laid out non-geometrically in response to topography and pre-existing features.

Source: Menghani (2000).

In this way, Ahmed Shah's Ahmedabad may be seen as an object lesson in combining the living vitality of an organic process with the formal clarity given by a thought-out concept.

AHMEDABAD IN THE NEW MILLENNIUM: THE STREAMLINED MACHINE IMPOSED

We now jump across centuries. Ahmedabad became a leading industrial city in the subcontinent in the twentieth century, and also became a major centre of Gandhi's activities during the independence movement. Yet in the last decades of the century, a new form of economics along with a new politics took hold.

Like other cities across the world, Ahmedabad felt the need to attract attention and investment through large, visible gestures. Politically, the centre of attention shifted from the basic needs of the poor to the well-off and their aspirations. In a media-saturated world, seductive images became the tool for revving up desires for a materially lavish way of life. Everyone became a consumer rather than a citizen.

The Sabarmati Riverfront Project was for India an early and very prominent action to get traction in the new politics. Immediately visible, large enough to be unmistakably recognised throughout the city, and involving flows of hitherto unimaginable funds—this project fitted perfectly into the vision of a techno-managerial feat of 'futuristic' and 'world-class' proportions.

In essence, the riverfront project celebrates the supposed supremacy of human will over capricious nature. The 'River' is regularised into a satisfactory simplified shape, with the additional benefit that new lands for sale are created by this straightening of the banks. Water can be poured into this dry, canalised bed from another mega project, that is, the Narmada irrigation project. A seductive, photogenic image becomes available. The water is visible but not usable. The 'order' of man-made geometry is visible but has no effect on the city hinterlands (see Figure 5).

Unseen is the massive displacement of thousands of slum dwellers, who occupied the edges of the original river course. Unseen is the destruction of many livelihoods that depended on the open space and the sandy bed of the river. Or the livelihoods that were possible

Figure 5 *The seductive image hides the reality*
Figure 5 shows what the spanking new riverfront looks like.
Source: Author.

because of the slums' proximity to nearby residential and work areas (see Figure 6).

The natural surface drainage of the city is now replaced by massive, expensive, engineered systems that require energy for pumping. In the first two sections of this chapter, we saw how the earlier city configurations respected the lay of the land and were sensitive to the flow of rainwater. That 'soft engineering' response has been now replaced by an arrogant assumption of absolute mastery over the forces of nature. Recent flooding of the riverfront project in 2015 challenged that assumption, and, with climate change, may challenge the engineering assumptions further (Figures 7a and 7b).

In sum, the project supersedes and 'streamlines' irregular, 'disorderly', capricious nature and replaces it with an efficient and obedient machine. More ominously it streamlines erratic and inconvenient humans and transforms them into efficient and obedient consumers of visual delight!

Figure 6 *The wall closes in: The retaining wall and the slums that were replaced*

Source: Author.

7a   7b

Figure 7 *Challenge to man's hubris*

Figure 7a shows the riverfront project in good times. Artificial walls and imported water create the 'perfect' artifice displaying human ingenuity. Figure 7b shows the flooding of the riverfront area in 2015. Notice the partially submerged light poles of the lower walkway.

Sources: Figure 7a: Photo by Iampurav, https://upload.wikimedia.org/wikipedia/commons/c/c7/Riverfront_sabarmati.JPG (https://creativecommons.org/licenses/by-sa/3.0).

Figure 7b: Photo by WIKIJIMMY, https://commons.wikimedia.org/wiki/File:Flood_at_Sabarmati_Riverfront.jpg (https://creativecommons.org/licenses/by-sa/3.0).

PARTICIPATION OR CONTROL?

I have used the riverfront project as an illustrative example. However, the Gujarat government began several mega projects in a similar mode.

In order to actually implement such a vision, a degree of top-down authoritarian governance is needed. Ways must be found of insulating the project from the rough-and-tumble of long-drawn indecisive democratic processes that can achieve similar results. So a 'special purpose vehicle', which is a company that operates under company law and is independent of political processes, is formed.

However, such a project inevitably becomes the subject of public discussion. Such discussion can be troublesome for the powers that be. It may then become necessary to bring into action a more fractious and corrosive politics. Ultimately the city can no longer be a democratic inclusive space, but has to become the arena of an elite expert culture. Such a culture may or may not have the wisdom to accept unpredictability and diversity as the essence of the urban contribution to civilisation. The danger of the streamlined machine is exactly this: it replaces civic complexity with administrative simplicity.

REFERENCES

Laheri, Niketa. 2005. 'Factors Affecting Urban Patterns: A Study of Ahmedabad'. Unpublished undergraduate thesis, SA, CEPT University.

Mehrotra, Shagun. 2001. 'Indian Urban Space: Making Boundaries and Centres: A Study of Amdavad'. Unpublished undergraduate thesis, SA, CEPT University.

Menghani, Jitendra. 2000. 'Understanding the Notion of Place: A Study of the Jami Mosque Complex and Sarkhej Roza, Ahmedabad'. Unpublished undergraduate thesis, SA, CEPT University.

Tayyibji, Riyaz. 1996. Undergraduate Studio Study, SA, CEPT University.

Chapter 7

Lucknow Unrestrained
Palimpsest of Incongruous Possibilities

Sonal Mithal, Arul Paul and Fahad Zuberi

History of architecture has more often than not been relegated to its formalist format, and 'lessons from history' translate to stylistic emulations in architecture. This chapter describes the premise of—and methods developed in—an architectural studio[1] attempting to shatter that constricted viewpoint. The studio expands the application of historiography to include spatial concerns of materialism/technology/post-humanism/re-appropriation/erasures/identity/sexual orientations/economics. The studio further examines agendas of history, revisiting the historicity of architectural objects as a function of their archivability, and a function of erasures. For this the studio critiques the processes of archiving itself to highlight the politics of inclusions and exclusions of identities and agendas. Following a historiographical method of archival inquiry, the studio accesses the history of Lucknow as a palimpsest and creates a series of thematic maps and illustrations of the city to re-present it as a palimpsest.

Figure 1 *Lucknow during the 1857 uprising*—Lieux de mémoire

Source: Prepared in the CEPT studio 'Architecture by History: Case Example of Lucknow', conducted by the authors in 2018.

THE PALIMPSEST CONTESTS THE HEGEMONY OF LINEARLY TEMPORAL AND FORMALIST HISTORY

Palimpsest refers to a writing material on which several layers of writing have been superimposed. It is a mid-seventeenth century Latin word deriving its origin from the Greek *palimpsēstos*, combining *palin* which means 'again' and *psēstos*, which means 'rubbed smooth'. Usually that writing material would be animal hide—an expensive material that was difficult to produce, and hence was recycled. The old writing was scraped off or effaced, and new writing was layered over it. However, the older writing—being in ink—was never fully erased. It would still be visible under the new text. Sigmund Freud (1979) used the qualities of palimpsest to model the structure of the human mind, prompting the understanding that all earlier historical developments continue to exist along with the present. Such an understanding disrupts the static nature of formalist histories of architecture that are fixated in time and fixated on monumental examples of architecture. Reading an architectural history as a palimpsest extends agency to the contents of the palimpsest that assert their existence. The old and the new texts occur as layers on a palimpsest and obscure each other's clarity, occasioning emergent histories. The palimpsest exists precisely in the way each layer asserts its distinct identity despite its obscurity. In that assertion, the other layers become obscured. Thus, a palimpsest is that re-cycled surface where the constituent layers simultaneously keep becoming available to and departing from the vision, memory and intellect of the reader—depending on who is reading or what they want to read.

A palimpsest has usually been produced as a result of erasing by scraping off, collating and/or stacking. The fact that a palimpsest is a product of such actions makes an understanding of architectural histories palpable from the point of view of erasures, dominance, appropriation, re-territorialisation and resilience. Palimpsest mediates time. Hence, content-wise, a palimpsest could be a layering of temporal events and/or a layering of sensorial experiences. Physically, a palimpsest could be one of the following forms: a stack of layers of historical evidences superimposed one on top of another, and all layers equally visible but indiscernible; a layer of historical evidence added, then erased, then another layer added, then erased, and so on; several layers condensed into one image, and then careful obliteration revealing underlying layers.

In its valorisation of history's multiplicity, a palimpsest allows for a de-privileging of a unique or an originary moment of history. It ruptures the 'cult of the monument' (Riegl 1996: 72) premised solely on age-value and historical-value of an architectural object. Histories on a palimpsest are independent of the connoisseur or the archivist who curates historical events carefully to further an agenda—either of the state, or of the one who employs them.

SUBVERTING THE ARCHIVE

The studio projects take cognisance of the availability of a vast reposi-tory of information on Lucknow and its visibility across disciplines and discourses available in archives, newspapers, maps and active librar-ies. The projects access the archives—mostly colonial in nature—to subvert the narrative. In locating the absence of the voices of the colo-nised in the colonial archive, the projects problematise the archive. The resulting thematically illustrated maps—produced by layering information from various sources—emulate the properties of a palimp-sest. Mapping allows for standardising by way of uniformising and spatialising information without being reductive. This information-based inventorying method facilitates the researcher in searching the archive for that which might not be visible. Hence the researcher acquires the means to access that which might have been absent, hidden or even erased.

RADICAL CITY LUCKNOW

When presented as a palimpsest, Lucknow reveals itself as a 'radical city', a city that does not conform to conventions of polity, gender, religion, education, entertainment and revolt. During the 1857 mutiny, Lucknow protests took on the form of guerrilla tactics using the obscurity of loyalties of British-employed messengers and lack of city planning strategies to their advantage. The nawabs actively fur-thered a cultural environment which not only included but rather centred *rekhti* poetry—a form of Urdu writing that relied heavily on homosexual desire and pan-sexual encounters which the British dismissed as inappropriate for a ruler. The city has served as an active platform which each successive government has used to exhibit its political presence, power and agenda, visible in the numerous public parks. Lucknow is a city that has bred liberal-minded, educated and highly skilled women with an adaptable spirit, women who defied the heteronormative gender stereotypes and took charge of not just their identity, but also wealth, profession and sexuality. The city has transi-tioned from being a seat of institutions promoting employment-based education to becoming a hub of research facilities post-independence, to housing subaltern forms of education for the underprivileged that make them empowered to question and demand. These are some of the many versions of Lucknow.

PALIMPSEST-IC AND COUNTER MAPPINGS

The process undertaken in the studio develops two sets of illustrations. The first, titled 'Working with Archival Evidence', develops palimpsest-ic maps of Lucknow using archival evidence, followed by a counter map using evidence—collected on the ground—that does not make it to the archive. The counter map de-constructs the palimpsest-ic historiographical map using artistic methods of erasure to create another illustration (map) highlighting the narratives of exclusion. This way, the module privileges the archives, and later problematises the connoisseur's curatorial approach of selective archivability of events which biases the reading of a history. The second set of illustrations is titled '*Lieux de mémoire*'. Pierre Nora, in his essay 'Between Memory and History', describes *lieux de mémoire* as a physical site which is created to invoke a collective memory of a history (1989: 19). It uses the potential of individuals to live, remember and nurture their own memories in a fluid erratic form so as to create a collective memory of a past event which is driven by state-institutionalised modern history. Taking the case of the 1857 mutiny in Lucknow, illustrations in this section explore this politics of memory. Here, architectural design is treated as a tool to satisfy a political history agenda of memorising. The city is imagined as a futuristic venue for an immersive urban engagement to critically access its history, and make it available for the larger citizenship. The process is twofold—first, to create critical content of the mutiny; and second, to design the physical environment for exhibiting that content. The projects in this module occupy a wide spectrum of design interventions, both spatial and discursive—highlighting alternate voices of mutineers using British texts, curating informative trails, creating subtle physical markers in the city, inserting stylistic architectural interventions, and exploring virtual reality as a means of immersive and detached experiential environment of the place.

CONTESTING THE CURATORIAL AUTHORITY
OF ARCHIVAL INFORMATION

Presented in the following paragraphs are a few illustrations that respond to Eric Hobsbawm's explanation of the curatorial authority that is exercised while creating archives. Hobsbawm (1983: 13) states, 'history which [becomes] the ideology of nation, state or movement is not what has been preserved in popular memory, but what has been selected, written, pictured, popularized, and institutionalized by those whose function it is to do so.' In presenting the city as a spatial palimpsest, the city is acknowledged and accessed in the present as a container of multiple histories—both institutionalised and marginalised, both available and popularised by invoking the collective memory lying dormant in individual experiences. The obscurity of the earlier layers reveals the working of those conditions that obscured them.

Figure 1 uses the present-day map[2] of Lucknow as its base layer. This layer is superimposed with several other archival maps, namely, '1857 Lucknow: Intrenched position of the British garrison (1911)', 'Lucknow, 1857 (1858) by Edward Weller, with original hand coloring', 'A plan of Lucknow before the mutiny (1880)', 'Lucknow in 1857 (1898)', and 'A map of the siege lines in March 1858 (1897)'.[3] Three different routes were adopted by three different generals to reach the Residency and fight the uprising. All those routes are extracted from each map and located on the base layer. Superimposing the various maps makes those areas stand out which occur consistently, and hence are strategic to the colonial memory. The variations in scale and orientation have to be addressed by careful distorting of each layer, keeping the present-day layer unchanged. This is an example of presenting archival information in reference to the present day, anchoring in the specifics of forest cover, river, road networks and such. What is now a chaotic and dense road network might have been a garden precinct during the 1857 uprising. In those cases, the footprint of the historical precinct is kept on top, in others the chaotic road network. Yet, all layers are visible even though obscured. The ways in which the various layers deviate from each other become a commentary on the flaws and inconsistencies in the original maps themselves. There have been a few instances of archival maps on which places have been marked incorrectly or inconsistently. Those instances have been either highlighted or removed—depending on the content of the map. Each map is accompanied by a timeline. In cases where the events on the timeline have a spatialised presence on the city map, they have been marked accordingly on the map.

The map in Figure 1 serves as a demonstration for the other illustrations which use the same present-day map as the base layer at the same scale. Such juxtaposing of archival maps, archival text, with on-ground study has revealed new emergent histories of Lucknow. For example, Figure 2 presents the colonial imposition of moral prejudice on the erstwhile courtesans to exercise power over these financially independent, culturally rich and politically influential women of Lucknow. The map uses the current layout of the city as a backdrop, carefully erasing, revealing and spatialising the relevant geographical locations based on archival evidence such as old maps, photographs, excerpts from records, tax records, and legal documents that show the transition of the courtesan culture. The maps used over the current city layout depict the eighteenth-century layout of the city highlighting the Chowk area which was the centre of the courtesan culture and the Kaisarbagh area where the texts reveal there once existed the lavish apartments (*kothas*) built for the courtesans during the reign of Nawab Wajid Ali Shah. A layer is added to represent the layout of the city during colonial times when the addition of areas such as the cantonment and the Residency caused a significant change in the profession of the courtesans.

Figure 3 represents the anxieties of the British soon after the 1857 uprising. Despite their victory, they acknowledged lack of hygiene, safety, and ease of movement as the biggest threats to their assertive presence in Lucknow. To address those concerns, the British administration employed Robert Cornelius Napier—a military engineer—to reshape the city so as to make it defensible, safe and sanitised for the British. Napier envisioned a new road layout connecting the city's prominent areas, and razing several areas along the river for ease of movement and clarity of vision across the city and hence for greater control over the city. This map uses Napier's plan and texts from documents of the British administration to construct an argument about large-scale demolition organised by the British in Lucknow.

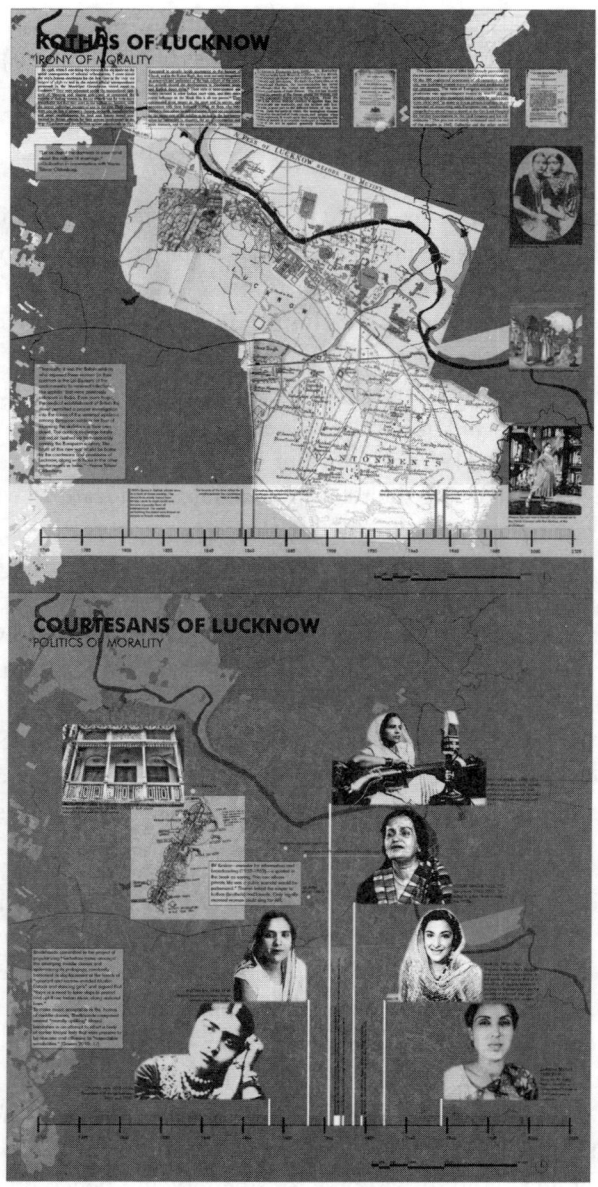

Figure 2 *The* kothas *of Lucknow*

Source: Prepared in the CEPT studio 'Architecture by History: Case Example of Lucknow', conducted by the authors in 2018.

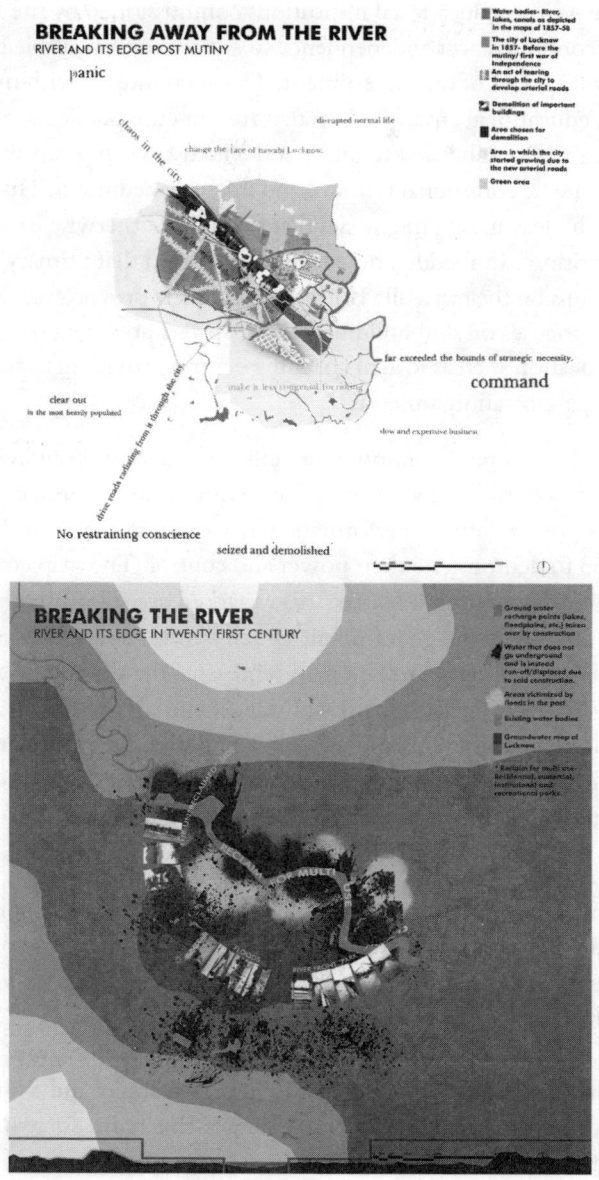

Figure 3 *Breaking away from the river*

Source: Prepared in the CEPT studio 'Architecture by History: Case Example of Lucknow', conducted by the authors in 2018.

Figure 4 maps educational institutions commissioned by the British, and later continued post-independence to create youth available to serve in the civil services of the government. This is countered with mapping subaltern educational environments that run obscure publication houses publishing well-established feminist and Marxist writings on women's empowerment, communal tension, and fascist nakedness in Hindi—to spread such ideas among the masses that might not otherwise have access to such writings. Embedded here is the assumption that primary education that runs on the erstwhile British model deters provocative thinking and solely focuses on skill building. The map also presents sites of alternative education such as formal coaching centres providing coaching to engineering education aspirants.

Figure 5 presents Lucknow as a centre of identity politics, legacy and political control. It locates politically commissioned projects which have been used as sites of performance by various state political parties since 1953 to demonstrate their power and control. The map comprises a timeline, the sites and a matrix. Also marked are subsidised housing schemes offered by the government which continue to grow irrespective of the party in power. The map represents the dominant role the government plays in changing the physical fabric of the city and selectively transforming it for political gain. The counter map brings out the paradox that the people's representatives occupy a huge percentage of the land, as their housing consists of sparsely populated, gated and guarded 'enclaves'.

The map in Figure 6 spatialises sites of queer inclusion, oppression, contestation, erasure and memory in the city of Lucknow, and provides archival evidence along a timeline. Figure 7 maps the sectarian violence in Lucknow using electoral data, demographic data of Shias and Sunnis, marking out the processional route of the tazias in Lucknow during Muharram, locating the mosques, *dargahs*,[4] madrasas and vulnerable neighbourhoods. In that mapping emerges the tense socio-political environment sustained because of the vested agendas of political parties, real estate dealers and sectarian leaders. The last two projects, 'Queer Lucknow' and 'Inglorious Lucknow' respectively, are detailed further in the following sections.

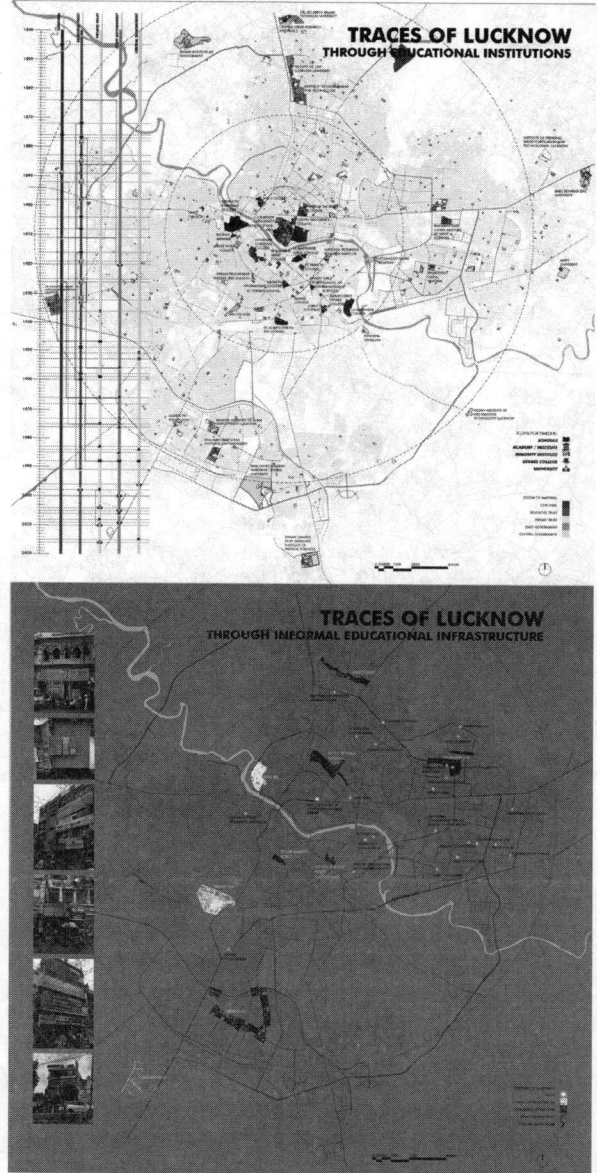

Figure 4 *Traces of Lucknow through its educational institutions*

Source: Prepared in the CEPT studio 'Architecture by History: Case Example of Lucknow', conducted by the authors in 2018.

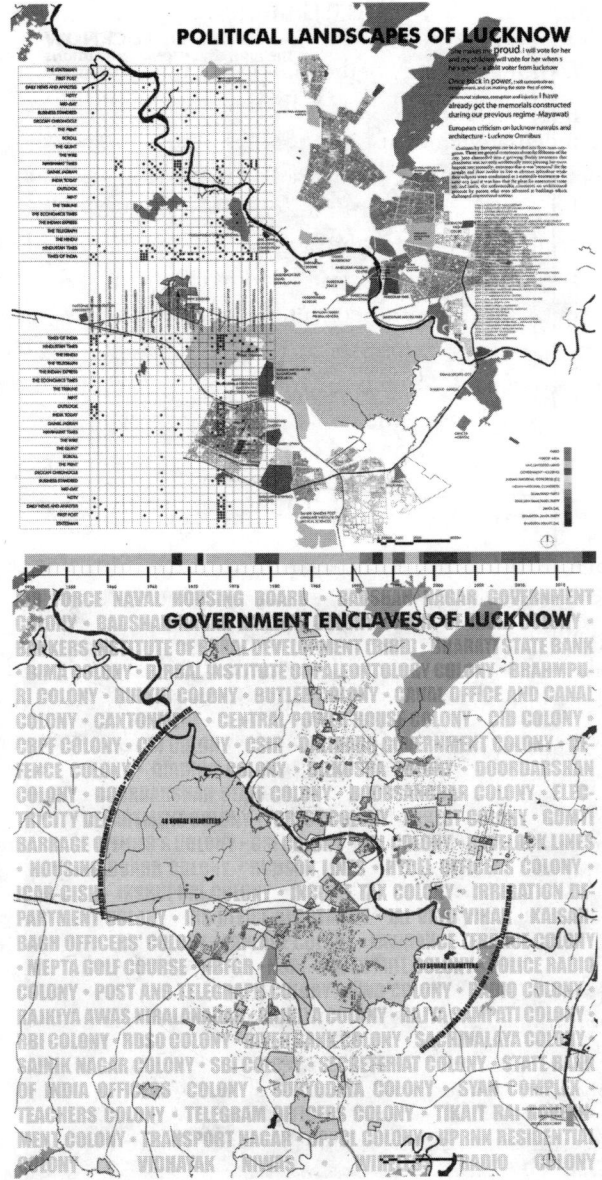

Figure 5 *Political landscape of Lucknow*

Source: Prepared in the CEPT studio 'Architecture by History: Case Example of Lucknow', conducted by the authors in 2018.

QUEER LUCKNOW

'Queer Lucknow' is a study of the LGBTQ+ histories of the city. When pieced together, the archives reveal queer histories that counter the formalist understanding of history and the dominant narrative of present-day queer life in Lucknow. The narratives translate spatially into physical sites that lie across space and time: sites that are appropriated by the community, often spaces that the dominant culture has abandoned; sites that are claimed against, or lost to, the dominant frame of heteronormativity;[5] sites of heterocentric containment;[6] politically activated spaces that short-circuit the exclusionary spatial systems of the city; temporal spaces that come and go with the queer bodies that inhabit them; and heterotopic spaces,[7] spaces that act as insular areas of change.

Palimpsest-ic Mapping

When pieced together, the fragments of queer histories from Lucknow's archives—books, biographical records, poetry, newspapers, photographs, paintings, illustrations, posters and digital references—counter the formalist understanding of the gendered and sexual histories of the city. The following sources have been pieced together to create a palimpsest-ic map: British writings that were critical of the fluid sexuality and the performance of femininity by male rulers and noblemen, and a general effeminacy of the male populace; *rekhti* poetry, where the male poet writes in a female voice, describing romantic and sexual desires, that include same-sex attractions; accounts of sexual activity among queens, noblewomen, servants and courtesans continuing well into the twentieth century; the founding of the first LGBT organisations in Lucknow; and the ensuing battle between these groups and the establishment, most evident in the actions of the police, who had made the gay and MSM (men who have sex with men) community a target of violence and exploitation.

These multiple narratives translate spatially into physical sites of queer inclusion, oppression, contestation, erasure and memory, and a palimpsest-ic method brings these sites that lie across space and time, together on a single map (see Figure 6). The physical sites dotted across Lucknow's landscape hold its stories, and its memories.

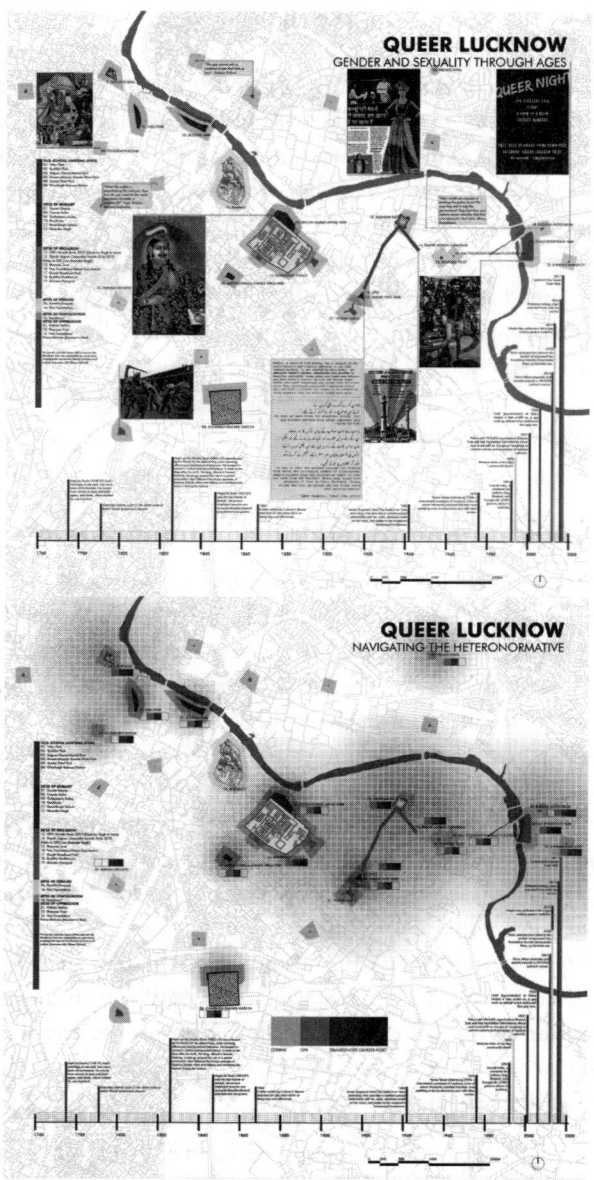

Figure 6 *Queer Lucknow*

Source: Prepared in the CEPT studio 'Architecture by History: Case Example of Lucknow', conducted by the authors in 2018.

Old-School Hunting Spots

These sites are *claimed spaces*, space appropriated by the community, often spaces that the dominant culture has abandoned (Campos 2014; Cottrill 2006; Reed 1996). An internet search for cruising[8] spots in Lucknow brought up a short list of spaces[9] that were known to be frequented by gay and bisexual men and MSM. By overlapping these spaces, spread mostly across the older parts of the city, a correlation between the historic sites categorised as *sites of memory* and these cruising spots emerged.

Sites of Memory

Historically, these spaces relate to the nawabs, their queens, courtesans and court culture, heterotopias of queer culture that were at times spaces of *heterocentric containment*, and at others, propagators of a culture that would appear queer in comparison to the rigid gender constructs of today (Foucault 1997; Grosz 2001). These harems and *kothas* were *homosocial spaces*;[10] designed to segregate genders and avoid sexual contact, they represent a heteronormative failure to recognise their homosocial potential (Bonnevier 2007). Lucknow's *sites of queer memory* are spread across time, from the eighteenth century when Asaf-ud-Daula moved his court to Lucknow, to the last decade of the twentieth century when Friends India[11] published its final volume.

Sites of Inclusion

These spaces, appropriated or claimed against the dominant frame of heteronormativity, are politically activated spaces that short-circuit the exclusionary spatial systems of the city, albeit temporarily (Cottrill 2006; Crawford 2016; Hutchison 1999; Reed 1996). They refer to the places where contemporary society permits, either temporarily or within spaces of *heterocentric containment*, the expression of queer identity. Queer pride, for example, is one such *temporal space* that comes and goes with the queer bodies that inhabit it (Ahmed 2006). Sites of inclusion are found in and around Hazratganj, in the heart of the old city, and also on the other side of the Gomti along its banks.

Sites of inclusion also include *heterotopic spaces*, spaces that act as insular areas of change, created by a crisis or deviance of the heteronormative (Cottrill 2006; Foucault 1997). Spaces such as the Naz Foundation and the Bharosa Trust—NGOs that work towards the betterment of certain sections of the queer community—act as safe spaces, spaces of queer expression, where queer identity may be expressed, and where gender and sexuality are performed, casting off heteronormative constraints (Campos 2014).

Sites of Erasure

Any deviation from or non-alignment with the field of heteronormativity produces a queer effect. But heteronormativity, in turn, is dependent on the renunciation of this other, what it is not (Ahmed 2006; Butler 2011). An example of a site of erasure in the city of Lucknow is the Ramlila ground, host to the Aloile Ka Mela of the hijra community, that was closed in 1994 due to objections raised by the residents of the newly built apartments in the vicinity (Hasnain 2016).

Sites of Oppression

Starting in the early 2000s, a dangerous trend of violence against gay and bisexual men, MSM and transwomen, perpetrated by the Lucknow police, comes to light. These incidents include raids on the offices of HIV/AIDS organisations and the arrest of their staff on charges of conspiracy to commit sodomy and the possession of obscene materials; the chief superintendent of police creating a fake profile on a gay hook-up website to lure and arrest gay men; the physical and sexual assault of outreach workers; and the entrapment, rape, theft and blackmail of male sex workers (Paul 2014). Tripti Tandon of the Lawyers Collective says, 'Rape, blackmail, violence and extortion by the police is pretty endemic,' and asks, 'When the police is perpetrating the violence, then how do you resort to the same machinery to make a complaint?' (ibid.).

Counter Map

Titled 'Navigating the Heteronormative' (see Figure 6), this map, in presenting the various groups within and NGOs working with the queer community, highlights the ways in which funding dictates agendas of such groups—each targeting specific segments and engaging with a range of issues. It represents the level of inclusivity in each queer site identified in the palimpsest-ic map 'Gender and Sexuality through Ages' (see Figure 6), and highlights the varied roles played by these sites in the experience of living in the city. In doing that, the map creates a counter to the dominant narrative of present-day queer life in Lucknow as a binary between celebration and oppression. It is through the representation of these zones of inclusion that the city's otherwise invisible heteronormative structures are made visible.

The Queer Archive

At this crucial time, when archaic laws are being amended, and the right to life and privacy has been extended to the queer community, might it not make sense to be cognisant of, and to curate and archive, the gendered and sexual histories of our cities? 'Queer Lucknow' is an archive. There are physical sites dotted across its landscape that hold its stories, and its memories. The 'Queer Lucknow' project serves to identify sites, traditions, and certain non-normative ways of being, and also acts as an archive of the violence perpetrated against some of the most vulnerable sections of society.

INGLORIOUS LUCKNOW: OF POLITICS AND SECTARIAN VIOLENCE

Lucknow is the only city in the country that has seen Islamic sectarian violence at various points in time. This research investigates the sectarian violence in Lucknow and its intertwining with the politics of the region, the events of the country, and the effects that international events have had on the city's ethno-religious divide.

Sectarian Divide in Islam: A Brief History

The ideological fault lines that are at the base of the conflict between the Shias and the Sunnis in Lucknow go back to the death of Prophet Muhammad in A.D. 632 and the contention about his rightful successor between Ali Ibn Talib and Abu Bakr (Haylamaz 2015). During the

Figure 7 *Inglorious Lucknow—Of politics and sectarian violence*

Source: Prepared in the CEPT studio 'Architecture by History: Case Example of Lucknow', conducted by the authors in 2018.

days of mourning in Muharram, Shias recite the *tabarra*—a doctrine that dissociates believers from those who are seen as enemies of Ahl E Bayt—people of Muhammad's house (family) (Gaborieau et al. 2007). This recitation appears as a provocation of violence in many instances in the context of Lucknow.

The Sectarian Violence in Lucknow

Azadari—mourning during the period of Muharram—has been observed in Lucknow at large scales since the Nawabi rule between 1732 and 1856 (Titus 2005). The conflict started when in 1888, a group of Sunni scholars moved court against the Shia call for prayer (*azaan*), terming it blasphemous and hurtful to their religious sentiments (Robinson 2003). The agitation was followed by minor conflicts that gradually escalated into the first riots in Lucknow in 1908 at Talkatora leaving several injured (ibid.). The city saw more violence in 1935, 1938, 1997, 2005, 2010 and 2013 with numerous deaths, self-immolations in protest, and protests against the prohibition and regulation of procession routes (Violette 1999; Ahmad 2014; Hasnain 2016; Piggott et al. 1908; Allsop 1935; Jones 2011).

As a consequence of every instance of violence, the city saw a shift of neighbourhoods between the two communities (Susewind 2017; Government of India 1961; Engineer 1991; Khan 1939; Ahmad 2014). The urbanity produced in Lucknow, therefore, bears the history of sectarian divide, creation of homogeneous neighbourhoods, and politics as layers in its imagination. Sectarian violence is, hence, an important lens in the context of the city.

Emulating the Layers: Palimpsest Map

The palimpsest-ic map represents the multiple layers that exist in the history of politics and sectarian violence in the city of Lucknow. It maps sites of violence, neighbourhoods (as they shifted between 1961 and 2012), prominent religious institutions, major routes observed by the tazia processions, and two timelines—of politics and of the history of violence. Clear nylon threads connect the sites of violence to the temporal context of politics and theological discourses—emulating the connection that exists between the two but requiring a closer analysis in order to be understood.

Evidence in the form of archival documents—legal papers, photographs and historical accounts—was laid over the city's map as a mirror image. The various layers show evidence, the city's map, timeline, context of the relevant historical photographs, and location of prominent sites on the canvas as a single plane—representing the city as being composed of layers of history where certain narratives get privileged over others and hence become dominant.

The first wash of photo colours forms the base for further layers of acrylic paints. Photo colours are a transparent medium and allow fluidity in strokes and free mixing of hues—a representation of the topographical and physical forms of the city that are then overlaid with the more dynamic and more volatile human elements of the neighbourhoods, sites of violence and those of provocation. Acrylic colour which is an opaque medium forms the final layer of paint. The thick opacity of acrylic paint allows for layering, scraping and merging of various spatial characteristics. Peering through these layers is the archival evidence or the grand design of history.

Counter Map: Developing the Game Board

The binaries of peace and war, of black and white, and of good and bad form the dominant tools of writing history in the modernist way of thinking. A city, however, operates in greys—with individual interests, capitalistic motivations, political rivalries, and context in history that is often silenced by the loud archival structures. Many such greys were revealed upon the visit to Lucknow, and the actors that the author identified through interviews were included in the design of the game. Using these interviews of various actors of the scenario as the basic tool, the research revealed a history of violence that had more to it than what the archives record. This is represented as an exercise in board game mapping.

The game is based on the structure of the board game *Monopoly*. The rules of the board game are as follows:

- A maximum of seven players can play the game.
- Each player assumes the role of an actor. The actors are as follows:
  - Shia Theocrat—Holding Shia Faith Schools
  - Sunni Theocrat—Holding Sunni Faith Schools
  - Shia Real Estate Developer—Holding Housing
  - Sunni Real Estate Developer—Holding Housing
  - Shia Politician—Holding Party Office
  - Sunni Politician—Holding Party Office
  - Social Activist—Holding Citizen Awareness Centres
- Each player rolls the dice and follows the number that appears as the total.
- Each area carries a value that the player must pay to the establishment in order to own the power there and build their respective holdings.
- In case of a player landing on an Event site, they draw a random card from the deck of Event cards (marked in yellow).
- Experience Points are gained or lost based on Event cards.
- Currency is gained or lost based on the regions controlled and the rent collected or paid.
- All players aim to cause sectarian conflict while the Social Activist aims at preventing conflict.
- A player can cause conflict if:
  - They hold power over more than 50 per cent (at least seven regions).
  - All such regions must have at least one holding each.
  - They hold a minimum of 1,000 XPs.
- The social activist can block a conflict by:
  - Holding power over at least four regions with all regions having one Citizen Awareness Centre each
  - Giving 500 XPs to the establishment
- The social activist wins if no conflict occurs by the end of six cycles from the start of the game.
- Other players win by causing three instances of conflict.

CONCLUSION

Palimpsest and counter mapping combined with tracing the timeline of historical events offer an opportunity for marginalised histories to surface, mobilise active contestations of curatorial archives, and include a non-linear temporality of history. However, the moment an event is placed on a timeline it becomes deterministic, again following the inventoried logic that the palimpsest seeks to defy. In that anomaly is the convergence of traditional historiographical methods of inquiry with newer ones, which insist on credible content creation. Mapping subaltern or hidden histories—such as histories of queerness—might invite questions of making visible the vulnerable to the powerful who might use this content to exercise their power over the vulnerable. However, the exercise is to challenge this very power by normalising the visibility of such hidden histories such that their subversion becomes difficult. The exercise has been to invite individuals to seize the opportunity and claim their own space to present their own versions of histories clearly, more often, and across more discourses.

NOTES

1   Architectural studio is a learning environment in architecture schools, where students share a collective workspace for a prolonged period of time in order to develop original projects to further an academic agenda. Students develop their projects through one-on-one interactions with the studio professor who engages by guiding, advising and critiquing the projects. This chapter particularly describes the process undertaken in the studio titled 'Architecture by History: Case Example of Lucknow in 2018' at CEPT University, Ahmedabad.

2   The map is in the form of an Autocad drawing created by Sushant School of Architecture, Gurugram. The drawing contains detailed urban features of Lucknow such as water bodies, road networks, green belts, gardens, orchards, parks, places of historical interest, residential areas, industrial areas, institutional areas, commercial areas, cantonment, simultaneously identifying whether the structures are high-rise or low-rise.

3   '1857 Lucknow: Intrenched position of the British garrison (1911)', Wikimedia Commons, retrieved from https://commons.wikimedia.org/wiki/File: Lucknow_Intrenched_Position_of_the_British_garrison_map_1911.jpg; 'Lucknow, 1857 (1858) by Edward Weller, with original hand coloring', Maps of South Asia in the Frances Pritchett Collection at Columbia University

(henceforth Frances Pritchett Collection), retrieved from http://www.colum-bia.edu/itc/mealac/pritchett/00maplinks/colonial/wellermaps/lucknow1857/lucknow1857supermax.jpg; 'A plan of Lucknow before the mutiny (1880)', Frances Pritchett Collection, retrieved from http://www.columbia.edu/itc/mealac/pritchett/00maplinks/colonial/lucknow1857/map1880max.jpg; 'Lucknow in 1857 (1898)', Frances Pritchett Collection, retrieved from http://www.columbia.edu/itc/mealac/pritchett/00maplinks/colonial/lucknow1857/lucknow1857.html; 'A map of the siege lines in March 1858 (1897)', Frances Pritchett Collection, retrieved from http://www.columbia.edu/itc/mealac/pritchett/00maplinks/colonial/lucknow1857/battlemap1897.jpg.

4   Tomb or shrine of a Muslim saint.

5   Heteronormativity is a structure, predicated on gender binaries, that privileges a default or normal form of sexuality—that between cis-gendered people of opposite sex (Paul and Mithal 2019).

6   Hidden spaces where the queer community can express themselves relatively freely (Grosz 2001).

7   *Heterotopia* is a concept used by Michel Foucault to describe spaces that deviate from the heteronormative (Cottrill 2006; Foucault 1997).

8   The act of visiting a public space in order to find a sexual partner.

9   Gay Cruising Spots, http://www.ohmojo.com/cruisingspots.aspx (accessed 29 February 2020); Gay India and Indian Gay and Lesbian Resources by Utopia Asia, https://www.utopia-asia.com/tipsindi.htm (accessed 29 February 2020); Lucknow Gay Cruising Places/Gayindiatourism.com, https://www.gayindiatourism.com/gay-cruising-lucknow (accessed 29 February 2020).

10 Single-gendered spaces that are potential spaces for homosexual activities.

11 Friends India, a newsletter for Lesbian, Gay, Bisexual and Transgender (LGBT) persons, was started in Lucknow in 1992.

REFERENCES

Ahmad, K. 2014. 'The Lucknow Connection'. *Indian Express*, 12 May.

Ahmed, S. 2006. 'Orientations: Toward a Queer Phenomenology'. *GLQ: A Journal of Lesbian and Gay Studies*, 12(4): 543–74.

Allsop, J. 1935. *Allsop Committee Report*. Allahabad High Court.

Bonnevier, K. 2007. *Behind Straight Curtains: Towards a Queer Feminist Theory of Architecture*. Stockholm: Axl Books.

Butler, J. 2011. *Bodies That Matter: On the Discursive Limits of Sex*. London: Routledge.

Campos, M. R. 2014. 'Queering Architecture: Appropriating Space and Process'. Ph.D. thesis, University of Cincinnati.

Cottrill, J. M. 2006. 'Queering Architecture: Possibilities of Space(s)'. Paper presented at 'Getting Real Design Ethos Now', 94th Annual Meeting of the Association of Collegiate Schools of Architecture, Salt Lake City, UT.

Crawford, L. 2016. *Transgender Architectonics: The Shape of Change in Modernist Space*. London: Routledge.

Engineer, A. 1991. *Communal Riots in Post-independence India*. Cambridge University Press.

Foucault, M. 1997. 'Of Other Spaces: Utopias and Heterotopias', in Neil Leach (ed.), *Rethinking Architecture: A Reader in Cultural Theory*, pp. 350–56. London: Routledge.

Freud, S. 1979. *Civilization and Its Discontents*. London: Hogarth Press.

Gaborieau, Marc, Gudrun Krämer, Denis Matringe, John Nawas and Everett Rowson (eds). 2007. *Encyclopaedia of Islam*. Leiden: Brill.

Government of India. 1961. *Monograph No. 03: Moharram in Two Cities, Lucknow and Delhi. Census of India* 1961.

Graff, Violette (ed.), 1999. *Lucknow: Memories of a City*. Delhi: Oxford University Press.

Grosz, E. A. 2001. *Architecture from the Outside: Essays on Virtual and Real Space*. Cambridge, MA: MIT Press.

Hasnain, N. 2016. *The Other Lucknow*. New Delhi: Vani Prakashan.

Haylamaz, R. 2015. *The Luminous Life of Our Prophet*. Tughra Books.

Hobsbawm, E. J. 1983. 'Introduction: Inventing Traditions', in E. J. Hobsbawm and T. Ranger (eds), *The Invention of Tradition*, pp. 1–14. Cambridge: Cambridge University Press.

Hutchison, J. M. 1999. 'Lesbian Space'. Ph.D. thesis, Department of Architecture, Miami University.

Jones, J. 2011. *Shi'a Islam in Colonial India: Religion, Community and Sectarianism*. Cambridge: Cambridge University Press.

Khan, K. U. 1939. Karim ur Raza Khan to Jinnah Madhe Sahaba file. Qaid-e-Azam Papers, Qaid-e-Azam Academy, National Archives of Pakistan, Islamabad. Also published in the compendium *Qaid-e-Azam Mohammad Ali Jinnah Papers*, ed. Z. H. Zaidi, Quaid-i-Azam Papers Project, Islamabad.

Nora, P. 1989. 'Between Memory and History: Les Lieux de Memoire'. *Representations*, 26: 7–24.

Paul, A., and S. Mithal (Guide). 2019. 'Queering Architecture: The Construction and Performance of Gender, Sexuality, and Space, in Popular Media'. Master's thesis, CEPT University, Ahmedabad.

Paul, S. 2014. 'Living in Fear: LGBTs in India'. Al Jazeera, 17 April. http://america.aljazeera.com/articles/2014/4/17/living-in-fear-lgbtsinindia.html (accessed 1 March 2020).

Piggott, T. C. et al. 1908. *The Piggott Committee Report*. Report on Madhe Sahaba issue commissioned by the Government of United Provinces under the chairmanship of Justice T. C. Piggott, judge at the High Court.

Reed, C. 1996. 'Imminent Domain: Queer Space in the Built Environment'. *Art Journal*, 55(4): 64–70.

Riegl, Alois. 1996. 'The Modern Cult of Monuments: Its Essence and Its Development'. *Historical and Philosophical Issues on the Conservation of Cultural Heritage*, pp. 69–82. Los Angeles: The Getty Conservation Institute. Originally published as *Der moderne Denkmalkultus, sein Wesen, seine Entstehung* (Wien: W. Braumüller, 1903).

Robinson, R. 2003. *Sociology of Religion in India*. New Delhi: SAGE Publications.

Susewind, R. 2017. 'Muslims in Indian Cities: Degrees of Segregation and the Elusive Ghetto'. *Environment and Planning*, A 49(3): 1286–1307.

Titus, M. T. 2005. *Islam in India and Pakistan: A Religious History of Islam in India and Pakistan*. Delhi: Munshiram Manoharlal.

PART III

Fractured Realities

Chapter 8

Art Deco Bombay
The Radical Re-imagination of the City through
Its Aesthetics

Mustansir Dalvi

From the mid-1920s onwards, the city of Bombay transformed, taking its first confident steps to becoming a metropolis. This was accomplished in two ways—first, by reshaping the city itself through the various reclamations (collectively, the Backbay reclamations), and second, by its paradigmatically new building programme that brought in a completely new set of images by which the city would, in time, be known and loved. These transformations, radical by themselves, also pervaded the sociocultural transformation by making a littoral and mercantile city into a business and entrepreneurial hub, inviting a new flush of migrants, educated and cosmopolitan, for new white-collar jobs.

This new English-speaking middle class needed places to live, work and play in, and through the 1930s and 1940s had their needs fulfilled in the new architecture that was now burgeoning in the city. This radical new urban landscape was one of good manners and planned precincts—a comfortable play of iconic buildings and street harmonies. A new aesthetic, the resultant of new materials and technologies and a new semiotic, was adapted to make Bombay Asia's foremost Art Deco city, all appropriated by the first generation of Indian-educated architects. Bombay, despite being a colonial city, from the time between the wars, transformed itself into a city made by and for the people.

This chapter is an attempt to chart a significant moment in the life of the city of Bombay, a very transformative moment because it was largely without precedent. When we think of Bombay, especially people who have grown up in the city, the mental image we have is of the city that emerged in the 1930s and 1940s. In a sense, it was where the whole notion of the public sphere developed, and that gave Bombay its particular public image. This was the one occasion where the *ex nihilo* came into play as a palimpsest over the existing city, completely transforming it into the kind of metropolis that we now hold in our imaginations.

THE CITY RE-IMAGINED

Bombay's architecture underwent a significant shift by the beginning of the 1930s. Several locations in the city were actively planned as precincts and neighbourhoods. The southern tip of the peninsula was the site of vast and city-defining reclamations. The Backbay reclamation was completed in two phases, in truncated versions of the ambitious W. R. Davidge plan that had intended to redefine the southern end of Bombay in a classical layout that provided '*side open spaces, recreational grounds, gardens, dignified civic centres and interrelated residential and commercial areas.... The street plan was laid out in a grid incorporating several broad tree-lined avenues, including a landscaped boulevard along the seafront*' (Batley 1944: 21–22).

But what happened was equally interesting. The areas west of the Esplanade were reclaimed by 1930, while the sweeping Queen's Necklace (Figure 1) was in place by 1940 (Jaffer 2010: 282–83). There was a catholicism in these developments that cut across the former boundaries of the colonial city and the native town. The former segregation of the colonisers and the subject populations that had shaped the first urbanisation of Bombay with stress on creating the monuments and public buildings that defined the Urbs Prima in Indus had been replaced with a mercantilism that made the city population soar in the

Figure 1 *The sweep of the Backbay reclamation: The Queen's Necklace at Marine Drive*

Source: Photo by author.

wake of the cotton boom of the 1860s and eventually transformed the city into a textile powerhouse.

After the plague of 1896, these new layouts were envisaged using the 'Garden City' concept with wider roads, green open spaces and buildings that were not so cramped in relation to each other. All in all, a healthier and a more hygienic city. What was perhaps not envisaged was the nature of the people's architecture that would come up in a manner that was paradigmatically different from the revivalist imperatives of the Raj. It was an architecture that looked to the future and was without precedent. It was practised everywhere in Bombay and for the first time darned the city into a comprehensible whole forming the backdrop for the arena of urban life, breaking down distinctions between colonial and native, weaving freely both amongst the extant monumental piles as well as along the newly resurrected seafronts.

These buildings, rather than being self-effacing like the vernacular architecture of the Konkan and native Bombay, tended to be open-faced, placing themselves squarely upon the streets on which they were built, calling for viewers and pedestrians to gaze upon their newness and novelty, speaking in signifiers that touched every citizen who very happily embraced them. The new public realm was being reshaped into one of cosmopolitanism and collegiality. We can see this in the form of new building typologies. Different types of apartment blocks came up, as well as office buildings and cinema theatres and so on which were not part of the imperial project of monumental buildings that had dominated the skyline up to that time.

THE RISING (AND ASPIRING) MIDDLE CLASS IN BOMBAY

The period between the two World Wars was also a time of consolidation for Bombay's middle class. In many families, the first generation of college-educated and English-speaking citizens were asserting themselves in the 'white-collar' workplace, finding jobs in offices, banks and insurance companies whose new buildings were now being erected in these planned precincts mentioned earlier. This generation was one step away from their migrant parents and grandparents who had sought to make their place in the city as workers in the harbours and in the mills. Finance and mercantilism now occupied centre-stage along with industry and trade. This potential middle class was also aspirational and aware of developments internationally. New professional architects educated in Bombay were also setting up practices. All these denizens now formed a great class of consumers who occupied the public realm and asked for their share of it.

Cinema was the new great art form. Both Hollywood as well as the movies made in Bombay's many studios were equally patronised in the many new cinema halls built during these two decades (Figure 2). The locations of these theatres of moving picture pleasure, built on prominent sites in the island city, soon made the cinema house the iconic architectural image of the times. Media publications from India and abroad also proliferated and were shared, discussed and internalised. So the 1930s and 1940s were a fecund period for domestic architecture in Bombay. Here affluent Indians, the influential elite of Bombay, shared a very different relationship with the British unlike elsewhere in India. They were much more equal and symbiotic in their dealings. The well-to-do elite, educated in the Western tradition, the upwardly mobile, globe-trotting and ocean-voyaging, cosmopolitan citizens of Bombay, made wealth and displayed it with ostentation. The most outward trappings were the construction and inhabitation of a better form of domestic space. Among those Indians who could afford to

Figure 2 *Regal Cinema, Bombay (Charles Stevens, 1933)*
Source: Photo by author.

patronise Indian architects, some even built to rent out spaces to English men who had settled down in Bombay to make lives and careers in the Urbs Prima.

Apartments were inherently cosmopolitan spaces designed for nuclear families who would now have to live cheek by jowl with possible strangers in terms of caste, religion, eating habits and education, and do so in a spirit of accommodation and cordiality. We can see this mixing concurrently with the increased occupation of the public realm. No longer were people limited to living within groups of a single identity, as was the case, say, of some of the chawls of Bombay. Apartment living would lead to the new formation, with new groupings and new

Figure 3 *The new apartments built along the Oval, photographed in 1936–37*
Source: Associated Cement Companies Limited (1937).

networks (Figure 3). The architecture of the apartment building also reflected this, for now there were no inner spaces like courtyards or deep-eaved roofs. Apartments were multi-storeyed and had facades with an outward aspect looking down into the streets and beyond, providing a piece of the sky, as Charles Correa would like to say, to every family in the form of boldly thrusting cantilevered balconies.

THE EMERGING ARCHITECTURAL PRACTICES IN THE CITY

By the 1930s, several architectural practices had also been established in Bombay. Amongst these were the first generation of Indian architects who had for the most part graduated from the Sir J. J. School of Art. The school itself had a separate department of architecture (from 1913 onwards) headed over time by some of Bombay's leading architects, including such stalwarts as Robert Cable, Claude Batley and C. M. Master (Figure 4). Among the influential teachers were city architects such as G. B. Mhatre, D. W. Ditchburn, P. P. Kapadia, S. H. Parelkar and Homi Dallas. They, along with their students and protégés, were

Figure 4 *Prominent members of the Indian Institute of Architects (1936–37), including Robert Cable, C. M. Master (seated, first and second from left), Claude Batley (seated, extreme right), and G. B. Mhatre (standing, extreme left)*

Source: Journal of Indian Institute of Architects (1936).

the home-grown architects who determined the course of Bombay's architecture over the next many decades. From the 1920s to the 1950s, the architects who were the principals of the biggest architecture firms in Bombay were also the heads and teachers at Bombay's architecture school. So there is a very direct correlation between academics and the profession and a very smooth movement across both.

Bombay's architects were educated in the Western tradition and were as forward looking and eclectic as their paymasters (Dalvi 2018: 62). They were aware of much of the influential literature that would later be accepted as part of the modernist canon. In 1942, in the pages of the *Journal of the Indian Institute of Architects*, Mistri and Billimoria proposed a future architecture for the city echoing the rational theory of Le Corbusier and other European modernists.

It is not enough that our architects are free from the vanity of 'styles'. They must learn to exploit and apply the fruits of scientific research in

> their day-to-day problems.... The building is a machine to live, work or play in.... Architecture has changed from the art of two-dimensional pattern making to the science of the relation of space and movement.... Orderliness is the beginning of everything. (Mistri and Billimoria 1942: 223)

We recognise this tone when we talk about the modernist period and the Bauhaus—this was the language of that time.

The architecture of their choice was what we now refer to as Art Deco. It must be remembered that this is a retrospective term popularised by the historian Bevis Hillier in 1968 to refer to architecture that came up between the wars in the United States and Europe, one that was synonymous with the hedonistic days of the jazz age. The name was derived from a 1925 exposition in Paris which celebrated living in the modern world. Today, of course, Art Deco refers to a very eclectic mix of building styles from the skyscrapers of New York to the hotels in Miami and so on. In Bombay, architecture at that time did not have a name beyond the occasional reference to it as Moderne. Claude Batley, in a lecture at the Indian Institute of Architects in 1934, spoke of these emerging trends simply as 'This New Architecture'.

> This New Architecture is in one sense the nudist movement in our profession.... Look at any facade on the West side of Hornby Road, in our own Bombay, and any reasonable man would agree that it would be transformed for the better if one of us took an axe and chopped off every bit of ornament ... surely it is more dignified for the architect to take his place in the vanguard of progress, serving his own day and generation, in its own spirit. (Batley 1935: 103)

He meant an architecture that was a return to primary essentials. In his speech, he was unabashedly critical of the revivalist neoclassical stylistics that were the hallmark of the architecture of officialdom until this time. Batley went on to speak of the changing ways of life that were the outcome of strange circumstances during World War I where a greater gender equality resulted and the plans of apartment houses started changing to reflect that.

NEW MATERIALS AND CONSTRUCTIONAL TECHNOLOGIES

Functionalism had been an inspiration for the new architecture along with new materials now available to contemporary architects like cement and its byproducts. Cement advertising was one of the very central reasons why these buildings came up with such large proliferation. The new architecture was also indexical with regard to the affluence that fulfilled the desire of Indian clients to imitate the lifestyle of many princes. The palatial homes of Manik Baug in Indore (1933) and the Umaid Bhavan in Jodhpur (1929–43) are examples of the appropriation of the Style Moderne as it emerged in America.

But this new architecture was freewheeling and eclectic and it had caught the fancy of the developed world at that time. It was not only the architecture of exuberance but also showcased architectural and constructional development.

Cement companies in India fuelled this rising popularity by the vigorous promotion of RCC (reinforced cement concrete). These companies had well-organised publicity departments that released bro-chures and folders that compiled photographs of newly finished buildings, both domestic and public, from the major cities and princely states in India, displaying a technology and aesthetics allowed by cement in their construction. The advertisements use a whole bunch of very interesting punch lines not only targeting architects but also targeting the general public. This is how the virtues of concrete were advertised by the Cement Marketing Company of India (Figure 5). They would say something like 'Concrete gives the maximum service for a minimum expenditure,' or 'Curved or square, it's equally easy for concrete' (Cement Marketing Company of India Limited [1942?]), which then started to reflect in the buildings themselves. They published examples of buildings that showed the popularity of this new form of architecture and the extensive spread of this new technology.

One of the more interesting publications was called *The Modern House in India*, which contained nothing except photographs of build-ings that were built in that year, comprising a wonderful archive. A single year's collection of *The Modern House in India* in 1937 shows new buildings that were built that year, all more or less in this type of

Figure 5 *Cover of* The Modern House in India, *c. 1942*
Source: Cement Marketing Company of India Limited (1942?).

fashion, from Bombay, Poona, Ahmedabad, Surat, Morbi, Udaipur, Indore, Hyderabad, Secunderabad, Tuticorin, Bangalore, Lahore, Patna, Calcutta, Darjeeling, Kalimpong, Assam, New Delhi, Kanpur, Aligad, Karachi, Madras, Coimbatore and Alleppey, amongst others (Associated Cement Companies Limited 1937). The point is that although we tend to associate Bombay with being the Art Deco capital of India, this kind of building was happening everywhere in the country.

Architecture constructed in RCC would soon become the standard for bungalows, apartment blocks, office buildings, even palaces. It is through these publications that we can see the long reach of this technology and the popularity of the architecture that it engendered. Significantly, most of the architecture firms publicised by these cement companies were located in Bombay, which is more a matter of history than anything else. Art Deco did not rise out of a canon, nor did it ever get an authorial grammar for its stylistic understanding and dissemination.

THE NEW AESTHETIC OF ART DECO ARCHITECTURE IN BOMBAY

The buildings of that time were all a result of iterative practices rather than the express codification of design ideology, and in fact they grew in an ecosystem or a semiosphere of their own making. As they built more buildings, more buildings were built, and these buildings were built in that particular manner. Art Deco buildings of all types speak to each other in their uses and their facades, expressing their purpose and inviting the observer to participate in the process of signification, but in an open-ended way, rather than through any great codification. So it has always been very difficult to pinpoint what 'Art Deco-ness' is. One cannot say with precision whether it is the decoration, the soaring balconies, the steppe shape, the symmetry, the towers that pierce the skyline, or all of these things. The point is that at least at one level it is a complete negation of the revivalism that came before.

In my research, I looked at more than a hundred buildings from the 1930s and 1940s. There are essentially three types of features which one tends to see: the first is the larger form of the building; the second is the way the building structure is broken into a series of discontinuities; and third, the features that are superimposed on this, essentially building ornament. Thus these features can be best read as a series of family resemblances, in the words of Ludwig Wittgenstein (*Philosophical Investigations*, 1986 [1953]), for we can see its various expressions that differ from building type to building type, from locality to locality, and over time there is a certain consistency that is part of a larger commonality.

The common features that I identified in my research emerged largely out of semiotic analysis of the buildings. Putting back my findings into the chronology, I have come to conclude that Art Deco architecture in Bombay arrived full-blown in the 1930s (Dalvi 2017). There is no evidence of evolution from an earlier style. That is one of the reasons why we tend to look at the architecture of the city at that time through these intangibles, rather than in terms of any clear, stylistic kind of development. In the delineation of common features, what is best associated with Art Deco is not its decoration but more its physical form (the first and the second features mentioned earlier). The most common feature of Art Deco buildings is the flat roof, because in a city like Bombay, prior to this, the deep-sloping, eaved roof dominated the city skyline. Flat roofs were possible due to the technology of RCC. Starting with the flat roof, a series of changes in this new form of construction led to the building showing all the features of Art Deco architecture.

Looking at the proliferation of these self similar buildings, we recognise a paradigmatic shift, a radical intervention to a city which had earlier largely been a binary of the native town with all these sloping roofs and very densely packed buildings, and the monumental buildings associated with the Raj. This New Architecture infiltrated like a virus all over the city, but in the process brought the whole city together as well.

CONCLUSIONS

To conclude, here are some reasons why Bombay in the 1930s and 1940s can be called a 'radical city'. The first is this idea of a fully formed urbanity. It came because of that way that the plots were planned; there was a lot of planning in the city. It came because of this *ex nihilo* idea of the city which actually was brought out from the sea with these large amounts of reclamations.

Second, it had very easy acceptance by the citizenry at large. It is not so much a top-down approach but something that becomes part of almost a pop culture. Everybody wants their houses to be that way. For the first time, for example, you have colourful buildings, which emerge into the city. Today we associate Art Deco with much more

Figure 6 *Empress Court (G. B. Mhatre, 1937)*
Source: Associated Cement Companies Limited (1937).

muted colours, but during its time, the palette was much brighter (Figure 6). This is visible in examples of buildings, not in Bombay, but all over India.

Third, even as Art Deco goes into decline, it does so interestingly. The first feature to go is the ornamentation and yet it still looks like an Art Deco building. Such buildings have been referred to as 'stream-lined deco'. Even as features recede, the vestigial building still evokes Art Deco-ness (Dalvi 2017).

Finally, the essence of buildings like these and their position in the city is the celebration of public life. That is the central notion of Bombay's architecture at that time, which epitomised a living that was almost anti-gentrification. Bombay never had gated communities. It is only now that we start to see them. Even in the earliest phases, *waadis* and chawls were never closed off from the rest of the city.[1] The rich and the poor lived side by side. When these new buildings came in with the new planning, they were not gated either. Popular Art Deco precincts like Hindu Colony and Parsi Colony, despite their names, were never cut off by walls but integrated seamlessly into the larger life of the city.

Cosmopolitanism, inclusivity and an international style brought the citizen into the public sphere, whether it was living, working or playing—these three words which we now use quite freely when we talk about a new kind of design. That is why I consider this period a radical moment in time.

NOTE

1   A *waadi* is a residential cluster in Bombay dominated by a particular community. It is not normally gated, but would probably be entered through an open gateway.

REFERENCES

Associated Cement Companies Limited. 1937. *The Modern House in India*. Bombay: Associated Cement Companies Limited.

Batley, Claude. 1935. 'This New Architecture'. *Journal of the Indian Institute of Architects*, 1(3): 103–4.

———. 1944. 'The Architect's Sphere in Town Planning'. *Journal of the Indian Institute of Architects*, 11: 21–22.

Cement Marketing Company of India Limited. [1942?]. *The Modern House in India*. Bombay: Cement Marketing Company of India Limited (Publicity Department).

Council Members of the Indian Institute of Architects, Bombay, 1936–1937. *Journal of the Indian Institutes of Architects*, III (1), 148.

Dalvi, Mustansir. 2017. 'Buildings as Text: Developing a Semiotic of Bombay's Art Deco Architecture (1930–1949)'. Ph.D. thesis, Indian Institute of Technology Bombay, Industrial Design Centre, Mumbai.

———. 2018. '"This New Architecture": Contemporary Voices on Bombay's Architecture before the Nation State'. *Tekton: A Journal of Architecture, Urban Design and Planning*, 5(1): 56–73.

Hillier, Bevis. 1968. *Art Deco of the 20s and 30s*. London: Studio Vista.

Jaffer, A. 2010. 'Indo Deco', in C. Benton, T. Benton and G. Wood (eds), *Art Deco 1910–1939*, pp. 382–95. London: V&A Publishing.

Mistri, M. J., and H. J. Billimoria. 1942. 'Architectural Development in Bombay during the Last Twenty-Five Years'. *Journal of the Indian Institute of Architects*, 8: 216–23.

Wittgenstein, L. 1986 [1953]. *Philosophical Investigations*. Oxford: Basil Blackwell.

Chapter 9

Land(e)scapes of Utopia
Reconciling Old Ways of Living in New Towns in India

Rachna Mehra

Modern urban planning from its commencement was woven around the imagination of creating a just and orderly city which palpably remained counter-intuitive to inexorable social hierarchies. The predicament became more pronounced in the context of post-colonial India, where the surreal Utopia of independence was marred by the dystopic reality of partition and the destruction of towns and cities. While, on the one hand, the vivisection of the Indian subcontinent in 1947 caused havoc and destruction in many regions, on the other, it also ushered in urbanism and the growth of new towns and cities which offered opportunities to refugees to begin afresh. In this context, I will look at the creation of resettlement towns where 'development' became a 'synecdoche' for the rehabilitation of refugees (Zachariah 1999: 169).[1] This effort was further bolstered by the participatory paradigm of the cooperative movement where the refugees began to be moulded into the citizens of a newly independent nation.

As the dust of partition began to settle, the new nation donned the mantle of a welfare state and enhanced its socialist credentials by prioritising the developmental concern for its citizens. The planning ideas borrowed from the New Town Movement in Europe along with the adoption of the welfarist ideals of the Community Development Programme (CDP) became the hallmark of urban development in the initial phase. The rehabilitation accounts of the government in the post-colonial period were marked by celebratory overtones, lauding the building of new towns and capital cities alongside the reconstruction of old ones. Nehru's philosophical rumination regarding the creation of a perfect human in an idyllic space was embodied in these urban restorative and community development projects. For Nehru, the new town projects epitomised the vitality or emergence of a newly independent nation and not a partitioned one: 'To build a city is something happy to think of. To create a new town is itself a happy thing. There cannot be a greater joy than to create. To be associated therefore, with the construction of the city has been a thing which I appreciate the most' (Nehru 1991: 115).

Ravi Kalia (2006) suggests that Nehru's vision to induce modernism in urban planning had to contend with the dilemma of straddling the two worlds of Western culture and vernacular tradition. On the one hand the post-colonial nation had to move beyond the friction produced by a communal and a casteist society, on the other it had to strengthen the secular paradigm. This was not an easy task as the political, social and urban fabric of India struggled between the irreconcilable utopias produced by Nehru's ideas and Gandhi's rumination about creating an ideal society. According to Kalia,

> post-colonial India demonstrated two competing versions of history and ideology: Gandhi's vexed, sometimes mystical, attachment to villages as a source of ideals for building a new India competed with Nehru's inclination for cities. Gandhi had tirelessly campaigned in the hope that his life might help mediate the nation's treacherous journey between memory and expectation about villages, about religious violence and about the untouchables. Nehru on the other hand was illuminating the phenomenon of 'alternative' histories of India, especially with reference to the city and to religion. He spent much of his career as an intellectual and a political leader trying to confront traditional India, and his Western training placed him in an oppositional—and sometimes advantageous—position to comment on the struggle over memory in Indian society. In Nehru's writings and speeches, he was portraying a historical vision for India in which urbanism flourished,

where villages became citified and where modern industry thrived. (Ibid.: 152–53)

Nehru's personal involvement in planning the capitals and new towns was aligned with his romanticised notion of creating an ideal citizen in the newly independent nation. Therefore, a great deal of emphasis was laid on regeneration of human vitality by raising townships. It was not just a restitutive task of providing houses to refugees, but also an important mission, which could re-instil confidence in them. It was an attempt to help them overcome and heal the disruptions of their past by directing their collective energies into various township schemes. These urban experiments were also envisaged as models for future emulation. Nehru wrote:

> I love to have the city beautiful, the country beautiful, the world beautiful, so that our people in future may have a glimpse of a world where they will have cooperation, a sense of service for the common good, goodwill and love for each other and not violence, hatred, exploitation and misery. (1991: 95)

Nehru employed renowned architects and planners (Albert Mayer, Le Corbusier) to realise his vision of a new India and build aesthetically appealing cities where people would practise socialist principles of cooperative living. Gyan Prakash (2002: 4) suggests that Nehru's 'confidence in planning as an instrument to achieve progress' was evident in the building of Chandigarh where 'urbanisation' was seen as indispensable for ushering in 'modernisation'. Prakash further contends that Nehru was able to 'position' the state and its 'technocratic elites and experts' like Le Corbusier as 'agents of History, removing planning from the scrutiny of democratic politics' (ibid.: 5). Thus, people were participants in the planning process only to the extent of facilitating the building of new projects directed and finalised by the government.

According to Annapurna Shaw (2005: 51), 'three major influences' inspired the thinking and practices of the policy makers and urban planners in India: 'colonial planning', the 'International Style of architecture' (Le Corbusier) and 'the advice of international organisations' (the Ford Foundation). It is essential here to clarify that the New Town Movement in India drew its inspiration from the 'new towns' built in Europe. The impact of the ideas and institutions of colonial rule continued in the post-colonial period despite the attempts of the Nehruvian state to distance itself from its immediate past. The post-colonial welfare state applied the generic idea of 'development' to planning, which is accepted, and often undisputed, as an indicator of evolution and progress (McEwan 2009: 12). It is also utopian to the extent that it has the power to fascinate, seduce, spin dreams and create expectations without culminating in concrete results. It would be interesting to explore the extent to which the post-independence discourse differed from the 'development projects' conceived in the dominant and universalising discourse of the colonial world. At this juncture, it is essential to trace the trajectory of the New Town Movement which began abroad and found its way into India, albeit in a different scenario altogether.

THE NEW TOWN MOVEMENT IN BRITAIN AND OTHER PARTS OF EUROPE

The New Town Movement in Europe was largely shaped by the exigencies created by the housing crisis in the post–World War II period. In 1937 Britain, when the war was still impending, the government appointed a National Commission headed by Sir Montague Barlow to present proposals concerning the distribution of industry and of population. The Barlow Report presented in January 1940 advocated 'a policy of decentralization and de-concentration of industry' and reorganisation of congested urban areas (Merlin 1980: 78). In 1943, the London County Council under the direction of Patrick Abercrombie prepared a plan for the redevelopment of the metropolis. The idea of building 'new towns' at this stage was to plan 'a group of "satellites" which were to be developed upon existing towns within a fifty mile radius of London's center' (Crouch and Bigger 1950: 245). It is difficult to ascertain whether there was anything novel about these 'new towns', especially those built around London, which were clearly mentioned in the plan as 'satellites' meant to decongest the metropolis.

The 1944 draft of the regional plan for London incorporated the Barlow Report's suggestions. The plan included provisions for some workers to move from central London or from the suburbs and resettle beyond a 'greenbelt' stretching from 13 to 20 miles from the centre (Merlin 1980: 78). These settlements were placed in the outer ring where the proposed 'new towns' were to be created. A Royal Commission was appointed with Lord Reith as its chairman to outline the physical characteristics of the new towns and to prepare a law giving them official status.

After the adoption of the New Towns Act in 1946, the government appointed a committee and a development corporation for each town. Apart from the committee, there was an official in charge of implementation, and a general manager who had to recruit his own staff of planners, engineers and administrators. The development corporation was responsible for planning, buying and building a majority of housing units, shops and factories. Under the act, the British government built 28 new towns between 1946 and 1970 (Suge 2005: 148). The Reith Commission incorporated many of Ebenezer Howard's initial utopian views in the planning of the new towns.[2] These towns were proposed to be built in the vicinity of large cities like Birmingham, Liverpool, Manchester, Cardiff, Newcastle, Glasgow and Edinburgh. The ring towns were to be 25 miles from London (or 12 miles from other cities) and were supposed to cater to a population of 20,000–60,000 in an area of 5,000 acres (Merlin 1980: 79).

Some of the new towns built between 1947 and 1950 to alleviate the housing shortages were Basildon, Bracknell, Corby, Crawley, Harlow, Hemel Hempstead, Aycliffe, Peterlee and Stevenage (Crouch and Bigger 1950: 260). In the second phase (1961–64), other new towns, namely Telford, Redditch, Runcorn and Skelmersdale, were developed. The New Towns Act, 1946, was revised in 1965. In the last phase, which lasted from 1967 to 1970, some old towns were expanded to absorb the excess population from the major cities. During this third phase, Central Lancashire, Milton Keynes, Northampton, Peterborough and Warrington were developed. Thus, the New Town Movement in Britain, which at its onset planned to resolve the housing crisis, culminated in depopulating the congested cities by opening new avenues of employment in the peripheries of the older cities. This process of urban dispersal has led John Madge (1962: 210) to infer that the new towns did not embody any 'alternative forms of development' except for serving some distinct economic functions.

The New Town Movement which began in Britain had its variants in other parts of Europe. While Ebenezer Howard's 'Garden City Movement' was implemented innovatively in Letchworth, Welwyn and the new towns in Britain, the Athens Charter served as the preamble for developing suburbs in Stockholm and Amsterdam. In France, the housing crisis created in the post–World War II scenario spurred the government to invest financially in housing construction. In 1965, there was a proposition to develop Paris in a manner that broke the monopoly of a single centre by creating new urban centres or new towns in the suburbs. While much attention has been paid to the creation of new towns in the post-war period, of late the attempt has moved to understanding the social response of those who inhabited these towns.

The New Town Movement in England has been critiqued for gradually disavowing the principles of the Garden City Movement to accommodate the state's needs, which had become increasingly 'vulnerable to world competition' (Hardy 2002: 5). If the Garden City Movement was an offshoot of the 'altruistic' desire to socially improve the cities by developing the suburbs, it was the 'productive' need of the capitalist state of Britain which prompted the government to build new towns after 1945 (ibid.). Hence, the implementation of the garden city principle was waning in new towns, the human dimension of planning was missing in Stevenage, and the ideal of 'self-contained' communities was lacking in Basildon. Basildon was designed in 1949 as the seventh and biggest London new town, with a target population of 50,000 inhabitants (Suge 2005: 149). The social ideal desired by the planners was to create a 'balanced and self-contained community' within the township (ibid.: 162). This implied providing ample employment opportunities and community recreational facilities to the inhabitants, where people would live a life 'independent of nearby great cities' (Crouch and Bigger 1950: 254). But a 1971 census indicated that nearly a quarter of workers (mostly belonging to the second generation) preferred the white-collar jobs in London. There were frequent newspaper reports to suggest that Basildon was a 'social desert' and tenants usually suffered from 'loneliness and boredom' (Suge 2005: 167). Thus, Basildon, despite its autonomous creation, became dependent on the core city for its sustained existence belying the hope of creating a 'self-contained' new town.

Meryl Aldridge (1996: 23) has critiqued the Garden City and the New Town Movements for being only a 'demi paradise' for women as they did not offer women any opportunity to contribute to civic life. The movements reiterated the conventional role of women as homemakers who had to tend to their mundane domestic chores. Thus the 'physical and economic development strategies' were based on the 'unquestioned division of labour' interlinking the social life of women to family and household forms of economy (ibid.). Little consideration was given to any proactive role that women could play in the economic, social or cultural life of the new town.

While the basic premise for building new towns lay in creating an improved social milieu, which ruptured the vagaries of an industrialised city life, one way to gauge its success could be to unravel the experience of workers who were resettled in the towns. Did the housing facilities provided in the new towns drastically transform their erstwhile sordid living conditions? How amenable were people to their new surroundings, or did they resent the loss of earlier homes? These questions open up interesting avenues of research to understand the impact of new towns in the lives of different urban classes.

It is important to recall David Harvey's formulation for understanding the city, that is, by relating the 'social processes in the city to the spatial form which the city assumes' (1988: 23). According to Harvey,

> Any overall strategy for dealing with urban systems must contain and reconcile policies designed to change the spatial form of the city (by which is meant the location of objects such as houses, plant, transport links, and the like) with policies concerned to affect the social processes which go on in the city (i.e., the social structures and activities which link people with people, organizations with people, employment

opportunities with employees, welfare recipients with services, and so on). (Ibid.: 50)

Harvey dubs the socialist programme in post-war Britain as a failure as it did not have any impact on the distribution of real income in society. It was an attempt to 'alter distribution without altering the capitalist market structure within which income and wealth are generated and distributed' (ibid.: 110).

Despite its shortcomings, the New Town Movement, which had its roots in Britain, was widely accepted in many places in Europe and outside. The movement gathered momentum as it spread to France, Germany and Sweden in Europe and was later welcomed in the United States. It also filtered to other parts of the world, including British colonies like India, where new towns were built in the form of industrial, administrative and refugee towns.

NEW TOWNS IN THE INDIAN SETTING

The new towns in India were built in the twentieth century mostly by government agencies except in the case of Jamshedpur, which was planned under the auspices of the Tata industrialists. In the late nineteenth century, that is, prior to the development of these towns, the rural landscape in north India, especially Punjab, was interspersed with canal colonies, and urban growth was concentrated around railway colonies. The urban landscape of India was transformed with the vast network of railway lines which gave birth to railway towns. K. C. Sivaramakrishnan (1977) considers the railway towns as the harbinger of new towns in India. According to Sivaramakrishnan, these railway colonies initially consisted of employees' quarters and station buildings, but later became sizeable settlements with the inclusion of markets, schools, playgrounds, and so on (ibid.: 2). In 1941, about 30 railway towns with a population of 10,000 formed the 'nuclei of urban settlements' in India (ibid.). 'Kharagpur or Asansol in eastern India, Tundla or Itarsi in the north, Manamad or Bhusaval in the west and Arkonam or Waltair in the south are now familiar names of cities which originated as railway towns' (ibid.).

While the British government was involved only in building railway towns, the foundations of two steel industry towns (Bhadravati in Karnataka built by the princely state of Mysore and Jamshedpur in Bihar sponsored by a private capitalist) were laid before 1947. However, the New Town Movement in India actually gained momentum in the post-partition period when many administrative and refugee towns came into being. Otto H. Koenigsberger, the German architect, was closely associated with the building of new towns in India. Koenigsberger broadly divided the pre-colonial and post-partition new towns according to their functional significance. He classified the towns into three major groups: industrial towns (Bhadravati in Mysore and Jamshedpur in Bihar, which were built in the pre-colonial period), administrative towns (Bhubaneswar and Chandigarh), and refugee towns (Nilokheri and Faridabad in Punjab, Kalyani near Calcutta) built after 1947 (Koenigsberger 1952: 110).

The industrial towns, namely Bhadravati (1923) in Mysore and Jamshedpur (1944–45) in Bihar, built in the early twentieth century, owe their origin to the establishment of a group of factories in new settlement areas. They initially served as labour camps or colonies which were interspersed with a few bungalows for the executive class (Koenigsberger 1952). Jamshedji Tata envisioned the building of Jamshedpur, and his desire was subsequently fulfilled by Dorabji and R. D. Tata who employed engineers, architects and planners to shape the town. This town was built in many phases. In 1911, F. C. Temple, sanitary engineer to the Government of Bihar and Orissa, was appointed as the chief engineer in Jamshedpur. He broadly demarcated the residential, business and open areas of the city and also re-planned the bustees (Sivaramakrishnan 1977: 47). In 1944, when the population of the town exceeded its limit, Otto Koenigsberger was invited to make the first master plan. Thus Jamshedpur was 'incrementally planned' over a period of 34 years by the Kennedy Plan (1911), F. C. Temple (1920), the Stokes Plan (1936) and Koenigsberger (1944–45) (Sinha and Singh 2011: 264).

Administrative towns like Chandigarh and Bhubaneswar symbolised 'new seats of state governments' and housed mainly government employees (Koenigsberger 1952: 110). These administrative towns-cum-capitals were usually kept out of the purview of heavy industries. The focus in capital cities mainly veered towards building government offices, secretariats, legislative assemblies and so on (Sivaramakrishnan 1977: 43). Gandhinagar, the capital of Gujarat, was another important city built in 1960 which showcased independent India's 'attempted transformation to modernisation and self-sufficiency' (Kalia 2005: 4).

The new refugee settlements, also known as 'development towns', such as Rajpura in Patiala and Nilokheri and Faridabad in Punjab, began as tented camps for the training of artisans and used the construction work of the towns as object lessons in productivity and cooperation (Koenigsberger 1952: 100). The partition of the Indian subcontinent in 1947 and the resulting dislocation of the population necessitated planning fresh urban settlements for refugees. It also entailed involving people in building new townships as they had lost their former means of livelihood. But there were other exigencies as well which prompted the government to actively undertake the planning process. State intervention for building new towns in the decolonised world was accompanied by the evocation of pride as it reflected concern for the people (Sarin 1982: 3). Thus planning became a legitimate exercise of the Indian state to control and regulate urban areas in order to allocate land, relocate the masses as well as create work opportunities for them in the newly built towns.

FARIDABAD: A CASE STUDY

The city of Faridabad as it exists today largely encompasses the three distinct regions of Old Faridabad, New Industrial Township and the sectors developed by the Haryana Urban Development Authority (HUDA). The old Faridabad area (founded in 1607), about 17 km from Delhi, lies huddled between the Delhi–Mathura road and sectors which were later developed by HUDA. The New Industrial Township is the heart of the city which was developed in the post-partition period to rehabilitate refugees from the North West Frontier Province.

In the post-partition period, the socialist group within the Congress party deliberated on the uncertain future that awaited the refugees.

Kamaladevi Chattopadhyaya pertinently pointed out that the camps could not sustain the refugees forever. Self-help appeared to be the most feasible alternative to establish them firmly. It led to the affirmation of the cooperative principles: one person, one vote, and democratic control of members over management, that is, both equity and accountability. The head office of the Indian Cooperative Union (ICU) was in Delhi, and it became a registered society on 27 December 1948.[3] The ICU was closely involved with the rehabilitation work in Faridabad. The cooperative principle of organising work was also in tandem with the socialist ideals of planning supported by Nehru in the 1950s.

The idea of cooperation embodied the ideals desired in the newly conceived economy, polity and society—namely, to distribute the benefits of capitalistic production without suffering its ill-effects. Cooperation was described as a 'cornerstone of the welfare state' (Ministry of Information and Broadcasting 1951: 56). Ideologically it combined the advantages of private ownership with the public good, which became the blueprint for organised and democratic units of civil society. It also aimed to serve as a vehicle for self-reliance, to disseminate values of mutual aid and provide protection for the weaker sections.

The ICU was ideologically similar to the Community Development Movement, which was associated in the West from the 1930s to the 1960s with social organisation, rural extension and democratic empowerment. The Community Development Programme (CDP) was adapted in the Indian scenario to rehabilitate the disarrayed refugees. Among the various projects under the CDP in India, some focused on building new towns, but the main thrust was on encouraging rural development schemes, which aimed at narrowing the gap between the town and the country with the proclaimed ideal of urbanising the rural and ruralising the urban areas to achieve a symbiotic balance in the socio–spatial relationship.

The ICU aided rehabilitation endeavours at Faridabad by structuring cooperative farms, initiating community development and rural credit, and developing and managing large marketing networks such as the Central Cottage Industries Emporium and the Super Bazaar. Faridabad particularly became a nursery for the cooperative approach and its practical application. It proved to be an experimental ground for government and voluntary organisations to work in a constructive harmonious partnership (Jain 1998: 6).

Political leaders like Jayaprakash Narayan and Kamaladevi Chattopadhyaya envisioned cooperative institutions infusing a profound value change in the society by a slow permeation of the spirit of democratisation, self-governance, mutual assistance and social concern. Cooperative enterprises aimed at promoting self-reliance among citizens. The ICU started with specific projects like building rehabilitation sites for refugees on the fringes of Delhi. Later it broadened its scope by expanding into other areas of national development including rural cooperation, small industries, handlooms, handicrafts and social welfare.

The CDP and ICU appealed to the vision of a modernising state that wanted to introduce a participatory model which would galvanise the communities inhabiting refugee towns. However, the abiding ties of kith and kin were stronger and did not make way for any nascent citizenly bond to emerge which would have possibly facilitated a seamless transition to this model of development. Those inhabiting the refugee towns participated in the cooperative movement driven by the exigency of ensuring their resettlement. Since they had been forcibly and violently removed from their place of origin, this arrangement was accepted as a fait accompli or an exception rather than as a long-term solution. Initially the people actively engaged in building houses and derived their means of income by working in small-scale cooperative units. But gradually as they settled in the new towns, they disavowed the enshrined principles of community participation promulgated by the ICU to retreat to their own trading community instincts by building independent shops to hone their business skills. While the ICU and CDP upheld the dignity of manual work and self-help as virtues to be inculcated in ushering in transformation, yet the democratisation process cascading from above was unable to bridge the gap between town and the village dweller as envisioned.

CONCLUSION

Urban planning, apart from facilitating the resettlement of populations, was also deployed as a policy lever to reflect the prerequisites of 'economic growth and social change' of a newly independent nation (Kalia 2005: 2). People were encouraged to proactively participate in building the new capital cities and towns. Annapurna Shaw emphasises the functional significance of the new towns whose development was linked with the 'location of heavy industries and power projects' (2005: 5). According to Medha Kudaisya (2009: 940), the generic idea of planned development signified the leadership's intention 'to accomplish what they had critiqued the colonial state for not being able to do, that is, to bring about the benefits of material progress through scientific means to be shared equitably among all its citizens'. Thus the 'welfare' state steered its utopian vision of building new towns in India to usher in social equality in order to counter the asymmetrical effects of colonial urbanism. But the 'dual city' of racial segregation was upstaged by the emergence of new fissures within planned development, which has not been able to resolve the socio-spatial inequalities or dissolve the kith and kin ties which continue to be the hallmark of post-colonial urbanism.

NOTES

1 According to Zachariah, 'development' served as a 'framework within to conceptualise a future or possible Indian nation, a nation in the act of becoming.... It was felt to be necessary by some to make explicit certain connections between economic regeneration and development and the wider processes of "nation-building", "national discipline", the "modernisation" of the masses, or forms of government' (Zachariah 1999: 169).

2 Ebenezer Howard was a social visionary, an influential thinker on urban planning and founder of the Garden City Movement in England. He inspired the imagination of an idyllic city where humans lived in harmony with nature. This was illustrated by his 'Three Magnets' diagram representing town life, country life, and the proposed 'Town-Country' settlement which symbolised the prospect of blending the best of opportunities, amusements and wages present in a city with the scenic beauty and affordable housing possible in the countryside (Hall 2014: 96).

3 'Report of Indian Cooperative Union Limited, New Delhi for January 1948 to May 1949', *Formation of Cooperative Federation in Delhi*, File No. 3 (20)/1948, Chief Commissioner, Delhi State Archives, p. 53.

REFERENCES

Aldridge, Meryl. 1996. 'Only Demi Paradise? Women in Garden Cities and New Towns'. *Planning Perspectives*, 11(1): 23–39. https://doi.org/10.1080/026654396364916

Crouch, Winston W., and Richard Bigger. 1950. 'Metropolitan Decentralization: Britain's New Town Program'. *Western Political Quarterly*, 3(2): 244–61.

Hall, Peter. 2014. *Cities of Tomorrow: An Intellectual History of Urban Planning and Design since 1880*, 4th edn. Malden, MA: Wiley-Blackwell.

Hardy, Denis. 2002. *From Garden Cities to New Towns: Campaigning for Towns and Country Planning, 1899–1946*. Oxford: Oxford University Press.

Harvey, David. 1988. *Social Justice and the City*. London: Blackwell.

Jain, Lakshmi Chand. 1998. *The City of Hope: The Faridabad Story*. New Delhi: Concept.

Kalia, Ravi. 2005. *Gandhinagar: Building National Identity in Postcolonial India*. Delhi: Oxford University Press.

———. 2006. 'Modernism, Modernization and Post-colonial India: A Reflective Essay'. *Planning Perspectives*, 21(2): 133–56. https://doi.org/10.1080/02665430600555289

Koenigsberger, Otto H. 1952. 'New Towns in India'. *Town Planning Review*, 23(2): 94–132.

Kudaisya, Medha. 2009. 'A Mighty Adventure: Institutionalizing the Idea of Planning in Post-Colonial India, 1947–60'. *Modern Asian Studies*, 43(4): 939–78.

Madge, John. 1962. 'The New Towns Program in Britain'. *Journal of the American Institute of Planners*, 28(24): 208–19. https://doi.org/10.1080/01944366208979447

McEwan, Cheryl. 2009. *Postcolonialism and Development*. New York: Routledge.

Merlin, Pierre. 1980. 'The New Town Movement in Europe'. Special issue on 'Changing Cities: A Challenge to Planning', *Annals of the American Academy of Political Science*, 451(1): 76–85. https://doi.org/10.1177/000271628045100108

Ministry of Information and Broadcasting. 1951. *Facts about India*. New Delhi: Government of India.

Nehru, Jawaharlal. 1991. *A Construct of His Sayings on Art, Architecture, Heritage, Cities and City Planning*. New Delhi: National Institute of Urban Affairs.

Prakash, Gyan. 2002. 'The Urban Turn', in *Sarai Reader 02: The Cities of Everyday Life*, pp. 2–7. Delhi: Sarai, Centre for the Study of Developing Societies.

Sarin, Madhu. 1982. *Urban Planning in the Third World: The Chandigarh Experience*. London: Mansell Publishing House.

Shaw, Annapurna. 2005. *The Making of Navi Mumbai*. Delhi: Orient Longman.

Sinha, Amita, and Jatinder Singh. 2011. 'Jamshedpur: Planning an Ideal Steel City in India'. *Journal of Planning History*, 10(4): 263–81. https://doi.org/10.1177/1538513211420367

Sivaramakrishnan, K. C. 1977. *New Towns in India: A Report on a Study of Selected New Towns in the Eastern Region* (Homi Bhabha Fellowship Award Project with support from the Indian Institute of Management Calcutta).

Suge, Ikki. 2005. 'The Nature of Decision-Making in the Post-War New Towns Policy: The Case of Basildon, c.1945–70'. *Twentieth Century British History*, 16(2): 146–69. https://doi.org/10.1093/tweceb/hwi015

Zachariah, Benjamin. 1999. 'British and Indian Ideas of "Development": Decoding Political Conventions in the Late Colonial State'. *Itinerario*, 23(3–4): 162–209. https://doi.org/10.1017/S0165115300024645

Chapter 10

Ruinous Imaginations

Pithamber R. Polsani

The focus of this chapter is threefold. Firstly, to frame the transformation of Indian cities and neoliberal urbanism by employing 'ruin' as a conceptual category. Secondly, to focus on the aesthetics and architectural typology of gated communities that offer home ownership as a picturesque lifestyle. And thirdly, to explore the anxieties experienced by residents of gated communities due to the contradiction between the idyllic world of their enclaves and the perceived chaos of the street.

I

The buildings don't fall into ruin after they are built
but rather rise into ruin before they are built.
—Robert Smithson, 'The Monuments of Passaic'

The philosopher George Santayana's often-repeated apothegm 'those who forget history are condemned to repeat' (1905: 84) is nowhere more visible than in Indian cities in the last two decades. The old cities are being refashioned, new cities are being built and sprawling suburbs extended ignoring the two-hundred-year experience of building modern cities and, moreover, repeating not only all the mistakes of the past, but also creating new ones that are socially and culturally specific to India. Complacent in wilful ignorance of history, architects, builders, planners, politicians, and the public in general, engendered shambled urban conglomerations that are condemned to be ruins, to distinguish themselves only as the most polluted cities in the world.

Reflecting on the possible critique of philosophy in the wake of Auschwitz, French philosopher Lyotard wrote, '[a] critique builds an architectonics of reasons, but it is impossible to build anything whatsoever from or on this debris. All one can do is thread one's way through it, slip and slide through the ruins, listen to the complaints that emanate from them' (1988: 43). In the absence of reason both as rationality and as causality at the core of this new urbanism in India, what can be done as a critique is to sift through the debris and drift through the ruins following some tenuous threads.

The newness of new urbanism—a perceptible phenomenon across all metropolitan areas in India—resides in its sharp differentiation with the older models of urbanism rooted in modernity and modernism that the Indian State embraced immediately after independence from the British in 1947. The postcolonial history of India can be divided into two separate and distinct phases of modernity. The first phase that begins and ends in the four decades following independence is grounded on the ideals of modernity and political zeal to build India as a modern nation with a secular polity, democracy, equality, strong institutions, a vibrant public realm and, above all, the State as the arbitrator of competing interests between the people, the bourgeoisie and the capital. Economically, it is driven by belief in science and technology as the harbinger of modernity and large-scale industry and irrigation dams as the path to alleviating the poverty of millions of Indians.

The 'Temples of Modernity' is how Jawaharlal Nehru characterised the factories, industrial towns, institutions, cities and hydroelectric dams that were feverishly built in the first two decades of independent India. These monumental structures, way beyond human scale, largely invisible and inaccessible to ordinary Indians, were memorialised as national patrimony through State-sanctioned photography and documentary cinema, contemporaneously recorded and produced. These structures and buildings were framed, notably by photographer Sunil Janah, in a dual and contradictory role: as the harbingers of modernity and as monuments for a modern India. This incongruent coupling of past and future—commemoration and expectation—in the present, is reflective of how the India of that time came to be defined by the political and intellectual leadership: a modern nation with a rich tradition. Janah's photographs attempt to suture this fissure—modernity and tradition—through a sponsored pathos of new monumentality. Following in the footsteps of Margaret Bourke-White, Janah perfects the heroic mode of documentary photography: very low angles to accentuate the vertical structures of factories like smoke chimneys, electrical transmission tower; sharp contrasts between light and shadow in black and white to add drama; and long shots to aggrandise the expansiveness of the industrial campuses. What is inherent in Janah's photographs, probably unintended, is the dialectical tension between industry and infrastructure conceived as civic and laic memorials in a culture of idol worship with the hope that the profane structures of modernity would subsume the religious icons to emerge as a new sacredness. Moreover, the photographs, through visual and rhetorical strategies and the discourse that surrounded them at that time, monumentalise industrial architecture. But these heroic Monuments for Modernity lie in real and conceptual ruins while the 'Temples' flourish in India and the memories of Nehruvian modernity have become an overbearing nightmare for neoliberal India.

The second modernity that started in the last decade of the twentieth century is driven by the neoliberal dogma of market fundamentalism, financial deregulation, worship of technology and salesmanship as an endearing human quality, and the withdrawal of the State from the social contract and its obligations for providing services to the citizens such as health, housing, education and infrastructure. The neoliberal Indian State, like any other in the world, is engaged in transferring public wealth into private hands through private–public partnership models or outright gifting of public lands and, often, acquiring individuals' land by invoking eminent domain to transfer them to private companies. The financial deregulation has led to easy availability of home mortgages and consumer credit, which in turn has resulted in exponential growth in urban areas. In only a generation, the aspirations of the middle class for owning a home have changed from a lifetime dream realised at retirement, to a first investment of a newly employed.

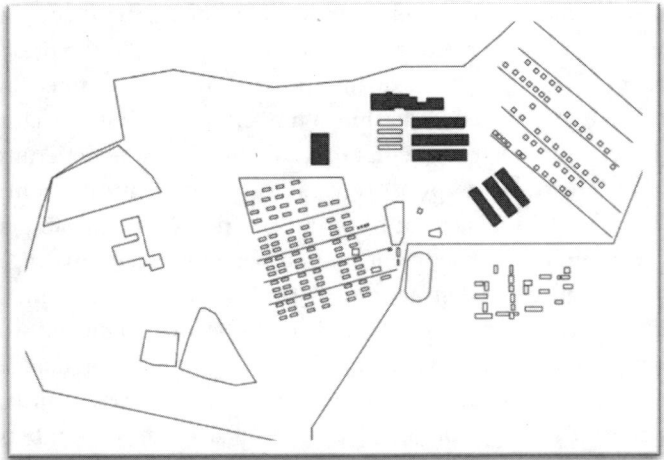

Figure 1 *Hindustan Machine Tools Company Town, Bangalore*
Source: Drawing by Priya Joseph based on Google Maps.

Spatially, the ideals of the first modernity were fulfilled not in the existing cities, but in the newly built company towns, new towns and model towns, which were, ideologically, horizontal reflections of vertically monumental factories and dams. In the 1950s and 1960s, the townships built around large industrial public sector undertakings were designed to embody, in their spatial arrangement, and at the same time fulfil, in their functioning, the ideals of Indian modernity (Figures 1 and 2).

Intended primarily for the employees of these companies, the towns were planned as shared space for Indians from different regions, religions, belief systems, castes and classes living and working in harmony as the citizens of modern India. Rational arrangement and managerial functionalism were the primary organising principles of these towns. Although housing was segregated according to the hierarchy in the workplace—managers, foremen and workers—the services, education, health, recreation and commercial, were common to all. The conceptual framework that informed these planned towns is the same as that which was intensely debated in the first three decades of the twentieth century across Europe. Today most of these company towns of

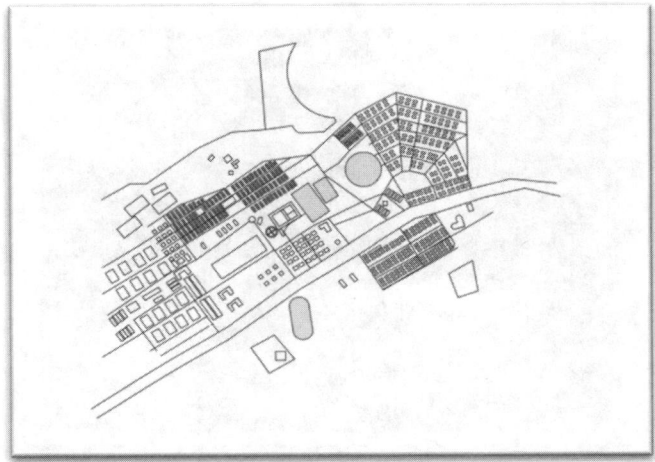

Figure 2 *Indian Telephone Industries Township, Bangalore*
Source: Drawing by Priya Joseph based on Google Maps.

mid-twentieth-century India lie, both metaphorically and literally, in ruins (Figure 3). They are the remnants of an unfinished dream; founded on an idea of the modern that would propel a new nation born at the stroke of midnight to a new dawn. It is on top of these ruins of unfulfilled utopia that the neoliberal urban conglomerations have risen up (Figures 4 and 5 here).

Figure 3 *Hindustan Machine Tools Township, Bangalore, in ruins*
Source: Photos by author.

Figure 4 *Hindustan Machine Tools Township, Bangalore, with new gated communities*

Source: Drawing by Priya Joseph based on Google satellite image.

Figure 5 *Hindustan Machine Tools Township, Bangalore. The built and visible structures are some of the new gated communities. Under the green cover lie the ruins of the old township.*

Source: Image by Priya Joseph based on Google satellite image.

The urban phenomenon of the second modernity in the last two decades in India has neither the rational organisation of growth nor the charms of idiosyncratic urbanism. It is driven neither by a pragmatic plan nor by an architectural ambition. Instead, it is an uncontrolled proliferation of built environments, groupings of fenced enclaves connected by roads. They are not cities, but a collection of gated communities of townhouses and apartments, secluded office complexes and special economic zones (SEZs), and privately controlled shopping malls and recreational spaces. They are built as fragments to be sold as commodities on pieces of land acquired as currency in a land bank. In Lefebvrian words, it is neither representation of space—planned, architectural symbolic of power—nor is it the space of representations—that of resistance and everyday life. Instead, this new urbanism lies at an intersection of pure commodification facilitated by a neoliberal State that functions as an agent of financial capital. This phenomenon that defies all forms of understanding urbanism, including the vernacular, can only be comprehended as ruin.

II

... everything to me becomes allegory
—Charles Baudelaire, *The Flowers of Evil*

Since they became for the first time objects of contemplation for the Renaissance humanists, ruins have persisted in the imagination of artists, philosophers and thinkers alike. As Brian Dillon (2011), a leading scholar of ruinology observes, for the humanists the ruins were fragments of code to be deciphered. For the eighteenth-century mind, ruin was the destiny of history and of all human creation. The romantics in the nineteenth century valorised decay as artistic symbol (ibid.: 55–56). For example, in the picturesque aesthetic, which I will highlight a little later, the ruin was a vital element of visual appeal. William Gilpin, one of the greatest exponents and practitioners of the picturesque, explains the importance of ruins in painting, writing, 'we must use the sledgehammer, instead of the chisel: we must beat down one half of it, deface the other, and throw the mutilated members around in heaps. In short, from a smooth building we must turn it into a rough ruin' (Gilpin 1792: 7). To the moderns, ruins are the emblematic state of the present that the living bring upon themselves. T. S. Eliot wrote in the concluding lines of *The Westland*, 'these fragments I have shored against my ruin' (2004: 75). The postmoderns ruminate on the ruins of modernity without realising that after cannibalising the past we can play only with the rubble.

In order to employ ruin as epistemological category, it is important to delineate the ontological characteristics that are relevant to my purpose here. The ontological features of the ruin are the following.

First, *fragmentariness*: Once a whole, the ruins come to us as dismembered and disconnected pieces that are impossible to be assembled into a cohesive totality. Each ruin in its dereliction is a totality in itself. A fragment is neither related to what lay adjacent to it nor is it a piece that would complete a whole. It stands on its own, singular and insulated.

Second, *presentlessness*, that is the absence of 'now' as an existential time. Ruins reside in a disjointed temporality—past and future—neither of which can be phenomenologically accessible. Ruins are testimony to a collapsed dream of the past's future and projections of an inevitability of the present's future. For example, Gustav Doré produced an engraving in 1872 based on what Thomas Babington Macaulay had written 32 years earlier about a New Zealander contemplating the ruins of London. While Lord Macaulay, in his reverie, fantasises about future London in ruins, his proposal in reality to introduce English as official langue in India replacing Persian and English as the medium of instruction in schools resulted in ruinous consequences for Indian vernacular education and systems of knowledge.

Third, *imaginaries*: Because of the fractured temporality and the oscillation between the past and future, the present can only be experienced as an anachronistic imaginary, a fetishistic fantasy and a delirium.

There is an indelible connection between the ruins and the rise of modern architecture and urban design as disciplines. As architect Robin Skinner asserts,

[the] accounts by British architect-travelers of ruins in the Eastern Mediterranean and Middle East were published as large folios between 1750 and 1850. In the published volumes, travelers presented the

surviving fragments and reconstituted them into reinvented larger works. In doing so, they changed the Western understanding of architecture and its day-to-day practice. (2002: 1)

However, these journeys, romantic and, at times, fanciful explorations, were framed by the picturesque aesthetic that dominated eighteenth- and nineteenth-century Britain. Following in this tradition, James Fergusson, a Scotsman who came to India in 1828 to make a fortune, which he did in indigo farming, undertook an extensive study of Indian temples, mausoleums and other structures many of which were in ruins. In writing the first history of architecture, he invented Indian Architecture with categories that even today remain uncontested. Ruins were at the heart, defining the past and future of architecture in the eighteenth and nineteenth centuries, and the ruins continue to be our horizon of urban imagination.

In the neoliberal reshaping of Indian cities, two phases are discernible in cities like Bangalore and Hyderabad. In the first phase, lasting about a decade and a half starting in the early 1990s, individual family houses in existing neighbourhoods were demolished to be replaced by small apartment complexes of 10–15 apartments each. In replacing single-family homes with multiple family units, the population density of the neighbourhood increased exponentially, and, combined with an increase in automobile density as well as support services, the cities, within a decade of liberalisation, were completely choked up. It is only from the early 2000s that the real estate companies began promoting large theme-based gated communities, enormous office complexes, SEZs and malls that have become a typology for neoliberal modernism. Since the land necessary for building large themed gated communities was in short supply within the city, the developers began to move to the outskirts along the major highways leading out of the city. All the new constructions were conceived as self-contained communities either as single-family homes, townhouses, apartments/flats, or office buildings and malls.

The major distinguishing characteristic of these new neighbourhoods is their boundedness, that is, they are encircled by a wall clearly separating them, firstly and most importantly, from the street and non-gated populations, and secondly from other similar communities or built structures. Each separated from the other, disjointed and dissimilar they stand as disconnected fragments. These walled communities are not only created as individual entities without any relation to others, but were created as a means of restricting the access and to clearly differentiate the inside from the outside. The inside/outside segregation is not only between the city and the gated community but also between neighbouring communities. It is nearly impossible for residents of different gated enclaves to come together as there is no shared space other than the street.

A street in India is no man's land. It is used for the movement of 'pure biological life without mediation', to borrow philosopher Giorgio Agamben's words (2000: 40). It is a purgatory that connects different paradises—gated communities for living, working, shopping and recreation.

III

> How fascinating is that class
> Whose only member is Me!
> . . . .
> Obsession with security
> In Sovereigns prevails;
> His Highness and The People both
> Pick islands for their jails.
> —W. H. Auden, *Bucolics 5. Islands*

It is not uncommon to be greeted in the morning with full, front-page advertisements promoting new apartment complexes or villas of luxurious living, security, serenity, unparalleled views of lakes and non-existing landscapes, and above all sexy, happy people discovering their repressed passions. What is offered in these full-page spreads is not a dwelling that can be made into a home, but *a lifestyle that can be called your own*. Lifestyle is a composite object that consists of structures and actions. The structures are material support for the presentation of a lifestyle; however, actions are aspirational. While the structures offer superior status, elitism and exclusivity to those who live in the gated communities, actions enhance their status within the community.

Unlike the images in shampoos, soaps and age-defying face cream ads that remain only as elusive ideals, real estate advertisements create a reconfigured and realisable domesticity. By colonising the quotidian and organising everyday life as a closed circuit of controlled consumption, they systematise thought and structuralise action (Lefebvre 1971). The 360-degree views, open expanses, swimming pools, gymnasiums, club houses and gardens are offered as consumables of good-life and the activities—long walks, gym workouts, playing with children, and frolicking in artificial lakes—as the very essence of domestic life. In real estate advertisements, the semantic complex of image/text obliterates the difference between the image and the object. And what is offered through this erasure is pure sign *qua* consumption. Therefore, living in these domestic spaces is consuming lifestyle and through consumption the lifestyle is attained.

This transubstantiation of *home* into *lifestyle* is achieved through consuming images. Consumption literally means ingesting. The consumption in this case is not oral but scopic. The dominant aesthetic frame that structures these consuming images is the picturesque. The picturesque is probably the most enduring aesthetic since its invention in eighteenth-century Britain as a mechanism for designing landscape gardens. Because of the use of simple visual devices, scenic arrangement of forms and florescent subject matter, the picturesque enjoys the greatest appeal among the general public. The picturesque lends itself naturally to a scenic arrangement of facilities in gated communities—the pool, the gym, play areas, walking paths, trees, bushes, plants, lawns and the people. It is not just in ads, but in reality, as a typology of a built form, that gated communities create spatio-visual experience. Hence, the architectural experience ceases to be bodies moving in space in relation to objects; instead it is a sequence of unfolding arrangements of built forms in a scopic field wherein space is a purely visual experience.

The picturesque as a dominant aesthetic frame for creating an architecture that unfolds as visual experience, renders a gated community as a picture. As a 'better life', this specular image coincides with the resident's imaginary, fulfilling a fantasy picture of lifestyle. However, this enclosed picture gives rise to anxiety and corresponding paranoiac responses because of a perceived threat from outside. As a result, the residents of these communities define extensive security procedures for entry and exit not only into the community, but also the individual buildings. Surveillance devices such as video cameras and biometric scanners are installed in the shared facilities. Moreover, the residential associations define elaborate rules, regulations and punitive actions to regulate the behaviour of residents. These rules have often led to major conflicts among residents resulting in police intervention and legal action. Gated communities often pretend to possess extrajudicial and extra-national status.

IV

There is no worse deprivation, no worse privation, perhaps, than that of the losers in the symbolic struggle for recognition, for access to a socially recognized social being, in a word, to humanity.

—Pierre Bourdieu, *Pascalian Meditations*

In India, cities as built environments do not consist of clearly demarcated territories of use and action. Instead, varied spaces—domestic, commercial, street, entertainment and shopping—overlap and intrude into each other. As a result, solitude, peace and quiet, and openness are inviting luxuries. Similarly, an absence of avenues for cultivating emerging ideas of health, body and beauty, and the notions of family life, senior living and others provides the impetus for offering a picturesque lifestyle as a commodity of consumption. In addition to images of domestic real estate advertisements, magazines and newspapers actively promote lifestyles through beauty, health and good housekeeping columns and advice. This picturesque lifestyle image as the new domesticity offered by gated communities stands at a confluence of the real (the outside) and the imagined (the inside), although the residents have an inverted view of this binary. They portray the inside as the real and the outside as a distorted reflection of the reality. As a result, the relation to the outside—the city, the surroundings and its habitants—and the inside—the residents and the picturesque setting—produces an interesting dialectic.

A gated community is an act of self-exclusion and self-segregation. Ironically, in practice, the exclusion from the rest of the city space rests on the active participation of cities' marginalised habitants who come to work as domestic help, chauffeurs, security guards, car washers, gardeners, plumbers, electricians and other maintenance staff. The domestic help and other service providers are the connection and at the same time the buffer between the new domesticity and the city they exclude.

It is in the treatment of the help and supporting staff that the exclusiveness of a gated community is continuously affirmed, because the excluded Other provides the necessary support for the fantasy. Paradoxically, gated communities reach out to the cities' underclass because the community can be sustained only through their labour. But at the same time maids and supporting staff are seen as the greatest threat to a carefully constructed domestic paradise. Therefore, close monitoring of staff through police verification, ID cards, entry/exit procedures, uniforms, use of separate elevators, body searches, collective punishments and other surveillance procedures as well as behavioural requirements are strictly imposed and any violations are immediately dealt with. Now mobile technology and apps have made monitoring residents, help and visitors more effective, but also more intrusive. These measure have led to hostilities.[1]

While the help and maintenance staff are confined to the margins of the gated community and subjected to monitoring, the residents themselves become mere actors in the idealised spaces. The desire to maintain an image identical to what was presented in the promotional brochure is so strong that the residents themselves are viewed as potential threats to the fantasy. In order to suppress any irruptions and disruptions in space, rules are formulated defining the use of different spaces; normative behaviours are prescribed for residents; rules of conduct are elaborated. The behavioural requirements, surveillance mechanisms and punitive measures used to control the supporting personnel and residents of the gated communities are similar, but the effects they produce differ based on which side of the dividing line the individual is located: inside or outside. These techniques of systematic control, discipline and punishment make constantly visible the non-belonging of domestic staff, both to themselves and to the gated community. For residents, on the other hand, the same procedures are accepted as necessary for realising the lifestyle and maintaining the image of idealised domesticity they have invested in. To the list of institutions—schools, prisons, clinics and mental asylums—that Foucault studied as mechanisms of control, surveillance and subjugation of the body, we should add new gated communities.

Thomas Whately, a proponent of picturesque landscape gardens, wrote in his work *Observations on Modern Gardening*, 'At the sight of a ruin, reflections on the change, the decay and the desolation before us, naturally occur; and they introduce a long succession of others, all tinctured with that melancholy which these have inspired' (1776: 155). If the ruins inspire melancholy in those who view them, the buildings that rise up as ruins provoke psychosis in those who live in them.

NOTE

1   See, for example, https://cdn.dnaindia.com/sites/default/files/styles/half/
    public/2017/07/15/592931-noida-case-pti.jpg (accessed 22 June 2020).

REFERENCES

Agamben, Giorgio. 2000. *Means without End: Notes on Politics* (trans. C. Casarino and V. Binetti). Minneapolis: University of Minnesota Press.
Auden, W. H. 1991. *Collected Poems*. London: Faber and Faber.
Baudelaire, Charles. 1993. *The Flowers of Evil* (trans. J. McGowan). Oxford: Oxford University Press.
Bourdieu, Pierre. 2000. *Pascalian Meditations* (trans. R. Nice). Stanford: Stanford University Press.
Dillon, Brian. 2006. 'Fragments from a History of Ruin'. *Cabinet*, 20: 55–59.
Eliot, T. S. 2004. *The Complete Poems and Plays*. London: Faber and Faber.
Gilpin, William. 1792. *Three Essays: On Picturesque Beauty*. London: R. Blamire.
Lefebvre, Henri. 1971. *Everyday Life in the Modern World* (trans. S. Rabinovitch). New York: Harper and Row.
Lyotard, Jean-François. 1988. *Heidegger and 'the Jews'* (trans. Andreas Michel and Mark Roberts). Minneapolis: University of Minnesota Press.
Santayana, George. 1905. *Reason and Commonsense*. New York: Scribner's.

Skinner, Robin. 2002. Introduction to *Unpacking Ruins* Exhibition. https://www. otago.ac.nz/library/exhibitions/ruins/about.html (accessed 10 December 2019).

Smithson, Robert. 1967. 'The Monuments of Passaic'. *Artforum*, December, pp. 52–57.

Whately, T. 1776. *Observations on Modern Gardening*. London: T. Pyne and Son.

PART IV

Material Manifestations

Chapter 11

City in Steel and Timber

Sankalpa

With the changing climatic conditions, the future of our cities rests on material and the way we use it.[1] In this light, the present chapter argues that building details become an extremely important aspect of the future design of cities. Details that can be dismantled and reused in the building's life cycle to reduce waste, that ease pressure on new demand for resources, are responsive to livelihood opportunities, and use less water in construction, will be the need of the future cities of India. A response to these conditions was sought through explorations undertaken within a studio conducted for the Master's in Architectural Design at CEPT University, which informs much of the discussion in this chapter. Here, building materials like steel, timber, earth and bamboo were used to work out an architectural possibility with dry construction as its primary system. The choice of these materials came out of their high reuse value apart from their being natural. The scope of the chapter is limited to a focus on the aspect of detailing explored within the architectural design studio. A detail matrix of the studio is provided to substantiate the process of arriving at assembly-based construction details.

'Increasing desertification of India's soil is a fundamental threat to agriculture,' according to the *State of India's Environment 2017*:

nearly 30 per cent of India is degraded or facing desertification. Of India's total geographical area of 328.72 million hectares (MHA), 96.4

MHA is under desertification. In eight states—Rajasthan, Delhi, Goa, Maharashtra, Jharkhand, Nagaland, Tripura and Himachal Pradesh—around 40 to 70 per cent of land has undergone desertification. More to it, 26 of 29 Indian states have reported an increase in the area undergoing desertification in the past 10 years. (CSE 2017)

The impact of this is not going to be small. Apart from large-scale impact on agriculture, it will put immense pressure on the building industry. Most of the bricks in Gujarat have salinity ingress resulting in efflorescence. Apart from the performance of the aerated blocks, the shift from bricks to blocks is driving the mining of river sand or crushed stone sand. This will widely further the overuse and depletion of a single resource. Demand for a particular range of pH and freshwater is another growing concern for construction. Many parts of Gujarat are using fresh Narmada water for construction.

The construction industry has the ability to relook at the craft of making buildings where industrial and artisanal modes can converge instead of becoming enemies for narrow economic gains. In the wake of the situation just described, the construction industry needs to respond to pertinent and imperative challenges such as innovation in construction with care towards resource utilisation, waste, long-term environmental impact and creating opportunities for artisans.

In light of this, the master's programme in Architecture Design at CEPT University focuses on furthering emerging methods in resource-efficient design, detailing and construction. It intends to be a leading studio in taking up innovation in design and detailing in a sustained and progressive manner suited to the Indian context. The present chapter employs the detailing outcome of an academic design studio experiment conducted as part of the Master's in Architecture Design at CEPT in July 2019 to discuss some of the aforementioned concerns.

According to Rather et al. (2017), 'food contamination is a matter of serious concern, as the high concentration of chemicals present in the edibles poses serious health risks.' High amounts of chemical compounds that are harmful for the human body have entered the food chain because of pesticides and other modes of processing our food. With the rise of the city, agriculture slowly and steadily got removed from it. Cities

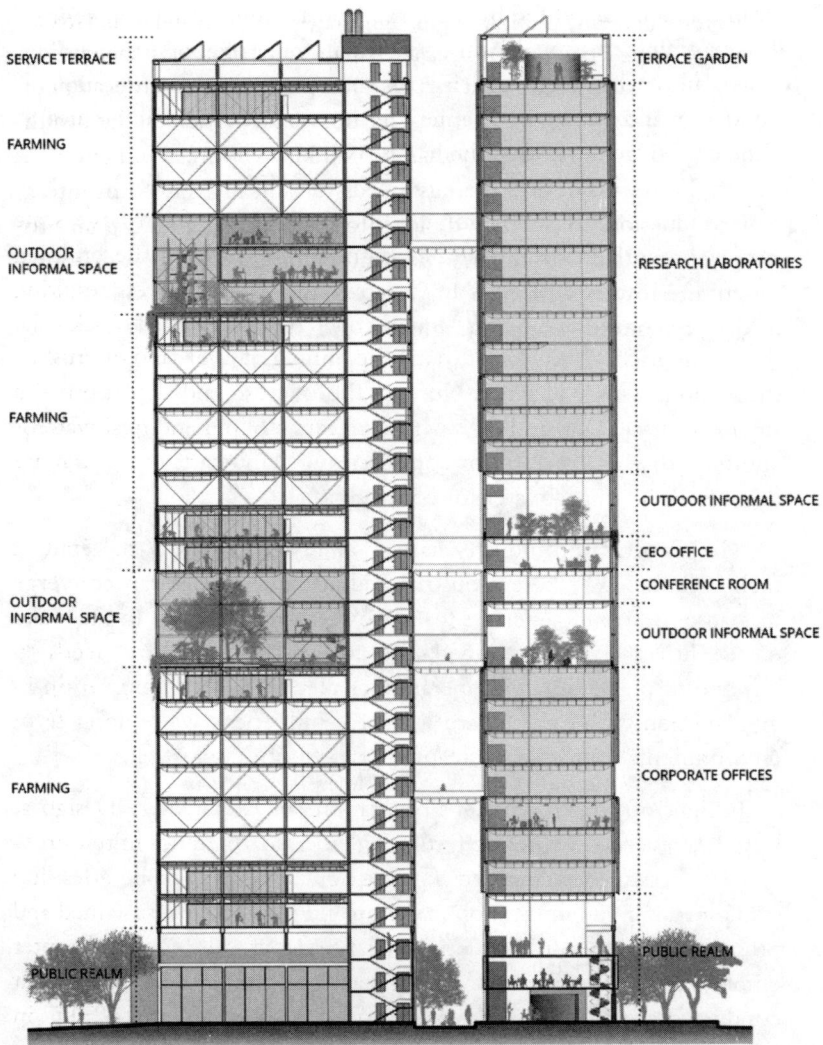

Figure 1 *Sectional drawing showing the overall spatial distributions of functions within the building*

Source: Drawn by Harshil Amin, Master's in Architectural Design, CEPT University.

became a focus supported by the hinterland as their production centre. Slowly, with increasing urbanisation, the number of people depending on agriculture has been reducing. With depreciating organic ways of production and inroads by chemical fertilisers and pesticides, the health of the city today remains in the hands of unknown forces and circumstances. To regain health, the city needs to radically transform into a semi–production house. The design project assumed a radical city to be a place overlaid with the new demand of localised food production. Agriculture towers within such a city were undertaken as one of the building types to investigate (Figures 1 and 2).

Figure 2 *Bird's-eye view of the site*
Source: Students of the Master's in Architectural Design, CEPT University, 2019–20.

The agriculture tower is like an experimental setup for the community which can be erected and later dismantled in the future. The idea of the tower is not only that it produces but constantly engages in

1. developing various retrofits that are required for existing buildings to have some level of productivity;
2. developing an entrepreneurship around agriculture where it can be maintained personally or can be leased;
3. working on various emerging building types that will house agricultural produce as part of a decentralised production facility.

PROVOCATION STATEMENT OF THE STUDIO

1. If the architecture of tomorrow has to respond to increasing demand for optimising the utilisation of limited resources, innovation in the construction process and details is a key factor in achieving this.
2. If innovation in construction and detail is a key way forward towards the future with increased pressure on limited resources, architecture needs to evolve out of availability of material, skills, tools and technology to recalibrate to the times.
3. If availability of material, skills, tools and technology needs architecture to recalibrate with time, experiments in detailing and construction materials that have either high reuse value or are natural like steel, timber, earth and bamboo need to be at the forefront of adaptation in emerging building types.
4. If experiments in construction and detailing in materials like steel, timber, earth and bamboo need to be at the forefront, the human agency involved in this process has to be a stakeholder adapting to emerging building types with an inclusive construction detailing.
5. If the human agency involved in this process has to work towards inclusive construction detailing, consciousness of effective methods of detailing as a response to resource utilisation needs to be relooked.

CONTEXT

Historically, there have been two dominant ways in which the process of building production took place in India pre-1991 or pre-liberalisation of the Indian economy. In traditional architecture, the choices of building materials have been usually more durable. The agencies involved in constructing these buildings have been different from the user of the building. The investment in the repair cycle of such buildings has often depended on choices of materials and construction systems. The vernacular buildings, however, have either worked with materials which have been slowly upgraded to be more durable, or worked with systems of connections and elements that require continuous repair and recycle. Every year in Indian villages, groups of artisans would visit to repair the tiles, put a new layer of thatch or change the tying materials. In a way, the cycles of repair time as a factor in traditional and vernacular buildings are what can be seen as a crucial difference between the two. However, the following learnings can be drawn in contemporary times from the perspective of environmental consideration as well as supporting small-scale livelihood opportunities:

1. Many durable structural forms have primarily employed compression-based systems. The earliest caves of Ajanta dating from around the second century BCE have vaulted roofs and only in the later period did flat roofs start emerging. In case the systems have been observed to be under bending stress, the ability of the detail to undergo ease of repair has worked towards increasing the lifespan of the building. Modan et al. (2006) in their study on systems of construction in traditional Ahmedabad houses point to ease of repair as one of the characteristics of the houses as compared to contemporary materials and construction technologies. The old city of Ahmedabad has survived with its single and double floor spanning system in timber as it has allowed the joist and binders to change, thereby stressing the ability of the details to undergo easy repair. This gives us a clue about the manner in which we need to address the building stock of the future where the scope of assembling building parts, taking them out and putting them back if convenient ensures buildings lasting more than a hundred years.

2. Details that account for repairs instead of complete demolition and discarding of materials are not only supportive of the environment but create a chain of less hazardous livelihoods around the life cycle of materials.

3. It is essential to compare the life cycle of various materials to that of RCC (reinforced cement concrete) to understand their performance over time. A *Guardian* report by Watts (2019) points out, 'If the cement industry were a country, it would be the third largest carbon dioxide emitter in the world with up to 2.8bn tonnes, surpassed only by China and the US.' The Indian story shall be no different either. The reinforced concrete uses very high embodied energy and is one of the most polluting construction materials. The lifespan of reinforced concrete is shorter compared to natural materials like timber or including industrial material like steel in a frame structure if it is used in an appropriate manner. Once the RCC is discarded and the concrete is separated from steel, the number of steps to reuse the discarded material again increases. The forms in which the material is available and the number of steps involved in the reuse of its constituents keep increasing, thus necessitating an assessment of the material's environmental impact.

4. From the perspective of the life cycle of a material, historical evidence has favoured brittle or denser materials in compression as a way to increase the lifespan of the building. These materials like stone or brick under transfer of load use its property fully. Most of the tensile materials do not last long and eventually give up in a short duration of time unlike materials under compression. The same materials under compression have been found to last longer than under bending.

5. Steel, timber and bamboo come in linear form and also use assembly as a method of construction. This is much in sync with many vernacular traditions where parts come together to make a whole and each part can be worked separately and then secured. The use of steel helps to achieve large span structure with less mass unlike timber and bamboo.

METHODOLOGY

The analogue methods of form finding as commonly used have their historical basis in Antoni Gaudí's work, later furthered in a much more explicit manner by Frei Otto at the Institute of Lightweight Structures,

University of Stuttgart. The method of form finding in a way is the derivation of the form by how forces are organised in an experiment for emergence of form, instead of a preconceived form.

The studio at CEPT takes up clues from various experiments conducted by Otto and his team to inquire into form and force relationships. The argument made by D'Arcy Thompson (1968) in his seminal work, that form is a diagram of force, is accepted as the basis of inquiry in this studio.

I was introduced to modelling experiments by Prof. R. J. Vasavada in 2012. He himself had developed his teaching method for the 'Form, Structure & Material' studio at CEPT University, Faculty of Architecture, in the 1980s. I happened to assist him in a course on surface structure to grapple with modelling experiments in understanding structural concepts. While working on this further, I made a departure from the form-finding process to form-deriving experiments using paper and threads, where the process of arriving at form uses the modelling experiment but does not necessarily produce form as emergence, rather as an articulation of the paper in a rule-based pattern. The shift to the form-deriving method has been a conscious one, to strive for fresh articulation while responding to the experimental condition of distortion in form as an application of various forces. In this manner, there is a departure taken up in the studio where form is derived by articulating the flexible and brittle property of the experimenting material before the introduction of building material.

From the perspective of pedagogy, a direct engagement of the body through experiments conducted by the students is a necessary step in form derivation. A choice of using tension members has been taken up consistently to allow the body to experience force while tying the cables of the model of the structural system.

The studio was conducted with a focus on exploring structural systems in tall structures using primarily timber, steel and bamboo.

STEPS TOWARDS THE DEVELOPMENT OF DETAILS

	Stages	Steps	Remarks
1	**Modelling and generating systems**	Identifying skills	Analogue & digital
		Introducing analogue method through series of experiments on form finding	The constraints imposed by the method should connect to the programme
		Integrating analogue with digital to expose digital knowledge form	*Identifying digital parameters to their analogue equivalent, introduction to basic algorithm in Rhino & Grasshopper*
		Deriving structural system using analogue method/ deriving further iterations using digital method	Using analogue method and digital method/*type of digital information/ input that can lead to several iterations*
2	**Testing**	Testing system under forces	Process of form optimisation (efficient, light)/translation of physical/analogue to a digital model with appropriate geometries
3	**Detailing & detail as a set of affordances**	Introduction of programme and choosing of structural system, material and detail appropriate to the programme; development of fenestration system	Evident relationship between system and programme/selection of detail on the basis of affordance, assembly sequence and production

MODELLING AND GENERATING SYSTEM

Students were asked to undertake a paper experiment in a vertical cantilever having a height of 2,100 mm. They were given a maximum area that they could occupy in order to stabilise the overall structure. The constraints imposed by the experiment were fixed sizes of the paper, all joints as pin joints and use of thread as a necessary condition for generating the structural system. The purpose of giving pin joints and thread was to ensure that students developed sensitivity towards the magnitude and direction of forces.

Once students arrived at various options, they were asked to simplify the rules of propagation as well as stabilise the system. The digital platforms of Rhino and Grasshopper were used to further study the model. The system is made out of parts instead of one single member as a constraint to the experiment. This ensured that the joinery and junctions were built into the structural experiment. This later became the basis of the bearing and spanning system of the proposed building.

The learning outcomes of this stage were following:

1. To create a modelling experiment to study the behaviour of force and stabilise the form based on the learnings.
2. To identify the role of each part in a joinery with respect to force and the possible property of material.
3. To design a joinery that was a combination of two different flexibilities resulting in a mutually strengthening combination of joints.
4. To be able to code information for computational tasks using Rhino and Grasshopper.
5. To be able to differentiate types of information required to process analogue and digital mediums of production (see Figures 3, 4A and 4B).

TESTING

Physical experiments were worked out with push, pull and rotation including basic shaking of the base to register distortion in overall form. The distortions were noted on a grid and further worked out to stabilise.

Figure 3 *Derivation of a vertical system as an outcome of stabilisation of paper strips*

Source: Subham Pani, Master's in Architectural Design, CEPT University.

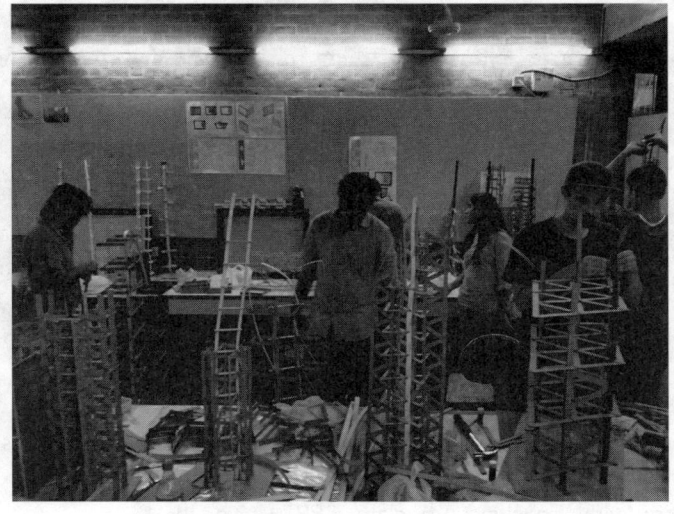

A

Figure 4 *(Continued)*

Source: Amod Shah, Master's in Architectural Design, CEPT University.

B

Figure 4 *Studio working methods of engagement and constant observation and iterative physical modelling using materials*

Source: Aviral, Teaching Associate, CEPT University.

A condition of 30 times the weight of the overall mass used to make the structure was assumed to be the beginning point of the test. Once the material was introduced, structural engineering help was taken for sizing of the members. The learning outcomes of this stage were following:

1. To identify forces working in various members of the spanning and bearing system.
2. To study and simulate the behaviour of the building under various forces.
3. To improvise configuration of various parts of the structure as a response to behaviour (Figures 5, 6 and 7).

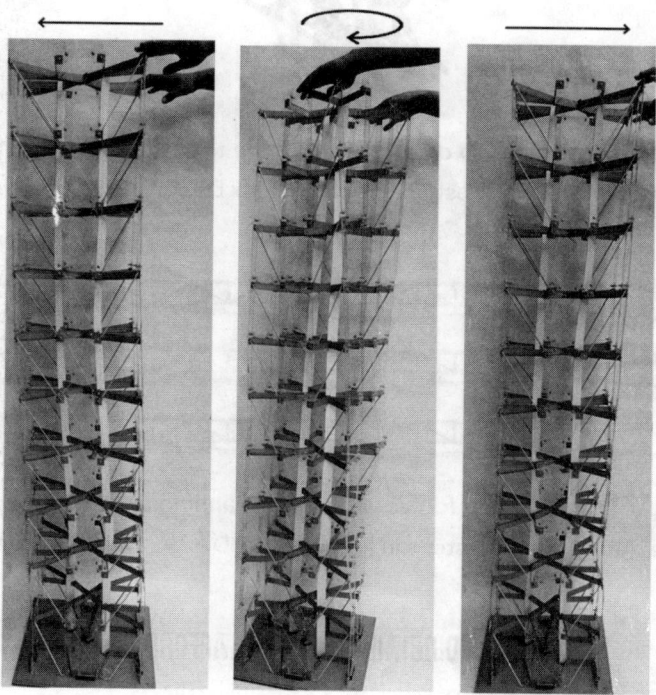

Figure 5 *Preliminary testing through models to understand the system's response to push, pull and rotation*

Source: Subham Pani, Master's in Architectural Design, CEPT University.

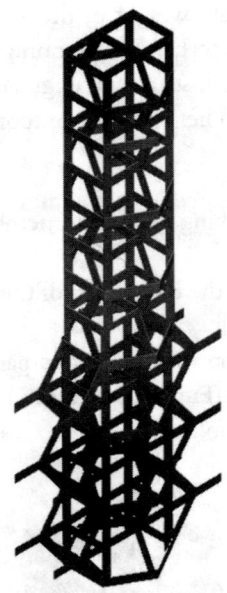

Figure 6 *Simulations to describe and refine the structural system*
Source: Subham Pani, Master's in Architectural Design, CEPT University.

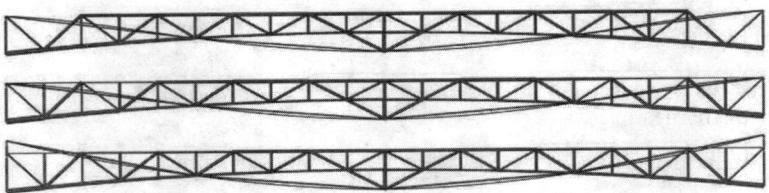

Figure 7 *Diagramming forces within the spanning systems*
Source: Amod Shah, Master's in Architectural Design, CEPT University.

DETAILING AND DETAIL AS A SET OF AFFORDANCES

In a conventional design process, detailing is usually seen to begin at
1:20 scale, where how materials come together is expressed through
drawings. The realm of detailing usually encompasses best practices or
standard details that are employed in a building. Allen and Rand (2009)

explain detailing as an opportunity to advance the concepts, symbols and aesthetic themes of the basic design. They discuss the thematic breakdown of details into function, constructability and aesthetics. Emmitt et al. (2004) discuss detailing from the perspective of ecology and enumerate the necessary stages in order to work out a detail. This work is of immense relevance as it touches upon essential parts of detailing as a method and not a solution.

The discussion on detailing in the CEPT studio acknowledges both these texts; however, the inception lies in the work of Frei Otto as mentioned in the section on studio methodology. This necessary bias is meant to lay the foundation of observation of measure and response to distortion of form on application of force as the beginnings of the derivation of detailing.

The studio introduced the architectural programme once the structural system was ready so as to decide simultaneously upon the choices of material. The choice of material and construction system added to the next level of expression. At this juncture, students were introduced to the idea of affordability of details on various accounts:

1. Details as an account of assembly.
2. Details as an account of water demand.
3. Details as an account of agency.
4. Details as an account of waste generated in making and in dismantling.
5. Details as an account of availability of skill and tools.

Out of the five affordances identified, four were taken into consideration while approaching the studio.

Details as an Account of Assembly

The choice of material is an important consideration for a number of agencies that will be involved in the construction process. This, unlike a single agency with a single material, has the ability to affect the building process, the sharing of resources in society and the environment in a large way.

Assembly as a method of construction allows visible tolerance on the following accounts:

1. The construction is the organising of materials having specific form in a geometry. The geometrical condition creates various points, lines and planes where there is change in continuity of shape. These points are the points that the construction process is trying to achieve. In a way, they become the regulator or governing condition to retain the desired form. The assembly-based construction allows correction by reversing the sequence of construction to achieve corrected form.

2. The involvement of two or more agencies calls for a careful and coordinated handling of the detailing process to reduce the likelihood of errors. The task of resolution of such errors would otherwise fall upon the agencies involved in further processes. This coordinating detail and demand for precision allow agencies to come together and find an informed resolution. Such conditions could also emerge out of change in geometry or change in direction of force.

3. Any condition that involves the coming together of two or more materials triggers a dialogue on compatible and incompatible properties of materials (Figure 8). These properties become a negotiation that gets expressed through geometrical adjustments to take care of each other while performing their tasks.

Materials like steel, timber and bamboo or materials having a better life cycle if detailed out in a way that they can be dismantled have a better chance for future use (Figure 9). These materials also score in involving fewer steps before being available for reuse, unlike many kinds of construction debris that have to be crushed and remade in order to be used. The debris of RCC or brick as construction waste merely provides raw material and requires several more steps unlike a mild steel section used as a joist.

The use of traditional materials interpreted and used in new buildings has the potential to ensure the continuity of artisanal tradition in a significant manner. The studio has pushed on to work with this idea of contemporary expressions in traditional materials.

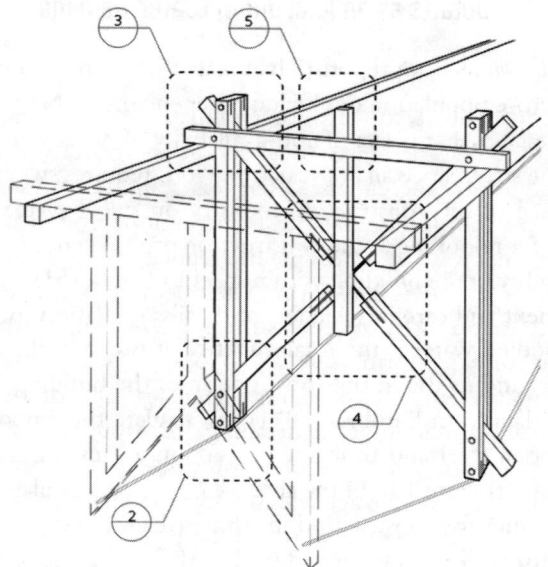

Figure 8 *Identifying critical conditions to explain the details*
Source: Subham Pani, Master's in Architectural Design, CEPT University.

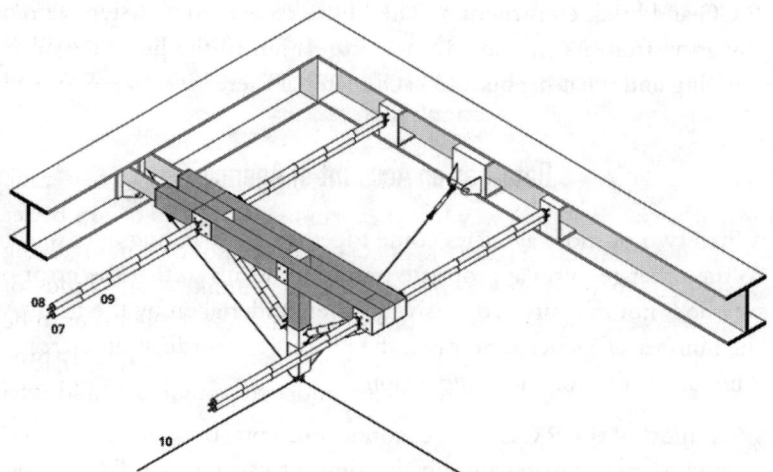

Figure 9 *Spanning system explained through sectional axonometric drawing*

Source: Amar Agarwal, Master's in Architectural Design, CEPT University.

Details as an Account of Water Demand

As per a *Down to Earth* report (Khanna 2019), almost 4.5 crore of the total 6.5 crore population of Gujarat is dependent on Narmada waters. This also establishes the fact of non-availability of sweet water in various parts of the state. Since all construction work requires sweet water, the dependence of the construction industry on sweet water is colossal. This calls for relooking at the construction process, choices of material and durability of the building with respect to embodied water, and also development and careful selection of details in relation to its lifespan. The embodied water is the total quantity of water in the production of material and its use in the construction of the building. The studio relied on data from Bardhan (2011) to calculate the embodied water for a floor in steel and timber construction against brick and RCC construction (Figure 10). In the absence of any data available regarding water demands for construction in Ahmedabad, the data produced by Bardhan for Kolkata was applied to the Ahmedabad conditions.

On calculation in one of the projects, it was found that the amount of water required for largely brick and timber construction came to 11.13 kl/sq m. This is almost half of the embodied water in regular RCC and brick construction. The future construction system cannot shy away from its embodied water in relation to the life cycle of the building and what happens to each material thereafter.

Detail as an Account of Agency

When two or more agencies come together, the handing over of one to the other requires appropriate transition details so that the error of one does not magnify progressively when undertaken by the next. As the number of agencies increases, the process of coordination increases. This affects the way detailing is done.

In most of the RCC to steel connections practised in Ahmedabad, instead of fixing plates during the time of casting of RCC, anchor fasteners are used later as a fixing detail. This happens due to three reasons. First, the agencies involved in casting are different from those that would be fixing plates. In order for these two agencies to

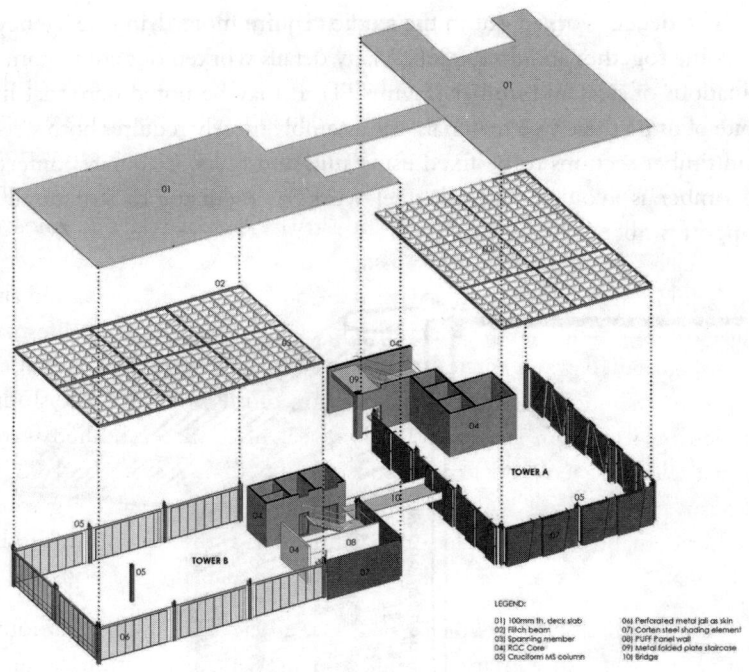

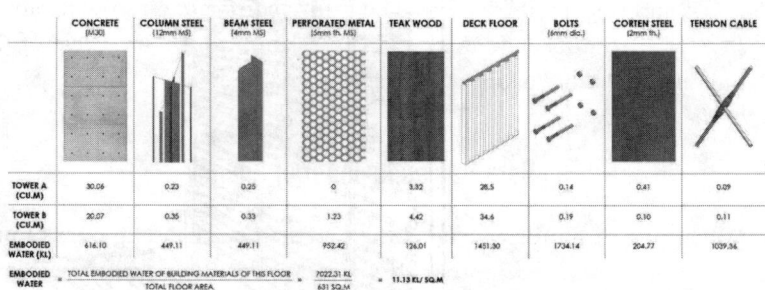

	CONCRETE (MXO)	COLUMN STEEL (12mm MS)	BEAM STEEL (4mm MS)	PERFORATED METAL (5mm th. MS)	TEAK WOOD	DECK FLOOR	BOLTS (6mm dia.)	CORTEN STEEL (2mm th.)	TENSION CABLE
TOWER A (CU.M)	30.06	0.23	0.25	0	3.32	28.5	0.14	0.41	0.09
TOWER B (CU.M)	20.07	0.35	0.33	1.23	4.42	34.6	0.19	0.10	0.11
EMBODIED WATER (KL)	616.10	449.11	449.11	952.42	126.01	1451.30	1734.14	204.77	1039.36

$$\text{EMBODIED WATER} = \frac{\text{TOTAL EMBODIED WATER OF BUILDING MATERIALS OF THIS FLOOR}}{\text{TOTAL FLOOR AREA}} = \frac{7022.31\ \text{KL}}{631\ \text{SQ.M}} = 11.13\ \text{KL/SQ.M}$$

Figure 10 *Material calculation for a single floor for water audit*
Source: Harshil Amin, Master's in Architectural Design, CEPT University.

come together, coordination and cooperation are a must. Often for small projects, such coordination is a financial burden on the client. So after the completion of RCC work, the fabricators use anchor fasteners to fix the plates.

The details worked out in the studio require more than one agency to come together and do the job. Many details worked out are in combinations of steel and timber (Figure 11). It may be noted here that in spite of using these two materials, the assembly merely requires both steel and timber sections to be fixed using nuts and bolts. Elaborate joinery in timber is avoided. Instead, steel works as mediator to structurally support timber.

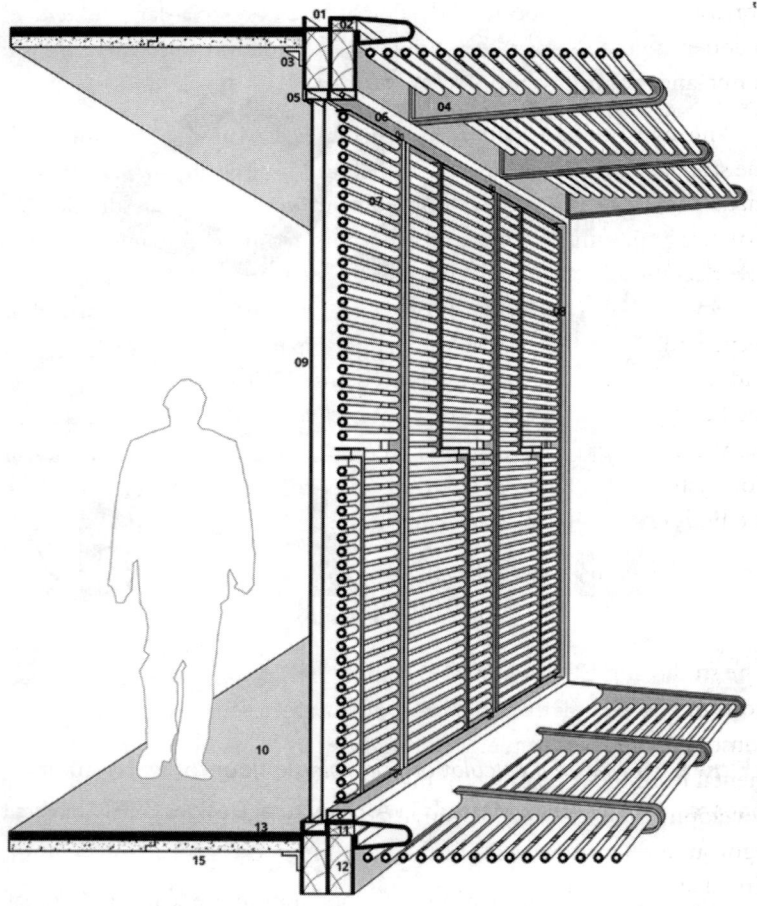

Figure 11 *Attitude towards detailing the building skin using bamboo and steel, described through a sectional perspective*

Source: Amar Agarwal, Master's in Architectural Design, CEPT University.

Details as an Account of Waste Generated in Making and in Dismantling

As per Broadbent (2016), 'Steel is 100 % recyclable and scrap is converted to the same (or higher or lower) grade steel depending upon the metallurgy and processing of the required product.' The steel which is part of a composite material like RCC requires process to be recovered. However, if the steel sections are protected from corrosion, they can be reused. This is also true to a large extent of wooden members. Bamboo, however, is difficult to use specially if it is nut-and-bolted.

The construction system in bearing and spanning developed by the students is made out of parts which can be assembled. The slabs are made out of decking sheet poured with concrete. This divides the principal spanning structural members from secondary members like decking sheet and slab. In such a system, the concrete debris can be recycled but with further processing. The decking sheet can also be recycled but the material of the primary spanning members like steel and timber sections is most likely to be used almost directly. Similarly, the bearing system made largely out of steel and timber in many cases has the ability to be dismantled and used again. Therefore, a construction system that generates less waste and can be reused is the future of the built environment.

CONCLUDING REMARKS

The studio at CEPT (Figure 12) is in its preliminary stage of investigation and is speculative in terms of environmental relationships to construction, for example, water demand in construction, or environmental feasibility of choices of building material in India, as well as the development of socially sensitive construction systems. However, a rigorous attempt to detail out the building in terms of construction is aimed at to investigate these possibilities of the city, which can factor in contemporary needs while reworking its conception.

Being an academic exercise, the studio needs to further systematically touch upon the following:

Figure 12 *Models of all designs displayed as part of the semester-end exhibition at CEPT University Campus, Ahmedabad*
Source: Sankalpa.

1. More rigorous data collection of water demands in construction specific to Ahmedabad.
2. Development of construction systems with the awareness that construction timbers will not be feasible in the case of India for some more time, unlike Canada or other countries where plantation is carried out to meet such demands.
3. A more detailed analysis of buildings in relation to social relevance with a focus on artisans.
4. A further study on the life cycle of buildings in relation to building materials and components recovery, reuse and recycling.

The radical city needs more coordination and cooperation instead of a singular idea imposed on a landscape.

NOTE

1   I am grateful to Neel Jain and Aviral for assisting me with the M.Arch. foundation studio. Neel has been an immense support in trying to work on the digital part of the studio as well as supporting me in the calculation of water demands in construction. I acknowledge and thank Freyaan Anklesaria for going through the entire document and helping me with editing. I am also thankful to Priya Joseph and Vishvesh Kandolkar for supporting me on various technical aspects of the chapter.

REFERENCES

Allen, E., and P. Rand. 2009. *Architectural Detailing: Function, Constructibility, Aesthetics*, 2nd edn. Hoboken, NJ: Wiley.

Bardhan, S. 2011. 'Assessment of Water Resource Consumption in Building Construction in India', *Ecosystems and Sustainable Development VIII. WIT Transactions on Ecology and the Environment*, 144(9): 93–101. doi:10.2495/eco110081

Broadbent, C. 2016. 'Steel's Recyclability: Demonstrating the Benefits of Recycling Steel to Achieve a Circular Economy'. *International Journal of Life Cycle Assessment*, 21 March. https://link.springer.com/article/10.1007/s11367-016-1081-1 (accessed 12 December 2019).

CSE (Centre for Science and Environment). 2017. *State of India's Environment 2017 in Figures* (eBook). New Delhi: CSE.

Emmitt, S., J. Olie and P. Schmid. 2004. *Principles of Architectural Detailing*. Ames, IA: Blackwell.

Khanna, Rajeev. 2019. 'Has the Narmada Dream been Oversold by Gujarat Politicians?', 26 March. https://www.downtoearth.org.in/news/general-elections-2019/has-the-narmada-dream-been-oversold-by-gujarat-politicians--63716 (accessed 2 December 2019).

Modan, A., N. Chhaya and V. Shah. 2006. 'Analysis of the System of Construction in the Traditional Ahmedabad Houses: Query in Seismic Resistance', in P. B. Lourenço, P. Roca, C. Modena and S. Agrawal (eds), *Structural Analysis of Historical Constructions: An Interdisciplinary Approach*, pp. 1347–56. New Delhi: Macmillan.

Rather, Irfan A., Wee Yin Koh, Woon K. Paek and Jeongheui Lim. 2017. 'The Sources of Chemical Contaminants in Food and Their Health Implications'. *Frontiers in Pharmacology*, 8: 830. https://www.frontiersin.org/articles/10.3389/fphar.2017.00830/full (accessed 12 December 2019).

Thompson, D'Arcy A. W. 1968. *On Growth and Form*. Cambridge: Cambridge University Press.

Watts, J. 2019. 'Concrete: The Most Destructive material on Earth', *Guardian*, 25 February. https://www.theguardian.com/cities/2019/feb/25/concrete-the-most-destructive-material-on-earth (accessed 15 December 2019).

Chapter 12

Death of Brick
Rise of the Vertical City

Priya Joseph

BRICK: THE BOOK OF HUMANITY

Bricks in vibrant colours, straw yellow, bright red and brown, with unexpected footprints of leopards, dogs and cattle, finger marks of the maker and more, have lain in the ancient city of Mohenjo-Daro for thousands of years (Marshall 1931: 266–67). Archaeologists and historians have been fascinated with the coins and pots they have found on site; they say these objects reveal the making of civilisations, while overlooking the humble brick, the unit block of architecture, cities and civilisations, that holds many a relevant trace of humanity. This story is of the brick, how it changed cities from low-rise to vertical skylines by transforming from a handcrafted object to a mechanised product of the construction industry and finally being replaced by steel and concrete. The burnt earth brick today is dying a death induced by the modular, the recyclable and the malleable forms of steel and concrete. The vertical city is here.

Starting as early as the time of the Indus Civilisation, the sites dated 2600 BCE have evidence of brick crafting in the region (Carlleyle 1877). Sites from Mohenjo-Daro's acropolis to the great bath and granary hold evidence of craft traditions, including metal work, seal making, carpentry and brick making. The houses in Mohenjo-Daro were mostly built with kiln-fired bricks. Brick remains and sizes ranging from as large as 360 mm to as small as 50 mm in length have been found in Mohenjo-Daro (ibid.: 73). The houses in Mohenjo-Daro were built in two to three storeys, all in brick. Walls above ground were made of burnt brick laid in mud or gypsum mortar (Marshall 1931: 15) (Figure 1). The wells were also made with burnt bricks. Researchers over decades have dwelt on the question of the roofing that may have prevailed in the region, as there is a large probability of corbelled brick spire roofing. As no tiles, slates, copper or brass roof coverings were found during excavation, it indicates the use of brick spire roofs. Excessively strong foundations and massive walls were built to take the load of the very heavy corbelled brick spire roofing systems (ibid.: 17).

The pillared hall with 20 brick piers and the great bath of the city were large structures in brick. Various sizes of bricks were discovered during excavation. The variety of sizes used in all these sections of excavation is a sign of extensive use, economising and employing of sophisticated brick-laying techniques in the region. The burnt brickwork was so extensive, especially in the Mohenjo-Daro site, that about 15 sizes of bricks were recorded from the excavation in the area in the twentieth century (Marshall 1931: 234) (see Table 1). Two distinctive brick sizes that emerged from the excavations were 28 × 13 × 8 cm and 25 × 13 × 6 cm.

The various ancient sites, from 3000 BCE onwards, like in the example of the Indus Valley, have extensive evidence of brick construction. This continues into the medieval epoch in India. The use of bricks is seen in stupas, temples, wells and ordinary houses too between the eighth and eighteenth centuries (Carlleyle 1877). From Tamil Nadu in the south to the Central Deccan region and the whole of the north and east of India, numerous examples exist of such structures in brick. The Kaveri delta in southern India especially had the right type of soil to produce high-quality bricks, which contributed to this development. The brick superstructures in the Madurai temple complex have pronounced central projections with openings on each of the nine ascending storeys. Free-standing colonnades distinguish the lowest of these openings, immediately above the eaves sheltering the entrance passageways (Michell 2008: 99). The Thanjavur brick *chatrams* (places

HR. Area, Section A.   Pl. V.

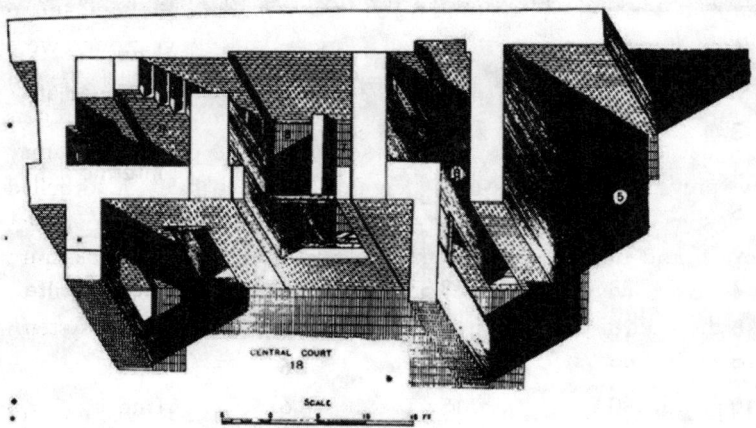

a) Oblique projection of southern chambers in House VIII, from north.

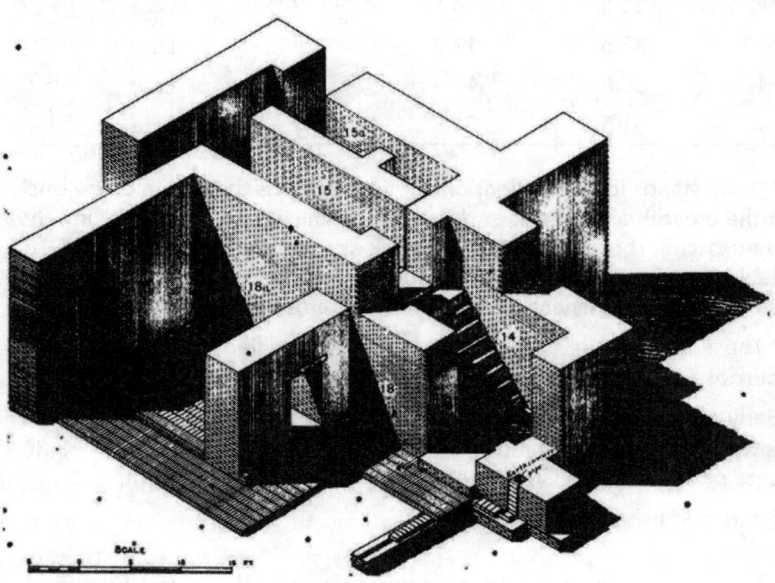

b) Isometric projection of steps in House VIII.

Figure 1 *Oblique and isometric projections of the brick houses of Mohenjo-Daro City*

Source: Marshall (1931: 19).

Table 1 *Brick sizes in Mohenjo-Daro*

No.	X-Dim in cm*	Y-Dim in cm*	Z-Dim in cm*	Period†
1	24	11	5	Late
2	25	12.7	5.7	Intermediate
3	25	12.7	5.7	Early
4	25.5	14	5.7	Intermediate
5	25.5	12.7	5.7	Late
6	25.5	6.4	5	Late
7	28	13.3	6	Intermediate
8	28	14	6	All
9	29	14.6	6	Late
10	30.5	15	6	Late
11	34	16	9.5	Late
12	35.5	16	9.5	Late
13	35.5	17.8	8	Late
14	36.8	18.5	10	Late
15	51.5	26.6	9	Late

* 'Dim' stands for the dimensions of the brick. X is the length of the brick, Y the breadth of the brick, and Z stands for the height of the brick in centimetres (cm). The dimensions of the brick were originally given in inches. This table contains the converted and rounded-off dimensions in centimetres, as it is the predominant method of measurement currently.

† The early, mature and late periods are classified as follows, for the purpose of Table 1:

Early period in Indus Civilisation: 3300–1300 BCE
Intermediate period in Indus Civilisation: 2600–1900 BCE
Late period in Indus Civilisation: 1900–1300 BCE

Source: Marshall (1931: 267).

of rest for pilgrims) are another example of sophisticated brickwork. The Vijayanagara Empire in south India, from the fourteenth to the seventeenth century, used brick fervently. Examples of brick construction from the sixteenth century include the Krishna temple, erected by Krishna Deva Raya in 1513 CE at Hampi, Karnataka, the Pattabhirama temple, a monument assigned to the period of Achyutaraya, built in the early sixteenth century, and the Hazara Rama temple and Anantashayana complex near Hospet. All these monuments have specific brick nuances that point out the sophisticated brickwork of the time. At the Krishna temple, the pyramidal tower or the *vimana* is constructed with brick and plaster (ibid.: 28).[1] Another example of a brick-roofing slab is in Anegundi. Anegundi was a part of the capital city of Hampi. Close to the Hampi site, it is on the bank of the Tungabhadra River and has many structures of the Vijayanagara dynasty. Gagan Mahal is one of them, which was built in the sixteenth century. It is a simple two-storey structure. The roof is a flat masonry roof 45 cm thick and with a 2.7 m span. Ananthashayanagudi temple, located about 5 km from Hospet, built by Krishna Deva Raya in 1524, is another interesting temple in typology. This is perhaps the only temple with a long *garbhagudi*.[2]

Brick was in extensive use in the Indian subcontinent from Indus times until the colonial forces arrived with western processes, cognition and practices. It is definitive that this extensive use of brick, especially the burnt earth brick, needed specialised knowledge of the material and making. This also meant that skilled masons and craftsmen were working with brick in complex forms of architecture. The use of 15 or more sizes of bricks found in the city of Mohenjo-Daro and the complex sculptural use of bricks in the Thanjavur *chatrams* are evidence of vast, sophisticated and widespread knowledge of the material and its use in architecture. It also meant that earth as a material was interpreted in different ways, through architecture.

The long epoch, from the Indus and Mohenjo-Daro to the Buddhist phase and then the arrival of the Islamic rulers, meant that various intersections in architecture styles, forms, use and techniques were employed in architecture. Though there was intersection, overlap and adaptation, there seemed to be a distinct way in which each region was unique in its interpretation of the basic material, that is, earth. The processes were decentralised and the elements of architecture were not standardised. The architectural elements constituting the structure and ornamentation were sophisticated brick details.

Bricks were used to create the distinctiveness in architecture of each epoch with great versatility. The tectonic use and working of the brick as a material was an important part of how architecture took shape. Details were imagined in brick, each changing with the social, climatic and political influences of the time. Whatever the changes in size, shape, process and technique in brick architecture, every variation strengthens the fact that brick was extensively used. This could be explained through the example of the brick *chatram*s of Thanjavur built in the early nineteenth century, which were featured in the exhibition titled *Material City* at the 'Radical City' conference.[3]

*CHATRAM*S OF THANJAVUR

The *chatram*s of Thanjavur are an example of smaller public buildings which used brick in a highly nuanced way until the nineteenth century. This was elaborated through the studio work and exhibition that formed a part of the 'Radical City' conference. The exhibition displayed the drawings and details of brick that were employed in the *chatram*s. There are 20 *chatram*s in the Thanjavur and Madurai districts of Tamil Nadu.[4] The *chatram*s were primarily built to be used as inns for pilgrims travelling long distances to visit temples in the area. The roofs, columns, walls and ornamentation are all detailed in brick. The vaulted and domical roofs of the Muktambal *chatram*[5] brick structure have a rise of 3 m, which covers most of the rectangular bays of the building. It is also a good example of the vaulting technique in brick in the eighteenth and nineteenth centuries, especially for a public building. Considering their origin in the fourteenth-century Muslim rule in the region and the adaptations by the Nayaka and Vijayanagara Empires, the innovations in vaulting techniques in Thanjavur require a mention. The Muktambal *chatram* is made by deducing from the basic geometry, almost like the whole building is a sculpture in brick. The masons used a very different technique to arrive at the structure of this *chatram*. Unlike contemporary buildings, walls were not built by stacking one brick over the other, nor were the ornate details, which form a part of the structure, dispassionately just pasted over the structure. The bricks were 3 cm in thickness and were stuck together with a thin lime mortar. The bricks were stuck vertically and placed in repetitive patterns and chiselled in some places to form the ornamentation. The structure and ornamentation were not separate but blended into each other. The fundamental feature of the structure is sculptural. The mass is sculpted to develop the structure in the Muktambal *chatram*.

The Muktambal *chatram* has ornamental details that fuse with the structure of the building. For example, the columns and brackets are a part of the structure. Such details in brick with intricate work are beautiful but more importantly are representative of the process that was adopted to create this structure—a complex and sophisticated one (Figure 2). The structure employs details of the Maratha architecture in the form of *chattri* roofs,[6] and imitates the stone architecture of the Cholas with details of chariot wheels, flower buds and so on, but its derivation is almost like a sculpture done by an army of artists. The terraced floors that were roofed with the *chattris* stand on a 1 m ornamental featured wall. The wall featured vertical series of floral and animal detail. The horses and the flower buds alternate as ornamental elements that are made by stacking the bricks vertically and chiselling them out. The masters set the guidelines but the artisans had to use their own judgement, innovativeness and awareness to create the details with a

Figure 2 Muktambal chatram *built in 1801 and its intricate details in brick*

Source: Author.

trace of their own skill. The craftsman or artisan was almost as important as the master, who would have conceived the details in totality. Detailed measured drawings and analysis of the building were undertaken through the studio. The exhibition at the 'Radical City' conference presented these drawings through 20 panels of extensive drawings.

Thanjavur *chatram*s or the numerous other examples from ancient and medieval India are testimonies to the nuanced use of the material brick. Brick was used sculpturally, in different sizes, in varied layouts and not just as an infill to create a partition or a wall. Neither the process nor the brick was standardised in the way we know it today. The cities that we know today are created with standardised modules of brick, which is no more than an infill to create walls. Brick is reduced to a mere infill in the cityscape, at best. The cityscape is influenced by the materiality. This change from a contextual, nuanced use of brick to its use as an infill was triggered by the industrial, mass-produced ways of building our cities. Today pre-cast concrete panels or steel frames with lightweight infills rise to the sky. This type of vertical construction requires mass-produced, standardised elements. Once the standardisation of elements set in, it changed how material was produced and used. Standardisation as a form involves shared concepts and meaning for a certain type of communication. Therefore, standardisation is an age-old process. However, in late-eighteenth-century Europe, standardisation was for the first time thoroughly systematised. Large-scale, systematic location of standards gained momentum. This changed the way built form was conceived, leading to the change in the way our cities were built, functioned and looked.

TAXATION OF BRICKS

Brick has changed from being a handcrafted object to a mechanically produced one. The mass production of brick inevitably led to its standardisation. The Indian brick sizes have been influenced by British colonial workings in nineteenth-century India. The nineteenth century saw the greatest changes in the history of brick manufacturing. The changes paradoxically were led by factors external to the technical world of manufacturing and lay more in the fabric of the Industrial Revolution and mass production. There was a great demand for bricks.

Bricks were used to make public buildings, factories, railway tunnels, offices and more, fuelled by the Industrial Revolution. What toppled this set-up was the brick tax imposed by the British government in 1784 (Campbell 2003: 189). The tax was levied per brick, so brick makers retorted by making much larger bricks, which meant fewer units were needed for the same wall. The tax was repealed in 1850, but by this time, many brick makers in England had changed their processes from handmade to machine-made bricks. Having invested heavily in machinery, it was not easy for the manufacturers to revert to smaller sizes, which meant the larger sizes stayed. As a result, the handmade bricks were replaced by standard sizes. Similarly in India, the British engineers who were trained in Britain came with a predetermined preference for standard brick sizes. This percolated into the Indian subcontinent very quickly through what we know as the PWD (Public Works Department) documents.

NORMALISATION OF STANDARD BRICK SIZES

Standardisation in architecture was a by-product of the on-going technological advancements and changes due to the onset of the Industrial Revolution in the nineteenth century. With the advent of printed books, and the aggressive development of the printing industry in the nineteenth century, there was a unique opportunity for the circulation and dissemination of ideas on a large scale. Books could be circulated in multiple copies across libraries (Carpo 2001). The printing industry made possible reproductions in a mechanised, fast mode. This meant that ideas, processes, specifications could be standardised and then circulated widely. This wide circulation of ideas normalised standards.

Ernst Neufert was a famous German architect whose efforts in the 1950s to normalise the use of architectural standards were inspired by the experiments of the Munich-based group Die Brücke, a German Expressionist group formed in 1911 (Vossoughian 2014: 37). Die Brücke's so-called *Weltformate* (world formats) laid the path for the release of the 'A' series paper formats in 1922, which endured as the norm alongside which all other standards in Germany were deliberated and understood (Vossoughian 2015: 676). As Vossoughian notes, 'The formats were based on the metric unit (the largest format [A0] is one square meter) and share the same proportions $(1:\sqrt{2})$ at all sizes. Likewise, larger formats create smaller ones by being folded in half along their longer dimension' (Vossoughian 2014: 38). This standardisation of A4 paper is used extensively today in the printing industry. Neufert was inspired by the standard paper sizes; his famous book on architectural standards is used by architecture schools all over India even today. Paper standards are the first set of standards discussed in the first edition of the *Bauentwurfslehre*, Neufert's famous book on architecture standards.

Neufert learnt through the concept of paper standardisation that the circulation of information is a powerful tool for standardisation of knowledge. He was also aware that this standardisation of knowledge would concentrate the production of information, which would change the construction industry. There is a connection between the paper sizes and standards in the construction industry, including the size of the brick. Although Neufert does not draw direct parallels with standard paper formats, the parallel is implied in the case of his 'Octametric' bricks, which he conceptualised. Neufert takes the idea forward that all bricks must have dimensions that are multiples of 1 metre, like in the case of paper standards, and called it the 'Octametric System' (Vossoughian 2014: 46) (see Figure 3). This system suggested universal norms derived from the subdivision of the metre into eight basic modules of 12.5 cm, because of which the concept came to be called 'Octametric'. Neufert's bricks have a length of 24 cm and a width of 11.5 cm (ibid.: 47). The uses of the Octametric System were driven towards efficiency in time and cost: it was devised to reduce fabrication costs and accelerate the design and construction process. It is essentially conceptualised to standardise brick sizes and eventually normalise them. Neufert knew that normalisation of brick sizes meant that the information was centralised. He hoped that Octametric bricks would become the foremost channel of design and construction for architects. To some extent this attempt was successful as many buildings adopted these standard bricks in Germany at the time. Thus, just as the standard-format sheet of paper produced a standard-format binder, the Octametric brick gave rise to an Octametric door (ibid.: 48). Standardisation of bricks reimagined architecture as a scheme for systematising dimensional models, which was calculated by architects.

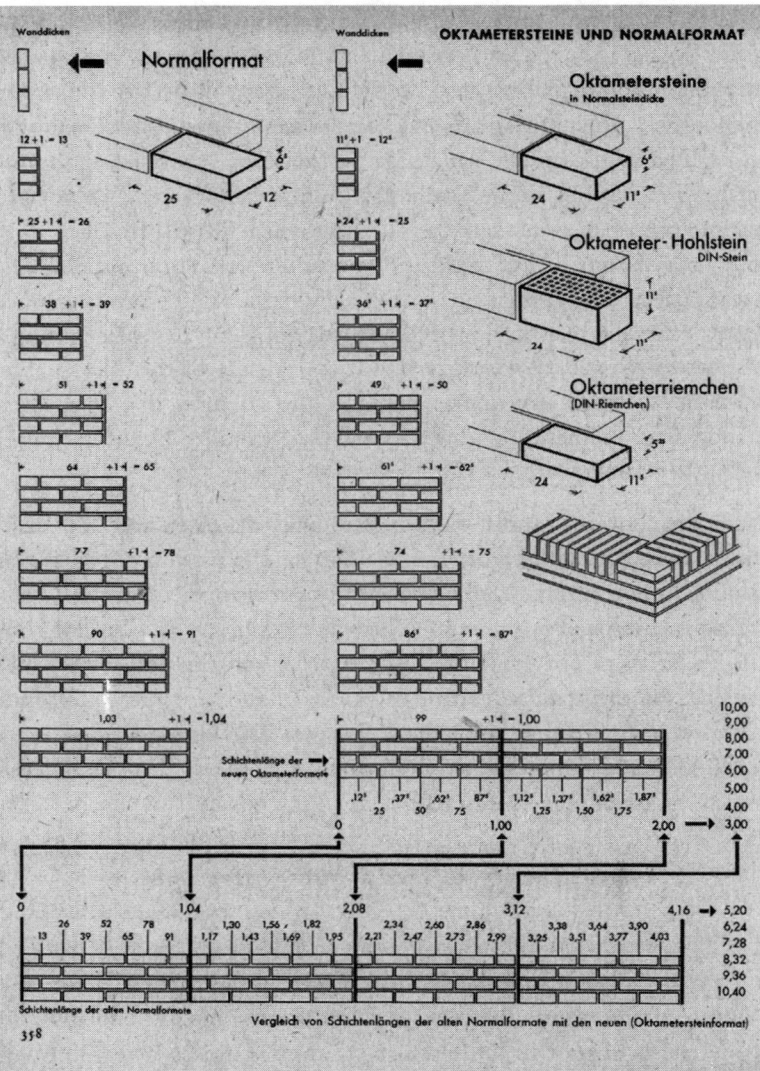

Figure 3 *Octametric bricks in Ernst Neufert,* Bauordnungslehre *(1943)*

Source: Ernst Neufert, *Bauordnungslehre*, 1943, Octametric Bricks [*Oktametersteine*] and Standard Format (Vossoughian 2014).

The processes in architecture thus tilted from memory to computation, or, in other words, from handcrafted bricks to mechanised modules. The digital became the new medium of design and, more importantly, the processes in architecture were more algorithmic with computed, standardised formats. 'Standardization is also linked to normalization, at least to the extent that both express social and not just technological aims and aspirations' (Vossoughian 2014: 49). The history of standardisation is thus the history of institutionalisation and normalisation (ibid.: 50). Design was intrinsically linked to the production of knowledge and manufacturing, and the case of 'A4' paper becoming a standard followed all over the world is evidence of this (ibid.). The Octametric bricks are one example of the attempts that formalised standardisation; there are others, such as the 'Modular' by Le Corbusier and others, which are not discussed here.

In the context of India, the British military engineers were the main agents who standardised brick sizes. The standardisation of bricks was sought in order to have greater control over manufacturing and centralising systems of production. This was often done by coercion, but the polemics of power, control and scale of construction were other reasons for the standardisation of bricks in India in the nineteenth century, apart from technological changes. The emergence of India from colonial rule and its entry into the age of new industrial material led to the brick being replaced.

DEATH OF BRICK—RISE OF THE VERTICAL CITY

The Industrial Revolution all over the world introduced new material and methods of construction. Iron-frame buildings came to define the skyline of the cities. Iron was frequently combined with glass in the construction of structures such as conservatories, like the Syon House (1830) by Charles Fowler and the Palm House (1847) at Kew Gardens by Decimus Burton. These led instinctively to the Crystal Palace, the peak of technological use of composite material possible in construction. In the design of the Crystal Palace, built for the Great Exhibition in London in 1851, Joseph Paxton employed timber, cast iron, wrought iron and glass. The Crystal Palace contained important innovations in the mass production of standardised materials and rapid assembly of parts. The new material of the time made it possible for the cityscape to rise vertically. Steel and concrete not only made it easy to let the city rise vertically, they expunged a system of valuing the characteristics, qualities and limitations of a material for building. Industrial material such as steel and cement made it possible to mould, mix, pour and stack architecture with reasonably fewer limitations. Brick was replaced. Even if it was used, it was as infill within a steel structure. From a nuanced, detailed and almost artistic use of brick, the industrial era changed the use of brick to a mere infill or it was replaced by composite material, which could give rapid verticality to the concentrated mega cities. Even in the smallest of neighbourhoods in Indian cities, we see cement and steel growing vertically from the ground.

The most obvious features of the modern epoch were industrialisation, standardisation and the modular. Standardisation meant that the construction industry had to shift to modularity in its production. Modularity and geometric spatiality were major attributes of this industrial epoch, linked to machine-made material. There is an implicit connection between geometric spatiality, the machine forms and the verticality of the city. The standardisation, mass production and overall industrialisation of architectural construction were thus one of the avant-garde's foremost preoccupations, leading to the death of brick, metaphorically.

NOTES

1   A *vimana* is the structure over the inner sanctum in the Hindu temples of south India.

2   Inner sanctum of a typical Hindu temple.

3   The detail drawings of the *chatrams*, exhibited under the title *Material City*, were a part of the 'Radical City' conference held at Bengaluru on 20–21 December 2019. The drawings were contributed by Priya Joseph, as a part of her on-going Ph.D. research at the Manipal Academy of Higher Education, and by CEPT students in the master's programme in Architectural History and Theory, Monsoon Semester 2019, Pruthvi Thakur, Roshini Kannan, Eva Thomas and Aishwarya Padmanabhan, tutored by Priya Joseph. The conceptual ideas for this article crystallised through discussions over the years with Dr Pithamber R. Polsani. The conceptual ideas for the studio, from which various drawings and ideas were generated, included a team comprising Priya Joseph, Dr Gauri Bharat and Fahad Zuberi.

4   Document dated 1908, consulted in August 2018 at the Chatram Committee
     Office, District Collectorate, Thanjavur.
5   Built in the late eighteenth century and early nineteenth centuries, the *chatrams*
     are elaborately detailed examples in brick in the region and illustrative of the
     confluence of European and Indian techniques in the making of their architec-
     ture. The early nineteenth century was a time of influence from European
     emissaries. The native, local influences mixed with European ways that per-
     suaded the patrons of architecture of the time to think in varied ways. Serfoji
     II was educated under the influence of a Danish priest, who was his mentor.
     He was greatly influenced by his perception of the West. He studied foreign
     languages and art and had large collections of artefacts from around the world.
     This background led him to imbibe European ideas for the architecture of
     chatrams and experiment with varied typology and details. The result was that
     the *chatrams* are unique; they intriguingly mix the sensibilities of the local
     and the imported and they represent the epoch when colonial rule created
     hybrid interpretations of architecture in south India. Each of the *chatrams* seems
     to be an experimentation with the idea of the indigenous and the Western idea.
     The Maratha rulers were already creating dappled architecture in the southern
     region, which was ruled for centuries by the Cholas. The strong Chola and
     Nayaka influence, the Maratha details and then the recent European cognition
     mixed to create the *chatrams* in locally manufactured brick, constantly and
     deliberately used as the material.
6   *Chattri* is the elevated, dome-shaped roof of a pavilion in Indian architecture.
     The word *chattri* means umbrella in many Indian languages. The shape of
     these roofs resembles umbrellas.

REFERENCES

Campbell, J. W. P. 2003. *Brick: A World History*. London: Thames and Hudson.

Carlleyle, A. C. L. 1877. *Report on the Tour of the Gorakhpur District*, vol. XVIII.
    New Delhi: Archaeological Survey of India.

Carpo, M. 2001. *Architecture in the Age of Printing: Orality, Writing, Typography, and
    Printed Images in the History of Architectural Theory*. Cambridge, MA: MIT Press.
    http://hdl.handle.net/2027/heb.05835

Marshall, J. 1931. *Mohenjo-Daro and the Indus Civilization*, vol. 1. London: Arthur
    Probsthain.

Michell, G. 2008. *Architecture and Art of Southern India: Vijayanagara and the Successor
    States* (The New Cambridge History of India I:6). Cambridge: Cambridge
    University Press.

Vossoughian, N. 2014. 'Standardization Reconsidered: Normierung in and after
    Ernst Neuferts Bauentwurfslehre (1936)'. *Grey Room*, 54: 34–55.

———. 2015. 'From A4 Paper to the Octametric Brick: Ernst Neufert and the
    Geo-politics of Standardisation in Nazi Germany'. *Journal of Architecture*, 20(4):
    675–98. doi: 10.1080/13602365.2015.1072232

Chapter 13

Advertising RCC
Material Mainstreaming in Pre-independence India

Gauri Bharat

In the popular imagination, and indeed, even in dominant architectural discourses, building practices are categorised using labels such as colonial, modern or industrial. These labels are associated with certain physical forms and often imply mutually discrete bodies of architectural work. The transitions in architectural production in the late nineteenth and the early twentieth centuries and the overlaps between colonial, modern and industrial modes of architectural production remain largely obscure and understudied though recent scholarship has begun to problematise this static imagination. Rao (2013), for instance, offers a close reading of the spatial, material and social developments in suburban Bombay to reveal the complicity of colonial development in producing what we recognise as modern domestic space in the early twentieth century. Scriver and Srivastava (2015) tread the more familiar path of examining iconic architectural works, but expand the narrative by including a wider range of architectural examples and drawing out diverse actors and trajectories of architectural production in the colonial and post-independence periods.

In a slightly different but related vein, Ramnath (2017) offers a historical overview of engineering which emerged as a profession in the interplay of industrial development, the colonial state, and the rise of Indian nationalism. Though his emphasis is on engineers, the trajectory of technology and patronage makes this a possible parallel to the rise of architecture as a profession during the same period. These works highlight the emerging directions in scholarship which seek to revise the contours of architectural history in the Indian subcontinent as a multivalent and complex set of shifts that took place across time and different geographies.

This chapter adds another voice to this growing body of work by exploring the shifts in building materials, particularly reinforced cement concrete (RCC), in terms of the increasing popularity of its usage among professionals and non-professional people. The rise of RCC entailed many aspects such as technological shifts, aesthetic developments, changing resource and labour networks, to name just a few. In this chapter, I focus on the popular cultural imagination of RCC as a way of understanding its currency in mainstream architectural production. I analyse advertisements of cement and reinforced cement concrete from the 1920s to the 1940s, after which it was well entrenched in the building industry. By examining the advertisements in technical journals and printed news media, I probe some early claims that the producers and suppliers made, which reveal how some of the early architectural potentials of concrete were considered desirable and marketed. Considering that advertisements are primarily intended to persuade customers and influence their choices, the analysis of their architectural content reveals some of the underlying requirements and concerns of various architectural 'consumers'. In doing so, I draw out some of the aspects that underpinned everyday architectural production and its transformation in the pre-independence period.

THE EARLY DAYS: 1910s AND EARLY 1920s

Concrete as building material that uses some form of aggregate and a binder has a very long history (Forty 2012). Modern reinforced cement concrete uses steel reinforcement bars and, for the most part, employs cement as a binder.[1] Globally, RCC construction was becoming popular as an alternative to stone construction. This is illustrated by the magazine titled the *Cement Age—A Monthly Magazine Devoted to the Uses of Cement and Concrete* published out of New York. It was first published as the *Cement Age* in 1904 and combined with the *Concrete Age*, another magazine that began publication in 1907. The articles in the magazine outline the then current uses, state of technology of the material, and examples of projects across the world as a way of situating cement and concrete as contemporary building materials that were growing in popularity. While an analysis of the articles is the subject of a longer project, the advertisements offer a brief but pointed snippet of the extent of use and perception of the materials. Three advertisements related to RCC are noteworthy—from suppliers of Portland cement of different brands, machinery for crushing aggregate, and for waterproofing compounds to be mixed with concrete for water resistance and 'increased strength'. If we consider these advertisements as targeting current use and concerns, it is evident that these are related to the basic attributes of RCC, namely, cement strength, quality of aggregate, and water resistance in the final structure.

In the Indian subcontinent, steel and cement began to be locally manufactured in Jamshedpur in 1910 and in Porbandar in 1914. During these years, we find early indications of RCC use, especially in infrastructure and industrial projects. The *Cement Age* magazine, for instance, describes a masonry bridge in Hyderabad which collapsed during floods in 1908 and was rebuilt in RCC.[2] The same magazine in 1913 reported that 'reinforced concrete structures are now seen in different sections of Bombay, and are likely to be the basis of a new system of building.' This rising popularity of RCC occurred against a backdrop of increasing prices of stone and timber, which were the common building materials of the time. It was simultaneously made possible by the increase in imports of cement and steel, which were required for RCC construction. In terms of publications and advertising, in this early period, we find trade publications such as business directories and a very limited number of engineering journals which hint at the state of building technology and the beginnings of cement use for reinforced construction. The journal *Indian Engineer*, published from Madras (now Chennai) in 1915 and 1916, ran on its front and back pages recurring advertisements for Indian cement brands and building contractors who advertised themselves as 'specialists in reinforced concrete' (see Figure 1). In parallel, there were advertisements

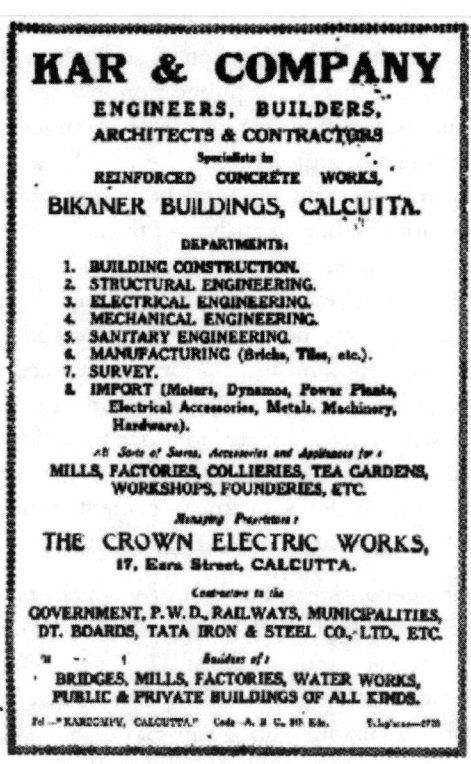

Figure 1 *Advertisement for construction company with multiple departments*

Source: Thacker's Indian Directory, 1920.

from timber stockists as well, which suggest that earlier modes of construction also continued.

Prior to this period, both cement and steel were imported from Britain but also other countries such as Germany. This continued for the next few years but the quantity gradually reduced in relation to the consumption of locally manufactured cement.[3] By 1929, cement manufacturing was established across the Indian subcontinent, from plants in Wah and Lahore in the north to Shahbad and Madras in the south, and from Porbandar and Karachi in the west to Japla and Calcutta in the east.[4] Imported and locally produced cements were advertised alongside each other. The shift to local production and the gradual increase in cement consumption were clearly an index of increased building activity and RCC use across the subcontinent. What is also interesting to note is the tone of adjectives in the advertisements. The imported cements are advertised in terms of ease of availability and for being well known across India, while the local brands claim parity with the imported brands in terms of quality and strength (Figure 2). The imports referred to in the advertisements usually indicated British brands of Portland cement which were known for their quality, and were intended to reassure the buyer about the quality of the cement. The references to strength and quality recur through the following decades, though the contexts for invoking these features vary in relation to the other developments taking place at the time.

Figure 2 *Advertisement for locally produced Portland cement*
Source: Thacker's Indian Directory, 1925.

INSTITUTIONALISATION AND MARKETING:
CEMENT AND RCC IN THE 1930s

A watershed moment in the use of RCC and the publicity of the material came with the formation of the Concrete Association of India in 1927. The roots of this institution lay in the marketing interests of the cement producing companies, but it was instrumental in generating and actively circulating a vast amount of literature on cement and concrete use for both technical and public audiences. A journal titled the *Indian Concrete Journal* (*ICJ*) was published each month and circulated to vast audiences across the subcontinent. As the editorial piece in the first issue of the journal, published in 1927, states,

> The engineer, the architects, the contractors, the builder and the concrete product manufacturer in India has in the past had to turn to foreign papers for that information.... up till now there has not been any paper dealing exclusively with this subject in India. It is hoped, therefore ... that here the cement consumer will be able to read of modern progress.[5]

Interestingly, the association positioned this as a public service. They ran advertisements in the trade directories where they stated their intention in reaching out to the public. They claimed: 'Believing that the full advantages of the use of concrete and the resulting economies are not fully appreciated nor understood by the public, the Association has been founded to give free practical assistance and advice in the uses of cement. Thereby it is hoped a public service will be rendered' (Figure 3).[6] The journal was published regularly every month and routinely included material ranging from articles on technical developments, lessons for students on design and use of reinforced concrete, reports from engineers, users of cement and RCC, suppliers, and advertisements for cement and a range of associated products. Compared to the earlier announcements on availability and the references to quality of cement, a more complex public discourse with multiple facets pertaining to the use, advantages, possibilities and various technical aspects of RCC was emerging.

The advertisements in the early years of the *ICJ* were for cement companies, concrete mixers, companies specialising in pile foundations,

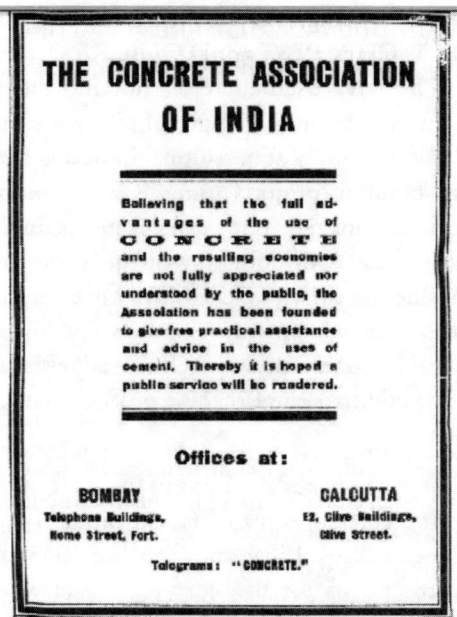

Figure 3 *Advertisement announcing the Concrete Association of India*
Source: *Thacker's Indian Directory*, 1928.

ready-made reinforcement sheets, and specialist machinery for building roads and breaking concrete, among other things.[7] At first glance, this is obviously a wider array of products and services compared to the previous decade. Analysed more closely, however, it offers subtle indications of the developments in RCC practice. The concrete mixers or the ready-made reinforcement sheets, for instance, are positioned as replacements for tasks which would have otherwise had to be carried out using manual labour. The advertisement for reinforcement sheets suggests that the '[f]abric is ready for cement to be applied, fixed in a moment, and fixed permanently. This means a saving in labour, as you will know from your experience of a gang of coolies trying to get similar results with loose rods, loose wires and their own fingers.'[8] Considering the largely informal nature of the construction labour force, these machines offered the promise of more uniform and consistence performance. In a different vein, one company advertised that they were a 'pioneer in cast-in-situ concrete piles—Over 260,000 lineal feet of "SIMPLEX" piling was installed LAST YEAR IN INDIA alone—The BEST, CHEAPEST AND QUICKEST method for heavy foundations."[9] The advertisement does not indicate the buildings where the piles are used, but the length of piling mentioned together with the reference to 'heavy foundations' indicates the possibility of more ambitious building projects using RCC. Compared to other foundations such as footings, piles can support larger structures or structures built in areas with poor or inadequate support due to soil conditions. Considering these indicators, we can conjecture that RCC technology had advanced, but more specifically, the advancements were now reasonably widely known such that advertisements could be used to persuade people to employ these products and technologies.

This continued for a few years, following which came the next watershed. Major earthquakes occurred in the west of the Indian sub-continent with the epicentre in Quetta (in modern-day Pakistan) in 1934, and in the east across Bihar and Nepal in 1935. This prompted a series of advertisements for the next few years where RCC was highlighted as a technology with higher seismic resistance. Specific advertisements showed houses, bridges and water tanks that remained intact alongside similar structures built in other materials that were damaged or had collapsed. Building contractors and companies also shifted their advertising pitch to align with the need for more stable buildings. In one example, the company labels the advertisements as 'earthquake proof bridges and buildings', and the accompanying image is titled as an example of a 'strong and inexpensive bridge'. The additional claims in these advertisements are 'economy' and 'ease of maintenance'. This is a clear shift from the earlier decade when companies identified themselves as 'specialists in RCC' to now implying their capacity to produce stronger, earthquake-resistant buildings. That this is a claim and not a simple statement of technical strength is evident from some of the other advertisements where the reference to the earthquake is invoked in an almost unrelated manner. An advertisement from a paint producing company, for instance, states:

The earthquake has passed—and the time has come when—You must face the facts and figures. An earthquake has shaken the country and it is natural that with the unforeseen expense of rebuilding to cope with, you should worry about the essential question of the preservation of your new building by using Good Quality paints.

Paints have very little direct relationship to earthquakes especially when compared to cement or RCC more generally, but it highlights that the earthquake was instrumental in generating a cultural climate where strength and stability were sought, and therefore nearly all building-related products advertised as such.

The geography of use of RCC was rapidly expanding during this time. A brief article in October 1930 describes the use of precast RCC elements by the railways. It states that both 'plain and reinforced [concrete have] certainly come into extensive use during the past few years.'[10] It further mentions that a number of railway companies had set up their own yards to prefabricate RCC elements such as 'platform copings, benches, name boards, signals, water tanks, hydrants, lamp posts, even booking halls and passenger overbridges'.[11] These yards were set up in otherwise small cities such as Asansol, Chittagong, Secunderabad, Trichinopoly and Bangalore. Considered together with the fact that larger cities such as Bombay, Lahore, Calcutta and Madras already had buildings built using RCC in parts if not more substantially, the technology had clearly percolated beyond the metropolitical urban centres into the provincial interior parts of the subcontinent as well.

Around the same time as the introduction of the *ICJ*, in 1929, the Indian Institute of Architects was consolidated from an earlier association of architecture students and professionals.[12] This body too began to publish a journal, the *Journal of the Indian Institute of Architects* (*JIIA*), which was circulated amongst its institutional and individual members. The institution was conscious that through the journal, intended primarily for its members, it was shaping the practice and discourse of architecture, as much as it was acting as a medium for the circulation of the latest developments in the field. The articles ranged from reflections on architectural examples ranging from the 'lesser' to the monumental, the pressures faced by practising architects, developments in town planning, technical developments and regulations.[13] With regard to RCC, in the 1930s, for instance, one article outlines the increasing use and architectural potential of RCC. It states:

> One finds that the Architect is following the lead of the modeller with
> his clay and is now moulding concrete—a material which is easily
> plastic—in a truly artistic and colourful manner into any shape that
> may be needed to see the structural requirements of the building under
> construction, or to suit its environment and the artistic tastes of the
> most critical clients.[14]

Though outside the scope of this chapter, these articles offer a distinctive set of insights into the status of RCC use in the early twentieth
century.

Returning to the discussion on advertisements, the journal carried
a wide range focusing obviously on technologies and products that
typically fell within the ambit of an architect's work. The advertisements
ranged from building contractors and the Concrete Association of India
to products such as coloured cements, ready-made mesh reinforcement,
insulating materials such as chemicals and concrete blocks, and even
weather-proof containers for storing cement. Interestingly, products
that dealt with the details of construction such as cement mixers or
specialist machinery were largely absent from the journal. Even when
technical things like pile foundations were advertised, the nature of the
visuals and text is different. Compared to the *Indian Concrete Journal*
where piles were advertised in terms of quantity and economy, *JIIA*
advertisements included photographs of buildings where the pile foundations had been used. One recurring advertisement is that for Franki
Pile Foundations, where the image of the New Customs House in
Calcutta is shown, possibly with the idea that the visual might appeal
to the architect.[15] This difference is not very obvious but significant
within the context of this chapter, since the advertisers were clearly
gauging their audience and pitching products and technologies in
specific ways, and it is this underlying motivation that turns the advertisements into a register of the aspirations and state of technology at
a given moment in time. More importantly, though the *JIIA* and *ICJ*
were initiated within and intended for professional bodies, the journals
both recorded examples and developments from across the subcontinent
and were subscribed to by individual and institutional members such as
libraries and educational centres at various places. The advertisements
and information were thus reaching diverse audiences, and arguably

marked a turning point in the increased and institutionalised circulation of architectural ideas.

NEWSPAPER ADVERTISING AND RCC IN THE POPULAR DOMAIN

Until the 1930s, the advertisements were limited to trade directories and journals of professional bodies, as discussed in the previous section. This, I argued, was linked to the early stages of use of RCC, where it was primarily tradespeople, building contractors, architects and engineers who were being persuaded through the medium of advertisements to employ the emerging technology. In the early 1930s, advertisements begin to appear in newspapers, which on account of their diverse readership may be considered representative of the space of the popular. The nature of the advertisements is, however, quite diverse within the same newspaper. In the *Amrita Bazar Patrika*, for instance, we see advertisements for architects and civil engineers who announce themselves as specialists 'For Re-in-Forced Concrete Structures & Artistic Modern Buildings'.[16] Around the same time, the same newspaper carries an advertisement for building material suppliers, which states, 'Building a House! Come to us for - Iron and Steel, Joists, Tees, Rods, Rounds, Angles, Flats, Corrugated Iron Sheets, Etc.... Mufasil customers can get advantage of our services by simply sending a post card stating their requirements.'[17] This second advertisement clearly indicates that the average house builder in Calcutta (and in other provincial, or *mofusil*, towns) was still using these materials, even though RCC construction was practised and being advertised. The simultaneous advertising of these different building technologies suggests a period of lag or transition between the use of steel and wood and the eventual ubiquitousness of RCC as the staple method of constructing a building.

Within a few years the situation changed. By the beginning of the 1940s, advertisements for cement, RCC and related processes and products began to occur more frequently in newspapers at various places such as Calcutta and Madras, if not more widely across the country.[18] These advertisements included brands of cement, independent building contractors and companies specialising in RCC, water-proofing compounds, and advertisements by the Associated Cement Companies

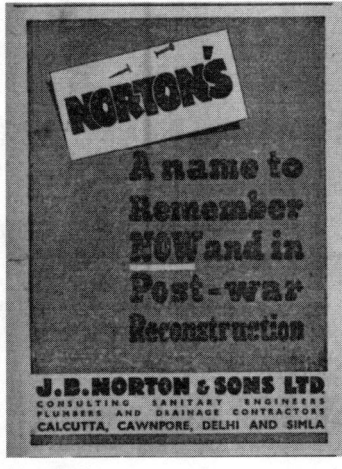

Figure 4 *Newspaper advertisements referencing the World War in Amrita Bazar Patrika in 1941 (left) and 1943 (right)*

Source: *Amrita Bazar Patrika*, vol. 73, no. 281 (12 October 1941) and vol. 75, no. 357 (28 December 1943).

extolling the various virtues of the cement. As discussed earlier, the range of advertisements indicates a possible increase in familiarity and widening of use of RCC. Then, in 1939, war broke out and disrupted, to some extent, the on-going expansion of the building industry. Advertisements from the war years nearly always invoke the event and hint at the nature of disruption (see Figure 4). The Concrete Association of India, for instance, stated that '[i]ts technical staff is at the moment assisting Civil and Military authorities on essential works in connection with the War Effort,' but sought to assure people that '[t]heir services are in addition available to all road building authorities in their post-war road development schemes.'[19] Other companies advertised similar assurances to individual customers. One advertisement read: 'At present the company is fully occupied with the government and railway works. But during the post-war period, the company will be at your service for your requirements in all sorts of construction work.'[20] Another advertisement intended to encourage people to make plans for the post-war period (see Figure 4). It claimed:

When peace returns, the pent-up energy of man and stored-up materials for industry will be released to create a happier and better world.... New Towns and villages will be planned, new houses built, new factories set up.... Let us submit plans, schemes, designs, estimates for your post-war reconstruction. Qualified foreign-trained engineers are at your disposal.[21]

What is interesting across these advertisements is the possible intent. Each of these companies sought to reassure the average customer that they were present and functioning, even though as the advertisements claimed, they were unable to supply material or serve the needs of private customers. It is also likely that their involvement in the war effort was being invoked as an emotive testimony of their professional status, particularly given that most companies were possibly less active in the general market.

CONCLUSION

The history of RCC in India is necessarily a complex and multivalent narrative. This chapter has introduced some of the key moments of its genesis and development in terms of the perception and use of the material in published media. Narrow as the scope of analysis is, it nonetheless provides some interesting cues. The advertisements of RCC see a subtle shift from trade directories and foreign journals in the early 1900s to technical journals and publications by professional bodies in the 1920s and 1930s. These appearances correspond to the spheres of familiarity and use of RCC. It begins with trade directories, since the earliest introduction to the material is through the import of Portland cement. It is only after the few initial decades of use by the Public Works Department of the colonial government that cement production and use percolate into wider audiences. And only after the beginning of local production of cement and steel does RCC use widen across the subcontinent. It is at this juncture that information through advertising shifts from the limited domain of the professional and business networks into popular consciousness. Some of the earliest iconic architectural uses of RCC take place during this phase; the Golconde House, for instance, was constructed in Pondicherry (now Puducherry) in 1939. It was possibly the first building to be nearly entirely constructed out of a combination of cast-in-situ and prefabricated RCC. From the perspective of architectural history, the important point to note is that RCC was, as evidenced through these advertisements, already ensconced as a popular building technology across the Indian subcontinent.

NOTES

1   I say 'for the most part', since there is evidence of lime being used as a binder as late as the 1960s.
2   *Cement Age*, May 1912, pp. 248–49.
3   In 1914, 150,530 tons of cement were imported while 945 tons were manufactured. By 1928 (when this information was reported), 74,700 tons of cement were imported and 557,951 tons were manufactured. Concrete Association of India, *Handbook and Directory of the Concrete Industry in India*, 1928.
4   Concrete Association of India, *Handbook and Directory of the Concrete Industry in India*, 1928, p. 1.
5   *Indian Concrete Journal*, vol. 1, no. 1, August 1927, p. 1.
6   *Thacker's Indian Directory*, 1928.
7   I refer to advertisements in the *Indian Concrete Journal* between February 1930 and May 1931. Most advertisements mentioned here recur in each monthly issue of the journal.
8   *Indian Concrete Journal*, February 1930, p. xiii
9   *Indian Concrete Journal*, March 1930, p. xii.
10 *Indian Concrete Journal*, October 1986, p. 286.
11 *Indian Concrete Journal*, October 1986, p. 286.
12 The first association to be formed was the Architectural Students' Association in 1917, which brought together graduates of the Sir J. J. College of Architecture. This developed into the Bombay Architectural Association in 1922, which became affiliated with the Royal Institute of British Architects in 1925. In the following years, a number of institutional changes were initiated and consolidated, and the organisation was officially registered as the Indian Institute of Architects in 1929. https://indianinstituteofarchitects.com/history/ (accessed 12 March 2020).
13 Through the 1930s, the journal carried a section titled 'Lesser Architecture of Bombay', which showed photographs and architectural drawings of buildings that were relatively quotidian compared to the monumental exemplars that dominated the narrative of Indian architecture.
14 *Journal of the Indian Institute of Architects*, July 1934, p. 79.
15 I refer to advertisements of Franki Piles, which appeared in the *JIIA* between 1930 and 1935.

16   Advertisement for N. D. Nandi in *Amrita Bazar Patrika*, vol. 67, no. 145, 21 June 1935.

17   Advertisement for Kuver Limited in *Amrita Bazar Patrika*, vol. 67, no. 141, 16 June 1935.

18   For the analysis of advertisements in this chapter, I have referred to the *Amrita Bazar Patrika* published from Calcutta and the Madras edition of the *Indian Express*. Though these places were important metropolitan centres even in the pre-independence era, the nature of the advertisements, especially those of smaller companies and material suppliers, suggests that similar advertisements may have appeared in local newspapers as well.

19   Advertisement for the Cement Marketing Company of India Ltd in *Amrita Bazar Patrika*, vol. 77, no. 159, 8 June 1945.

20   Advertisement for Indian Construction Company Limited in *Amrita Bazar Patrika*, vol. 74, no. 316, 13 November 1944.

21   Advertisement for British India Construction Company in *Amrita Bazar Patrika*, vol. 75, no. 357, 28 December 1943.

PART V

Potentialities and Probabilities

Chapter 14

Spontaneous Urbanisation

M. N. Ashish Ganju

In this chapter, I would like to bring to your attention a form of urbanisation which I have been studying for over 20 years. Not through the normal procedures of academia, but by actually living in a settlement at the edge of Delhi and discovering through sheer experience that this was a new phenomenon. I had been trained as an architect, but trained in a genre which believed that architecture was a kind of mother discipline and didn't need any further specialisation. So whether it was urbanism or landscape or parametricism, it could all be subsumed within the 'mother discipline' of architecture. It was only by an accident of history that I found myself living where it appeared that a new kind of urban form was confronting me, and I have been trying to understand this for 20-odd years. This is the counter form that I have been experiencing to formal descriptions of urbanism such as 'radical' or other forms of typological distinction.

I will preface my story with just a few remarks to put things in perspective. Urbanisation as a phenomenon goes back hundreds of years in the subcontinent. But I think today we can be quite clear that our urban thinking was illuminated by a celebration of variety and conviviality. It was not oriented towards celebrating technology. We have examples from all over our subcontinent which present a wonderful variety of urban types with distinctive features. Yet whether it was a river town, or one in the plains, in the desert, or on the plateau, the one thing common to all of these urban types was the notion of 'conviviality', that is, they had something to do with affirming life.

But something happens in the twentieth century and there is a shift in the paradigm. Pithamber Polsani in his introduction describes the rise of the CIAM (the International Congresses of Modern Architecture) which propelled this shift in thinking. The greatest exponent of this was the Swiss/French architect Le Corbusier, who came to India in the 1950s, and that started a parallel movement here. Figures 1 and 2 offer some examples of what was happening in Europe. Tony Garnier, from 1901 to 1904, while on a scholarship in Rome, drew a new urban type called the 'Industrial City'. In 1914, the Italian architect Antonio Sant'Elia was drawing visions of the 'Future City', while Le Corbusier was drawing the 'Radiant City' in 1931–34.[1] These were very powerful images of what would constitute the new form of the city in our times.

Figure 1 *'Industrial City' proposed by Tony Garnier, 1901–04*

Source: https://commons.wikimedia.org/wiki/File:Cit%C3%A8_Industrielle_(8157211736).jpg (accessed 7 June 2020).

Figure 2 *Italian architect Antonio Sant'Elia's vision of the 'Future City', 1914*

Source: https://arthistoryproject.com/artists/antonio-santelia/the-new-city/ (accessed 7 June 2020).

However, it's worth noting a significant point about this paradigm shift. After hundreds of years of predicating city design on the notion of public health as the feature that tied the whole design together, suddenly in the twentieth century, it became more important to stress on mobility, and transportation became the driving force of urban planning. This was a major shift. However, even in the West, this shift was never really digested, because less than half a century later, by the end of the 1960s, Ian McHarg was already on prime-time television in the US warning us about the environmental crisis being caused, among several other factors, by the indiscriminate burning of fossil fuels. By the end of the twentieth century, Kenneth Frampton, in his keynote address to the International Union of Architects Conference in Beijing in 1999, points out that perhaps the most significant technological change in the twentieth century is in fact the invention of the private motorcar. It has altered our lives completely, irretrievably. I used to think that the atomic bomb was the most important technological invention in the twentieth century, something which wrecked society and civilisation never to be the same again; but I think Frampton makes a better point, that the private motorcar is perhaps even more powerful than the atom bomb, because the private motorcar affects all of us in our daily lives. The bomb is very much present in our thoughts, with important leaders having their finger on the button, backed with great silos of armaments. But the motorcar affects our lives every day.

This major paradigm shift and the import of European urban models has distorted urban patterns in Asia and other ancient societies that are very different from Western Europe. Indian cities have been subjected to alien development parameters, resulting in urban distress, which is evident in most of our cities today. This is not something which has been studied carefully by policy planners and academics.

By an accident of fate, I had to go and live on the edge of Delhi in the year 2000. It was my millennial adventure. I have been living there since, and I discovered that a completely new kind of urbanisation was taking place here. It took five years for me to read the signs. It appeared that I had gone to live in a slum, because I couldn't afford anything else. Delhi is the capital city of the country, and it doesn't allow ordinary people a real housing alternative. There are very many kinds of apologies for residential development available in Delhi, but very few which are habitable and affordable. There are upscale residential neighbourhoods like Golf Links, for instance, but how many people can afford that? For an ordinary person it's very difficult to think of a housing provision in Delhi other than a slum.

I chose the slum very carefully. It was on the Aravali hills, at the highest elevation in Delhi, adjacent to the radar station on the western edge of the city. In about four to five years, I discovered that there was a city here being made by people themselves. Some years earlier while studying urban form, I came to the conclusion that there were three distinct kinds of urban reality in the country. I can't speak for other countries, but certainly in India we can distinguish these very clearly. There is the *organically evolved* city, which is the core of every city in the country. Then in the twentieth century, although there are earlier examples like Jaipur, there is the *planned* city, which is very different. Between these two kinds of urban types there is the *spontaneous* city. This is built by people outside the ambit of the plan and has no official sanction. In Delhi, the bureaucrats call it 'unauthorised colonies', and today we have about four million people living in such unauthorised colonies.

A survey on urban transformation that was carried out by the Centre for Policy Research in Delhi estimated that 75 per cent of Delhi's population now lives in 'informal settlements' (Heller et al. 2015). 'Informal' is another euphemistic term invented by bureaucrats and academics to obscure reality. The government lists eight types of urban development. Of these, one is the planned settlement, and seven are informal types, including *jhuggi jhopri* (handmade hutment) clusters, unauthorised colonies, slum squatters, and so on. Only 25 per cent of Delhi's population lives in planned settlements, and Delhi is the capital of this country. It is now well into the twenty-first century, and this is the reality today. What happens in Delhi, by and large, is replicated in other cities over time, like the first master planning exercise that happened in the 1950s and is being replicated in all cities. I will not go into the efficacy of the planning system, but the main point is that 75 per cent of the population is living in informal settlements. Of this the people who live in unauthorised colonies form a significant percentage, about one-fifth of the total population of Delhi.

I believe this is a new form of urban reality. I have lived in such a place for 20 years or so, hence I can subscribe to this view. The settlement is on the edge of Delhi, and Figures 3 and 4 provide ground-level pictures of the built fabric. There are about 200,000 people living in this settlement now. Its core, the organically evolved village, consists of about 30,000 people. The 'colony' around it comprises the rest of the settlement. When I went to live there 20 years ago, the proportions

Figure 3 *Aya Nagar, a settlement on the edge of Delhi*
Source: Author.

were about half and half, around 25,000 each for village and colony. The organically evolved core was an indigenous settlement of Gujjars, by and large, who allowed their agricultural lands to be sold off to the migrants coming in from different parts of the country. Today it lies on a highway which connects Delhi and Gurgaon, and is connected by the metro railway to both urban centres. It has most urban services except proper drainage. The twentieth century didn't believe in drainage being an essential part of urban infrastructure; all that was needed was a railway and a highway, and people could settle.

The village has a rainwater harvesting structure or *johar*, which has now become a sewage collection place. These *johar*s and other water-retaining structures in the rural areas of Delhi have mostly got filled up and destroyed, but in Aya Nagar we have kept this structure alive for two decades. The chief minister supported our efforts to try and redevelop the *johar*, which we are still doing for over 20 years. Figure 5 is a picture taken some time ago when the water was not yet fully covered with green matter.

Figure 4 *Aerial view of Aya Nagar*
Source: Author.

Figure 5 Johar *of Aya Nagar, New Delhi*
Source: Author.

Many students of architecture schools have visited this place to make academic reports. The chief minister visited in 1999 and wanted to convert Aya Nagar to a model village. I have tried to give a few illustrations of this living, proto-urban settlement between Delhi and Gurgaon. On one side we have Gurgaon with glass-encased towers, and on the other side is South Delhi, an upmarket part of New Delhi. In between is this spontaneous settlement, which we have been studying at first hand. This kind of development has many aspects which could provide very important pointers for city planners. We have been trying to read the patterns here, for which there was no methodology available, no precedent to act as a guide. We devised a simple system of four parameters for engaging in development work. *Community action* is what we start with; *habitat design* is our next important concern; and we *record the process* as we go along, because that will be our way of learning and critical assessment. There is no one who can tell us how to go about such a development task because nobody has done it before. Nowhere in the world has this magnitude of urban transformation taken place in such a short period. Everywhere planners are at a loss, and our cities are progressively becoming unliveable. I can testify that Aya Nagar is more convivial than Gurgaon. Its carbon footprint is perhaps one-fiftieth compared with Gurgaon's. Motorcars cannot drive fast through it, which is a great blessing, since the motorcar is quite enjoyable and safe when it is moving slowly. However, the greatest cause of distress is the lack of organised drainage.

Raising resources, the fourth activity, is equally important. It is no longer viable to expect the government to do everything for us. Aya Nagar is a real example of people actually building their habitat unsupported by any government programme. Residents raised resources, they went to their MLA (member of the legislative assembly) for help in getting electricity connections and water supply, getting a bus service, and now the metro has arrived as well. The process has been documented in a 52-minute documentary film called *An Outpost of Delhi* (Srinivasan 2011). A feature film maker worked with us to make the documentary. It gives you a good idea of the process of urbanisation. It was made in 2011, but it is still current and relevant. The film can be seen on YouTube. So with this very simple methodology, we are beginning to actually package our research into what we believe is a more sustainable and inclusive urban form in today's India.

The research has also led to the implementation of a pilot project to demonstrate that it is possible to provide a sanitation system which is affordable and sustainable, even in a densely built-up urban area. One neighbourhood of Aya Nagar has been the site for this demonstration exercise, recorded as a video entitled *Water Cycle Management in an Urban Neighbourhood: An Experiment in Environmental Technology* (Greha Delhi 2018). This is also available on YouTube. The project uses a decentralised system of bio-digestors for primary treatment of soil and waste water, installed below the roads. Secondary treatment is done by bio-remediation in a reed bed, and treated water recycled for use of the residents.

The most urgent requirement, as agreed by all, was drainage, which included sewerage, waste water and surface drainage. Water supply to the village and its extensions was inadequate, the traditional system of rainwater harvesting and shallow wells having been neglected and degraded. Spontaneous house building activity without environmental design or planning was rampant in all open spaces.

To design an effective drainage system in these conditions, it was evident that the centralised municipal system, which originated in Europe in the nineteenth and early twentieth centuries, was not appropriate. To convey sewage in underground pipes to treatment plants several kilometres away a large amount of water was required, and this was just not available at present or in the foreseeable future. Hence a decentralised model was required which could provide primary treatment contiguous to the household. This became feasible by using technology developed by the Defence Research and Development Organisation of the Government of India for bio-digestion of soil waste in discrete containers which could be minimised in size. The new technology was adapted to create a small-scale plumbing system which could be installed below the roads (even if they were very narrow) without entering private houses. The treated effluent from the bio-digestors would undergo secondary treatment through bio-remediation in a constructed wetland in the nearest suitable open space available.

The pilot project is funded by the Delhi Urban Shelter Improvement Board of the Delhi government. The primary sewage treatment system was installed by October 2017 and has been functioning satisfactorily since then. The secondary treatment system has become operational in

February 2020, and the resultant discharge is being monitored and tested to check compliance with public health norms. The project has shown that it is possible to instal a decentralised sewage and drainage system in a densely-built-up urban neighbourhood without damaging the built fabric, in an affordable and sustainable manner using local expertise and available technology.

The implications of this experiment in sanitation management need to be understood in terms of spatial planning. Decentralised sewage treatment and recycling of treated water within an urban neighbourhood allows us the freedom to design convivial built environments once again. Urban form which is not dependent on the tyranny of heavy engineering required for laying extensive piping networks can encourage building layouts which prioritise human needs over technological imperatives. City design may again become an exercise in promoting civic values, something we seemed to have lost in the twentieth century.

NOTE

1   See, for example, Le Corbusier's drawings for the 'Radiant City', 1931–34, at http://le-corbusierfullwork.blogspot.com/2015/06/058-plan-voisin-1925. html (accessed 7 June 2020), and https://i0.wp.com/writingcities.com/wp-content/uploads/2015/11/c85-la-ville-contemporaine-vista-de-la-zona-residencial-l.jpg?w=740 (accessed 7 June 2020).

REFERENCES

Greha Delhi. 2018. *Water Cycle Management in an Urban Neighbourhood: An Experiment in Environmental Technology* (YouTube video), December 2018. https://www.youtube.com/watch?v=oyGMm2Lkn8M (accessed 4 May 2020).

Heller, Patrick, Partha Mukhopadhyay, Subhadra Banda and Shahana Sheikh. 2015. *Exclusion, Informality, and Predation in the Cities of Delhi: An Overview of the Cities of Delhi Project.* Centre for Policy Research, New Delhi, August 2015. http://citiesofdelhi.cprindia.org/wp-content/uploads/2015/12/Cities_of_Delhi-Overview.pdf (accessed 4 May 2020).

Srinivasan, Sidharth (dir.). 2011. *An Outpost of Delhi* (film). Produced by PSBT in partnership with Films Division, Ministry of Information & Broadcasting, Government of India, New Delhi.

Chapter 15

Governance of Cities from the 74th Amendment to Special Purpose Vehicles

Tikender Singh Panwar

This chapter will talk about the 74th constitutional amendment, and how it is linked to city governance. I will focus especially on the journey that has taken place from the 74th constitutional amendment to the modern special purpose vehicles (SPVs).[1] I will also discuss something more, based on the experience of my five-year stint in the city,[2] namely, how cities are being governed, what is the driving force in the cities, what is the malaise in the cities. What are the real challenges? Architects view the city from one lens, but, coming from a political economy background and as someone who is an activist, how do I view a city? What does a city mean to me?

I will start by quoting one of my favourite poets, Percy Bysshe Shelley. Exactly 200 years ago, he wrote, 'Hell is a city much like London.'[3] And he speaks about the smog in London, the inequity that exists, and the final line of the stanza reads, 'Small justice shown, and still less pity.' Can we draw a similar inference about the cities we are living in now? Are these cities turning into hell, and if so, what is the reason for this? What is it that is actually leading our cities to a situation which is not really commensurate with the thinking or the imagination through which we envision our cities? One of the questions Pithamber raised was, '*Should* our cities survive?' But the point is also, '*Will* the cities survive?' While our cities have faced moments of extinction, rebellion and so on, the question of whether they will survive is often met with the whole idea of technology coming in through the cities and eventually leading us to the solutions. At a conference recently, participants were discussing how for the first time we know that if biodiversity in and around the cities finishes off, and especially if the honey bees die out, then we will all become extinct. In response, one of the technocrats suggested that robotic bees could provide the solution. Can you believe that? It's fundamentally ridiculous.

That's the way we are progressing. Why? Because cities are places and spaces for expropriating humongous amounts of capital. And I view the city from this lens. To me, a city is a place where massive surplus is getting generated, not only in the world, but in Indian cities as well. It is this surplus which drives the huge inequity that exists in the city. As an activist, I think it is important to democratise this surplus. So, I will use all my surplus in planning, all my efforts in politics and all my efforts in the overall realm of political economy to ensure that this 'democratisation of surplus' takes place. Now, what does that mean for the governance of cities?

Governance has been linked to the overall privatisation of the city, and increasingly with a kind of Haussmannisation of cities. We all know the story of Georges-Eugène Haussmann, but allow me to put it in context. Napoleon III brought in Haussmann primarily to ensure the extraction of an enormous surplus in France. If we were to draw a parallel with India, in a similar scenario, the current government led by Narendra Modi is building a corridor from Delhi to Mumbai, imagining that this will bring us to sustainability and sustainable goals. I was part of the UN Habitat III Conference in Quito in 2016, where Joan Clos, Secretary-General of Habitat III and former mayor of Barcelona, strongly emphasised the need for us to go back to the basics—the basics of planning. The last three to four decades of laissez-faire have taught us that its approach is not going to sustain. Returning to what Haussmann tried to do, the enormous scale of his operations could sustain Paris just for

15 more years, and eventually Haussmann was fired. Napoleon had to go to war with Bismarck, which he lost, and eventually his defeat led to the formation of the Paris Commune.

I am not saying that we will have a similar kind of situation arising now, but there are several similarities. There is a huge profit that is getting generated in the cities. Take this whole discourse about whether water is a need or a right. If it is a need, then even a private player can provide it, but if it is a right, then what accrues from its provision? Ursula Huws (2012: 63), in a paper concerning the political economy of the cities, mentions how, in the last three to four decades, things that had been counted as being of huge value to society—education, water, health and so on—have been converted into exchange value; in other words, they have been commoditised with a view to the generation of huge surpluses. According to a recent UNCTAD report (UNCTAD 2008: 3), the hundred largest transnational corporations of the world have shifted their domain from finance capital to services. There is enormous profit to be made, and cities are being forced to allow the entry of various multinational corporations in this sector. The figures are massive—7,900 transnational corporations—we can imagine the kind of profit that gets extracted out of all of these cities.

In this context, I should mention that the first file that came to my office when I joined as Deputy Mayor of Shimla was titled 'Privatise Water'. I have always fought against privatisation, even protested on the streets against it, so how could I allow such a thing to happen? We didn't allow it. Later in this chapter, I will share some of our experiences in Shimla in regard to what we actually did with water. The World Bank is now showcasing the Shimla model as a study in how the water utility should behave. This is because we were really able to bring in an alternative model, a 'radical' model, which I will speak about later.

As I had mentioned earlier, the question is not just whether the city *should* survive, but whether it *can* survive. There is something simmering inside the city, and that's what we call the 'rebellion'—from the 'radical' to the 'rebellion'. In all the dialogues regarding sustainability, all the discourses and nuances since 2008—I myself was part of the climate change talks in France in 2015, and then at the Habitat III conference in Ecuador in 2016—the focus has been on this whole discourse that we require sustainability—but sustainability of whom? From the lens through which I view things, from the perspective of the measure of inequity in the cities, it is clear that the city is not going to sustain. The happenings at JNU are not just about a small issue; similarly, the anti-CAA (Citizenship Amendment Act, 2019) protests are not just about one particular thing. Something is simmering in the cities—a huge disconnect and discontent.

Into this larger picture, I would like to bring in the story of the cities. What do our Indian cities reflect? Ashish Ganju in his contribution reflects on the experience of living in an informal settlement on the edge of Delhi—what we call the 'peri-urban'. There are some 9,000 urban agglomerations in the country, of which 4,500 are statutory towns while the others are non-statutory towns. All these places have developed through spontaneity, that is, first habitation moves, and then the planning moves. So, for instance, habitation precedes the planned apartment complex. This is a universal problem in all these non-statutory towns. The main point is that some 40 per cent of people live in these non-statutory towns, but they contribute about 66 per cent of the country's GDP and 90 per cent of government revenue. Just look at the inequity that exists in the cities. If the difference between the top 10 per cent and bottom 10 per cent of asset-holders in the countryside is 500 times, in urban India, the gap is 50,000 times! So the point is, *can* cities sustain?

This is where the role of the state is fundamental, and, as Joan Clos says, we need to 'go back to the basics'. The overall government expenditure on building infrastructure for urbanisation is 1.5 per cent in India, whereas it is about 25 per cent in developed nations. *Can* we sustain the urban infrastructure? The Isher Judge Ahluwalia report cites another startling figure for the amount of investment needed in urban infrastructure, and we are nowhere near attaining it. Small-scale approaches based on small interventions may allow us to develop some kinds of alternatives, but this cannot be an alternative paradigm for sustaining urbanism and urbanisation in the country.

Here lies also one of my problems with the planners. Allow me to share an anecdote in this regard. I teach fifth-year seminar students at the School of Planning and Architecture, and one batch of students was working on designing shelters for the homeless in Delhi. Now, 95 per cent of the people living in homeless shelters are workers. After their first visit to the shelters, the students, several of whom came from elite backgrounds, returned with stark 'us/them' narratives. I insisted that they stay at the night shelters for 24 hours before thinking about designing shelters for the homeless. This binary narrative is one that we find among planners as well. I host a TV show called *Urban Agenda*, on which I did a series of episodes on how unsafe our cities are. Many women told us that our planners do not even know what the demands of the women are when they plan a city, because there are hardly any women planners, and because the entire system is so patriarchal. Thus, there is a disconnect between planners and the people whom their interventions are intended to impact.

I now come to the question of the 74th constitutional amendment, enacted in the neoliberal period of the 1990s, and why it is also not sustainable. The 74th amendment, enacted in 1992, was supposed to empower the city governments. The Twelfth Schedule notified 18 items that were to be transferred to the city government. The latter, headed by the mayor, was to be formed by elections every five years. I am not a great votary of empowering the city mayor. What I am suggesting is empowering the people. I think that the era of Le Corbusier, when the city of Chandigarh was created—we cannot imagine the same kind of planning happening today. That planning has to be very collaborative with the people. To me, 'radical' means engaging with the people, and to do this you have to create not only nuances in the form of a new language of urban governance, but also structures in governance. Some of the critics of the 74th constitutional amendment believe that it's a dead letter because its aim was to mount certain user charges on the people to make sanitation, etc., sustainable. Nevertheless, at least it provided five years to every municipality.

I was a member of a task force headed by K. C. Sivaramakrishnan, set up in 2013 to review the implementation of the 74th constitutional amendment. We produced a very comprehensive report, which was however dumped by the new government that came to power in 2014. One of the suggestions that we had made, and which is very radical, is that 10 per cent of the income tax that is collected from the cities should be given back to the cities. Imagine what this would mean. I am not sure about the figures in Bangalore, but in Shimla we contributed some ₹2,000 crore in taxes, which means ₹200 crore would be returned to the city, which is a phenomenal amount. Similarly, we can devise ways of further democratising it back to the people.

The mayor has very little power to do anything, beyond largely ceremonial duties such as cutting the ribbon at inauguration functions. When my daughter used to ask me what my work was, I would say, 'Cut the ribbon, kiss the child—that's all.' In Haryana, in fact, there is an act by which the commissioner can seek the sanction of the government to remove the mayor. And the term of the Chandigarh mayor is just one year! What can you do in one year? On the other hand, the Shimla mayor was powerful because the Shimla Municipal Corporation is an old British legacy going back to 1851. Shimla is one of the oldest municipalities in India. At least in Shimla we had five years, but of course, that was for the first and the last time, because we were elected directly, and then the government amended the act because it didn't want directly elected mayors. So we have a situation in which the city government is not empowered, while there is this whole notion of extracting surplus from the cities. Once you have the empowerment of the elected people, at least their democratic aspirations will rise and this will mount pressure to give it back to the cities.

Currently, what we find in the cities is more of a project-driven approach. K. C. Sivaramakrishnan always used to say, cities are run by parastatals and by development authorities. This is not a sustainable model for the simple reason that these bodies want to extract the maximum profit from the cities. They don't want city governments or the citizen. Has the Delhi Development Authority (DDA) ever consulted the people? In 2017, the DDA commissioned the National Institute of Urban Affairs (NIUA) for revising the master plan for Delhi. We have led several delegations to the NIUA to request it to at least speak about migration, because migration was not even thought of under the 74th constitutional amendment. So the point is, who governs the cities? Is it the citizens? No. Is it the elected people? No. In fact, it is the parastatal, in conjunction with certain multinational corporations which have their consultants embedded in the cities.

Vice-President Venkaiah Naidu, who was then the minister for urban development, would come for meetings of the All India Mayors' Council, where he would say, 'Cities don't have money, they come to the state governments.' Out of 9,000 city governments, including both the statutory and non-statutory towns, just 10 per cent are able to pay the salaries and wages of their staff; 90 per cent are unable. Financially, they are completely disempowered; they do not have the authority to levy taxes, and have to seek resources from the state governments, with the exception of cities like Pimpri-Chinchwad.[4] But the state governments are also bankrupt, so they go to the central government, which also doesn't have the money, so they go to the multilateral institutions. The multilateral institutions intervene and create all these juggernauts in the form of the JNNURM (Jawaharlal Nehru National Urban Renewal Mission), Rajiv Awas Yojna, AMRUT (Atal Mission for Rejuvenation and Urban Transformation), and then the smart cities concept. The latest in this line is the National Urban Policy Framework. The Nobel Prize in Economics for 2018 was bagged by Paul Romer, who developed the notion of 'charter cities'—cities built in host countries in the developing world but administered by a guarantor from the developed world (for more on 'charter cities', see Idiculla 2018). So the next step would be, 'Charter it out!' If the people can't run the city, and the city governments can't run it, then beyond that is the chartered city. This is the new model, and it is unsustainable. The special purpose vehicle system also works along these lines. In many places, even the BJP-run city government has said that it doesn't want smart cities, because the SPVs (responsible for implementing the Smart Cities Mission at the city level) are in direct contradiction to the idea of empowering local administrations. Many experts have said that it is just like writing an obituary of the 74th constitutional amendment.

All of this is happening because the new model of extracting surplus comes in the form of the internet of things (IoT). According to a Bloomberg report, the global IIoT (industrial internet of things) industry is 15 trillion dollars. Our GDP is 2.5 trillion dollars. And according to Forbes, by 2020, the Indian market will be worth around 1.5 trillion dollars (Singh 2014). This is what they want to tap into. Now, I too want to use my mobile phone to switch off my electricity at home.

But the point is, some company makes money out of my act of switching off the electricity using my thumb impression. Can we democratise that? I think we can. It is extremely difficult, but some democratisation of that surplus can take place—not to bring in the Barcelona model of the 'urban commons' (Charnock 2018). Protecting the urban commons is also democratising surplus back to the people.

We tried to do this when Reliance Jio sent its team to lay cables in Shimla. We didn't allow them to dig in the city. They said, 'How is this possible? We are paying you!' We said, 'We want more.' We consulted with friends in the planning sector, who advised us to ask the Jio people to lay ducts free of cost in the city. So we asked Jio to lay two ducts free of cost to the city government while digging the city. This had not happened anywhere else in the country, and they were extremely unnerved. When we refused to budge, they went to the chief minister, who told them that we were directly elected office bearers who had pulled more votes than him, so they would have to listen to us. Ultimately, six months down the line, they accepted. Thus, the entire smart city infrastructure could be a win–win situation for the citizens and the city, and of course for the service provider. Huge amounts of money are going to be involved; the IBMs and the CISCOs are going to command the centre. Instead of the entire money getting extracted, the command centre can be with the people.

I would like to return now to our intervention with regard to the water utility in Shimla that I mentioned earlier. It is what we learnt through an accident. In all cities, there are multiple agencies that run the city. Water is a classic example. In Delhi, the Delhi Jal Board provides water, but they don't produce water. They buy water from somewhere else. This duality also existed in Shimla, whereby water was being provided by a parastatal of the government called Irrigation Public Health, and distributed by the Municipal Corporation of Shimla. Now, some engineers constructed a sewage treatment plant 5 kilometres upstream of a water-treatment plant. You can imagine what would happen. From 2005, every alternate year, there was an epidemic of hepatitis. Thousands would get infected and a few would die, especially pregnant women. The epidemic struck once while we were in office. We decided to do something about it and went to the government.

The government said that the contamination took place at our end; how could we suggest that the government was not providing potable water? Then we brought in the National Institute of Virology, Pune. They conducted a study and decoded the genome of the virus. Interestingly, the virus in the water samples, the human blood samples and the sewage was found to be the same. Yet we were unable to fix the responsibility for this on the government. I myself registered an FIR against the officials of the state government accusing them of negligence.

Then we started building block by block. We asked the government either to take the entire system and own responsibility for it, or to give it to us. The government said, 'It's a dead duck, let them own it.' So 300 people were transferred to us. We integrated the system, and through this integration, we created a utility and fixed responsibility. The beauty of the intervention is that, three years down the line, not a single case of hepatitis has been reported in Shimla. This is because now there is responsibility, there is transparency, and the backdoor privatisation that takes place in the form of ROs and water purifiers has been curbed; the tap water is potable now.

Look at the possibilities for democratisation of surplus. I have written an article on this issue recently (Panwar 2019). In Delhi, the National Green Tribunal had ordered that in areas where the TDS (total dissolved solids) in the water was lower than 500, ROs (reverse osmosis–based purifiers) were not required. The Supreme Court was to hear the matter. It was likely that ROs would be banned in the near future. So the RO companies in conjunction with the Bureau of Indian Standards (BIS) created a furore in Delhi around water samples having failed the tests for drinking water. These companies are representatives in the BIS. They wanted to create an environment to influence the Court so that the order banning ROs would be stayed. Eventually the Court refused to stay the order. In Delhi, we calculated ₹2,000 crore as the O&M (operation and maintenance costs) that the citizens pay every year to these companies—a huge amount. The main point is this excruciating inequity that exists and the surplus that is extracted from the cities. Under capitalism, of course, surpluses are going to get generated. If we are able to intervene in the form of democratisation, if we can democratise it back to the people, I think that is what will make the city more radical, and, of course, rebellion is simmering in there.

NOTES

1   The 74th constitutional amendment was legislated in Parliament in the year 1993 with the purpose of democratic decentralisation of powers along with functions to the cities in India. Regular holding of elections to the city government and the handing over of 18 functions to them were quintessential features of the amendment.

2   I served as Deputy Mayor of Shimla from 2012 to 2017. The deputy mayor in Shimla during this five-year period was a directly elected post, that is, the deputy mayor was elected by the people and not from amongst the elected councillors. But after 2017, elections to the posts of mayor and deputy mayor in Himachal Pradesh reverted to the indirect form.

3   P. B. Shelley, *Peter Bell the Third* (completed 1819; published 1839).

4   Pimpri-Chinchwad in Maharashtra is an exception to this rule, since until recently the city administration had the ability and the capacity to enforce octroi on goods, which comprised a substantial revenue for the city government.

REFERENCES

Charnock, Greig. 2018. 'Barcelona en Comú: Urban Democracy and "The Common Good"'. *Socialist Register*, 54.

Huws, Ursula. 2012. 'Crisis as Capitalist Opportunity: The New Accumulation through Public Service Commodification'. *Socialist Register*, 48.

Idiculla, Mathew. 2018. 'Castles in the Air'. *Hindu*, 16 October. https://www.thehindu.com/opinion/op-ed/castles-in-the-air/article25230289.ece (accessed 28 May 2020).

Panwar, Tikender Singh. 2019. 'Water Nexus and its Testing'. *People's Democracy*, 8 December. https://peoplesdemocracy.in/2019/1208_pd/water-nexus-and-its-testing (accessed 9 March 2020).

Singh, Sarwant. 2014. 'Smart Cities—A $1.5 Trillion Market Opportunity'. Forbes. com, 19 June. https://www.forbes.com/sites/sarwantsingh/2014/06/19/smart-cities-a-1-5-trillion-market-opportunity/#34963c2f6053 (accessed 28 May 2020).

UNCTAD (United Nations Conference on Trade and Development). 2008. *World Investment Report 2008: Transnational Corporations and the Infrastructure Challenge*. Geneva: UNCTAD.

About the Editor and Contributors

EDITOR

Pithamber R. Polsani is a faculty member and currently the Dean at the School of Advanced Studies and Research, Srishti Manipal Institute of Art, Design and Technology in Bengaluru, India. His education and work traverses diverse disciplines: philosophy, education, technology, management, literature, semiotics, media, psychoanalysis, art and Spanish language. Synthesizing insights from multiple domains, his research addresses conceptual and practical problems in the realms of the history of design ideas, vernacular design, urbanism and philosophies of urban design. Dr Polsani has led learning Academies for Royal Bank of Scotland and Nokia Siemens Networks, established a Virtual University at Satyam Computer Services and taught at the University of Arizona, Bates College & Delhi University. Some of his publications include, "Shadows Without Bodies: How was Modernism in India Art," *Indian Cultural Forum*, 2017, "From the Remnants of Reality: Art and Practice of Suresh Kumar G." *Unbound*, 2016, "The Image in a Fatal Kiss: Dalí, Lacan and the Paranoiac Representation", "Like A Lizard That Junks its Tail in Distress: Homer Simpson is no Antigone", *The Symptom*, 2003; "Use and Abuse of Learning Objects", *Journal of Digital Information*, 2003; *Bucknell Review*, 2001 "Riding the Satellite to the Millennium", *C-Theory*, 1998.

CONTRIBUTORS

Arul Paul: An alumnus of the Centre for Environmental Planning and Technology (CEPT) University, Ahmedabad, Paul is an architect, academic and educator. Drawn to environments that are avant-garde, creative and experimental in their approach and outlook, he has taught at several schools across the country and is currently an Associate

Professor at the Nitte Institute of Architecture, Mangalore. Situated at the intersection between architecture, queer theory, and media studies, his research uses the lenses of history and theory to critically examine pedagogy as it evolves in response to new advances and challenges. He is also an ardent campaigner for social justice and equality, regardless of gender or sexual orientation.

M. N. Ashish Ganju: An eminent architect, Ashish Ganju has taught at the School of Planning and Architecture and the Indian Institute of Technology in New Delhi, the University of East London (United Kingdom), and the Universita IUAV di Venezia (Italy). He is also the Founding Director of the TVB School of Habitat Studies, New Delhi and co-author of the book, *The Discovery of Architecture: A Contemporary Treatise on Ancient Values and Indigenous Reality.* At present, he builds with the Tibetan refugee community in Dharamsala to research the practice of a sustainable architecture in the Himalayas. He also lives and works on the urban fringe in New Delhi, demonstrating through practice the principle of urban renewal by citizens.

Fahad Zuberi: An architect, academic and writer, Zuberi currently serves as an Academic Associate with post-graduate and doctoral programs at CEPT University, Ahmedabad. Following a B. Arch. degree from Aligarh Muslim University and two years working in Delhi and Aligarh, he studied Architectural History, Theory, and Criticism at CEPT University, graduating in 2019 having won the CEPT Essay Prize 2019 for his essay about the challenges of dwelling in Asian cities. Zuberi is passionate about cultural theory, philosophy, architecture, music, literature, and human rights advocacy and actively participates in contemporary socio-political discourse, contributing columns to publications and journals such as *Domus India, Outlook Magazine, The Leaflet–Imprint of Lawyers Collective,* and Elsevier.

Gauri Bharat: An Associate Professor at CEPT University Ahmedabad, Gauri Bharat leads the postgraduate programme in architectural history and theory. Her research focuses on how people engage with built environments, ethnographic methods, and the relationship of architecture to popular culture. She recently published *In Forest, Field, and Factory:*

Adivasi Habitations Through Twentieth Century India, a volume on Santal Adivasi architectural history. Her current research includes ethnographic narratives of the city and a history of reinforced concrete in India, which is funded by the Graham Foundation.

Kiranmayi Indraganti: A filmmaker and teacher with interests in film direction, screenwriting and the writing of histories of women art practitioners, Kiranmayi Indraganti holds a PhD in Film Studies from the University of Nottingham, UK and an MFA in Film Production from York University, Toronto, Canada. At present, she teaches film across different levels and programs at the Srishti Institute of Art, Design and Technology. Her publications include a chapter in *Revisiting Star Studies* (2017, Edinburgh University Press) and a book titled *Her Majestic Voice* (2016, Oxford University Press).

Mustansir Dalvi: Professor of Architecture at the Sir JJ College of Architecture, Mustansir Dalvi research interests span architectural education, architectural history and heritage, urban transformation and architectural semiotics. He has been a member of the Academic Council of the University of Mumbai, the Chair of the Board of Studies in Architectural Education of the University of Mumbai, Chairperson of the Navi Mumbai Centre of Indian Institute of Architects and is currently serving on the Board of Governors of the MMRDA Heritage Conservation Society. Dalvi's work has been extensively published in architectural journals, magazines, as well as books, with the most recent publications being *The Past as Present: Pedagogical Practices in Architecture at the Bombay School of Art* (Sir JJ/UDRI, 2016) and *20th Century Compulsions* (Marg, 2016), a collection of writings about early Indian modernist architecture from some of the most important practitioners of the time.

Namrata Toraskar: Namrata Toraskar is an architect and independent researcher. She holds a Bachelor's degree is in architecture from Rachna Sansad's Academy of Architecture, Mumbai and a Master's in Interior Architecture and Design with a specialisation in Craft and Technology from CEPT University, Ahmedabad. She has since been supported by the Sahapedia Frames 2018 Fellowship and the Sahapedia-UNESCO

2018 Fellowship to further her research in the domain of Indian crafts and heritage which has predominantly been located in Himachal Pradesh and Maharashtra. Her research interests include the study of the building crafts, dwelling rituals and visual culture of Indian vernacular settlements. Currently, she teaches research methods in design and assists in architecture design studios for the undergraduate students at Wadiyar Centre for Architecture, Mysuru. Through an interdisciplinary use of illustrations, photography and writing she strives to evolve creative approaches to built environment and human habitations.

Neelkanth Chhaya: Neelkanth Chhaya has been a practising architect and academic since 1977. Emphasising the adaptation of built form to physical and social contexts and the innovative applications of local skills and materials, his institutional and residential projects have won major national awards as well as several architectural competitions. He is also deeply interested in the cultural factors that affect architecture, especially in societies of rapid change, and in traditional and artisanal knowledge in the area of built environment. He has taught at the University of Nairobi, the Institute of Environmental Design at Vallabh Vidyanagar, and was a faculty member at CEPT University, Ahmedabad for over twenty-five years, retiring as Dean of the Faculty of Architecture at CEPT University in 2013. He is currently Adjunct Faculty at Srishti School of Design and holds the position of Academic Chair at the Goa College of Architecture. A member of the Boards of Hunnarshala and Khamir Craft Resource Centre, both of which are involved in empowering traditional knowledge and sustainable practices, Chhaya has been involved in participatory rehabilitation housing projects as well as mass housing projects in urban areas.

Priya Joseph: An architect-researcher, Priya Joseph's research interests lie in the chronicling of histories of architecture, especially those revealed through a study of the material and tectonics of making. Her architecture practice called 'The Living Studio' focuses on designing with earth-based material. She was the Sahapedia-UNESCO fellow of 2017 and was also granted the INTACH Charles Wallace Research Scholarship 2018. Her recent work was presented at the University of California, Berkeley conference, IASTE 2018 and published in the working papers of Traditional Dwellings and Settlement Review. She has taught at the Faculty of Architecture, CEPT University, Ahmedabad and is currently a PhD Candidate at the Manipal Academy of Higher Education through the Srishti Institute of Art, Design and Technology.

Rachna Mehra: Assistant Professor in the Urban Studies programme at the School of Global Affairs, Ambedkar University Delhi, Rachna Mehra has a PhD in Modern Indian History from the Centre for Historical Studies (CHS), Jawaharlal Nehru University (JNU), Delhi. Her research interests include past and contemporary linkages of towns and cities, the history of partition and its impact on gender relations as well as the urban landscape. Her MPhil thesis project involved unravelling the relationship between gender and state within the purview of the Recovery of Abducted Persons Act of 1949. While her PhD thesis traced the urban history of the small town of Faridabad which later became a flourishing industrial city in the post partition period.

Sankalpa: An architect and urban designer, Sankalpa has been teaching construction and leading design studios for the last eleven years at the Faculty of Architecture, CEPT University, Ahmedabad. He is deeply interested in developing pedagogies that are bodily involved, modelling techniques that can be experienced and verified. His studios involve inquiries into structural principles and their articulation as a strategy for architectural design. In 2013, he co-founded 'Thumb Impressions Collaborative', a collaborative practice of young architects, civil engineers, photographers, urban designers and planners that is focused on design and build. Since then the practice has expanded into TiC furniture, TiC Execution & Detailing and TiC Design.

Savyasaachi: Savyasaachi started his explorations of different ways of life through long years of fieldwork with the Koitor forest dwellers in Chattisgarh in Central India and the forest people (Hill Kharias and Kutia Khonds) in Orissa in eastern India. He has since taught extensively at the Department of Sociology at Jamia Milia Islamia, New Delhi and has been visiting Faculty at the Department of Conservation Architecture, School of Planning and Architecture, the National Institute of Design, Ahmedabad and at the International Honours

Program, Boston University, USA. He has worked with conservation architects, notably with the Delhi-based Cultural Resource Conservation Initiative, a founding partner organisation of the UNESCO/UNITWIN (University Twinning) Network on Gender, Culture and People-Centred Development. Spanning the fields of Cultural Anthropology, Archaeology and Anthropological Linguistics, his work engages with issues of social life and culture, community-oriented cultural heritage preservation, decolonisation, and method. He has several publications including the Penguin book of forest writings titled *Between the Earth and the Sky*.

Sohail Hashmi: A noted historian, social activist, film-maker and very vocal heritage conservationist, Sohail Hashmi is a leading authority on the history of the city of Delhi. He is particularly well-known for his 'Delhi Heritage Walks', immersive tours through which he brings the history, architecture, culture, performative traditions as well as foodways of the capital alive in public memory. Passionate about getting children interested in knowing their city, its environment and its history, he also conducts tours exclusively for children and authored the book *Sanchi: Where Tigers Fly and Lions Have Horns* which forms part of the UNESCO World Heritage Sites of India Series. He is also an active member of the Safdar Hashmi Memorial Trust (SAHMAT) and Act Now for Harmony and Democracy (ANHAD).

Sonal Mithal: Sonal Mithal is a conservation architect-artist. She holds a PhD from the University of Illinois at Urbana-Champaign. At her conservation firm, 'People for Heritage Concern', her work prioritises archival and material research-based architectural conservation and artistic practice. She is also a Visiting Associate Professor at the Faculty of Architecture, CEPT University, Ahmedabad. She has created a number of artwork series based on extensive research which illustrate the palimpsestic nature of urban history—Kolkata, Lucknow, and Surat are some of the cities she has represented in her paintings. Her current projects include consulting on the restoration and adaptive-reuse of the Surat Castle and the restoration of CNI Church. She is invested in combining practice with teaching—bringing learning from either side to the other. Her artwork has recently been presented at the Venice Biennale 2019.

Sudhanva Deshpande: An actor and director with Jana Natya Manch, Delhi and a publisher with LeftWord Books, Sudhanva Deshpande is also involved in the running of Studio Safdar, Shadipur and the adjacent May Day Bookstore. In 1987, Sudhanva joined Janam, where he was mentored by Safdar Hashmi. Since then, he has held teaching positions at the National Institute of Design, Ahmedabad, and the AJK MCRC, Jamia Millia Islamia, New Delhi. He has codirected two documentaries on Habib Tanvir and edited two books, *Theatre of the Streets: The Jana Natya Manch Experience* (Jana Natya Manch, 2007) and *Our Stage: Pleasures and Perils of Theatre Practice in India* (Tulika Books, 2009). He cycles around town.

Tikender Singh Panwar: Was the directly elected deputy Mayor of Shimla city. Tikender was also a member of the national task force in the country to review the 74th constitutional amendment which speaks about decentralised governance. Apart from this Tikender has represented the city and the country on many international events.

Index